SETTLER SOCIETY IN THE
AUSTRALIAN COLONIES

Settler Society in the Australian Colonies

Self-Government and Imperial Culture

ANGELA WOOLLACOTT

OXFORD
UNIVERSITY PRESS

OXFORD

UNIVERSITY PRESS

Great Clarendon Street, Oxford, OX2 6DP,
United Kingdom

Oxford University Press is a department of the University of Oxford.
It furthers the University's objective of excellence in research, scholarship,
and education by publishing worldwide. Oxford is a registered trade mark of
Oxford University Press in the UK and in certain other countries

Published in the United States of America by Oxford University Press
198 Madison Avenue, New York, NY 10016, United States of America

British Library Cataloguing in Publication Data
Data available

Library of Congress Control Number: 2014948841

ISBN 978–0–19–964180–2

Printed and bound by
CPI Group (UK) Ltd, Croydon, CR0 4YY

For Carroll, Becky, and Matt

Acknowledgements

I gratefully acknowledge the Australian Research Council for the Discovery grant, which funded research for this project.

I am indebted to two stellar research assistants for their hard and painstaking work locating materials for this project: my warm thanks to Leigh Boucher and Carolyn Skinner for all of those hours of discovery; this book owes much to their efforts. Thanks go to Abby Waldman for some very useful early bibliographic research. I was also fortunate to have the assistance of an MA research intern from Gröningen University in the Netherlands; not only were Margriet Fokken's contributions to research for the sections on women valuable, it was a sheer delight to have her at the Australian National University (ANU) for a few months.

The project benefitted significantly from the allied doctoral research conducted by Catherine Bishop, and I thank Macquarie University and ANU for the scholarships that supported Cath's work. Her creative and wide-ranging research for her thesis shed light on issues central to Chapter 5, helping me to see that women's paid work in this period was ubiquitous and significant. Blake Singley kindly gave me the benefit of various aspects of his doctoral research on cookery books and settlers' cookery practices.

This book is much the better for thoughtful suggestions and insightful advice from anonymous readers and from Stuart Ward, and I am greatly indebted to them. The editors at Oxford University Press have all been a pleasure to work with. I thank Cathryn Steele for her assistance, and Marilyn Inglis for sharpening and tightening my prose. I thank also, for various pieces of collegial help and advice, Shaunnagh Dorsett, Cecilia Morgan, Heather Goodall, Frank Bongiorno, and Anne Rees. I have benefitted, too, from the comments and advice of audiences at many seminar and conference presentations over the past seven years. And more generally I thank my colleagues, both staff and postgraduate, in ANU's School of History for creating an intellectually supportive environment.

It is a joy to acknowledge that this book and I have been sustained on a daily basis by Carroll Pursell's wisdom and advice on matters large and small, his humour, and his superb cooking.

Contents

List of Illustrations

Creating Settler Society: An Introduction

Visiting Hobart in 1829 from India, East India Company official Augustus Prinsep found Van Diemen's Land surprisingly attractive and civilized: 'You have never supposed that it has a beautiful harbour, a fine metropolis, with towns, streets, shops, and pretty shopkeepers, like some of the larger towns of Devonshire or Sussex'. Moreover, he noted, there were counties and farms, the shops were well supplied with goods at reasonable prices, and there were not only several chapels but a number of schools, even a well-regarded girls' boarding school. Tasmania, in Prinsep's view, had wonderful prospects, so much so that he contemplated returning in a few years, and even concluded that 'I could willingly change India for Tasmania, and fall from diplomacy to farming with content'.[1] Prinsep was not the only Briton based in the Indian colonies who visited the Australian colonies in the early to mid-nineteenth century for reasons of proximity or as a health cure, only to discover their attractions.

For all of their unlikely penal origins and strategic imperial value, by the 1820s the Australian colonies had become a settler destination. Operating as largely open-air gaols, the settlements' foundation was the convict system that increasingly included assignment to private masters and mistresses, and thus offered settlers the inducement of unpaid labourers as well as the availability of land on a scale that defied and excited the British imagination. British settlers, to varying degrees, understood the expansion of imperial territories occurring through violence and forced acquisition in places stretching around the globe, as Britain used its naval and military power to build its global imperial ascendancy. With the wars against revolutionary and Napoleonic France finally over, and the massive consequent demobilization of soldiers and sailors, British aspirations for land, affluence, and salubrious climates leapt. Months-long voyages to start a new life became more imaginable. By the 1830s schemes for founding new kinds of colonies, not least those on the lines of Edward Gibbon Wakefield's (1796–1862) systematic colonization, gained attention and support. In Australia, these idealized and elaborate schemes meant new settlements in South Australia in 1836 and at Australind in Western Australia from 1840, settlements that were seen as uplifting new ventures for Australia, places for aspiring landowners and hard-working free labourers.

---

[1] Mrs A. Prinsep (ed.), *The Journal of a Voyage from Calcutta to Van Diemen's Land: comprising a Description of that Colony during a Six Months' Residence, from original letters* (London: Smith, Elder, & Co., Cornhill, 1833) pp. 55, 78, 89, and 107.

The decades from the 1820s to the 1860s constitute a foundational period in Australian history, arguably at least as important as Federation. Industrialization was transforming Britain, but the southern colonies were in a pre-industrial state, with economies driven by pastoralism, agriculture, mining, mercantilism including whaling and sealing, commerce, and the construction trades, as well as imperial government expenditure. Convict transportation had provided the labour on which the first settlements depended until it was brought slowly to a staggered end, first in New South Wales in 1840 and last in Western Australia in 1868. At the same time, the numbers of free settlers rose dramatically, surging from the 1820s and again during the 1850s gold rushes. In the 1850s most colonies achieved responsible government, a radical shift from penal settlements to self-governing societies that is at the heart of this book. Yet we know little about how inhabitants of the Australian colonies perceived the growth of a free settler society from its convict origins, how 'Australians' understood their rapidly evolving place in a profoundly changing world.

The core of this study is the rapid expansion of settler society in Australia in these crucial decades, when the weight of the British population shifted from unfree to free, when colonies dramatically expanded their territorial control (even though viewed in terms of the whole continent they remained small), and settlers and officials alike had grand plans for colonial possibilities. Knowledge, both tacit and articulated, of frontier violence in Australia shaped the settlers' lives; as also, for many, did more peaceful interactions with Aboriginal people. *Settler Society in the Australian Colonies* considers gendered conceptions of the free settler, along with ideas about what it meant to be a free 'white' settler in an empire based on racial hierarchies. A particular focus is the settlers' dependence in these decades on intertwined categories of unfree labour, including that of poorly compensated Aborigines, and indentured Indian and Chinese labourers, alongside that of convicts. My interest in gender includes the conception of political manhood (male suffrage)—by the 1850s men were endowed with political authority and the right to vote, and women were excluded from both. In order to understand contemporary perceptions of the colonies taking shape, I consider settlers' and residents' knowledge of and reactions to specific events around other parts of the British Empire, reactions to frontier conflicts and wars in other colonies, and commentary on political developments elsewhere. But perhaps above all, I hope to challenge assumptions that this was a clear and simple process of migration. Instead, I wish to evoke the ways in which settlers were mobile, often with short-term objectives, changing goals, and evolving conceptions of themselves and their societies.

From our own contemporary perspective, travel means the relative comfort of airplanes and airports that combine shopping malls and hotels. So it is perhaps surprising to realize that settlers in the early to mid-nineteenth century could be globally mobile. Despite the cramped and often smelly conditions on board wooden sailing vessels (the only choice until the introduction of iron steamships around the 1840s), the inevitability of seasickness, the poor quality of food, the danger of shipwreck, and the months it took to sail from Britain to its Antipodes, settlers not infrequently moved on, took trips, or returned to Britain for a visit or for good.

One story of extensive mobility was that of Captain Charles Hervey Bagot who, in 1840, emigrated to South Australia with his wife and children. Irish-born Bagot had already travelled the world during his career with the British Army. From 1804 for at least the next fifteen years, his military service took him to South America, the Cape of Good Hope (South Africa), Mauritius, and India. In South Australia, he became a sheep farmer and one of the first owners of a copper mine at Kapunda. Presumably the money he made from copper helped to facilitate his subsequent travel. In 1846 he took his wife on a trip to other Australian colonies, in which they visited Launceston, Melbourne, Sydney, and other parts of New South Wales. In 1853–54 they returned to England and Ireland for an extended visit, and after a further five years in South Australia returned to England yet again.[2]

The Bagots were not alone in this mobility, even if for others it was on a more modest scale. Kathleen Lambert, who arrived in Sydney in 1843 as a teenager with her parents, brothers, and sisters, lived in Australia for forty-five years before returning to England. Lambert experienced changes of fortune in her own material circumstances and those of her immediate family; for six different periods between the mid-1840s and early 1860s she worked as a governess (four in different parts of Sydney, one at Morpeth in the Hunter Valley, and one near Mudgee). For another stretch she served as her brother's housekeeper on his station at Montefiores near Wellington in central New South Wales, performing arduous domestic labour. While Lambert's mobility was on a smaller scale than Bagot's, during her decades in Australia she also visited Tasmania for four months. When she returned to England for good in 1888, she sometimes wondered whether she should not have stayed in Australia, commenting that other returnees had the same thoughts.[3] Some, indeed, returned again to the colonies. Chapter 1 takes up the theme of mobility and connections in order to establish the settlers' global conceptions, not least with regard to racial hierarchies and labour systems.

A point of departure for this book is the goal of taking a wide view of the Australian continent. Much of the history written about the Australian colonies for this period has focused on New South Wales, or Van Diemen's Land, or both. Thus Australian colonial history has revolved around the topics of the convict system, the battle to end transportation, the status of emancipated convicts, the gold rush, and political fights over land, as well as the urban agitations for self-government. When we widen the focus out to include the whole continent, the story becomes more varied and more complex. The wider lens compels us to consider how vast the Australian continent is, and how tiny, isolated, and tenuous the first British settlements were, even as the settlers used force to take land from the Aborigines. Frontier violence has increasingly been documented by historians and must remain central to our field of vision. Here, it is inextricably interwoven with the topics of land and labour.

---

[2] *A holograph memoir of Captain Charles Hervey Bagot of the 87th Regiment* (Adelaide: Pioneers Association of South Australia, 1942).

[3] 'Lyth' [Kathleen Lambert], *The Golden South: Memories of Australian Home Life from 1843 to 1888* (London: Ward and Downey, 1890).

In the period covered by this text, British colonialism spread out from the first settlements dotted along the east and south coasts and in Van Diemen's Land. Pastoralism pushed colonial frontiers west, north, and south from Sydney, and across the fertile regions of Van Diemen's Land. In 1829 the Swan River Colony extended the earlier small military bases in Western Australia with a fledgling settlement that would develop only slowly. In 1835 settlers in Van Diemen's Land crossed the Bass Strait and rapidly began to grab land in the Port Phillip and western districts of what in 1850 would become Victoria, against the wishes of colonial authorities. In 1836 the first Wakefieldian experiment was launched in South Australia, a systematic colony that sought to turn the messy processes of settler colonialism into an orderly political scheme of migration that would benefit landowners and labourers. If South Australia did not live up to its notions of its own moral exceptionalism, its sibling colony at Australind, begun in southern Western Australia in 1840, would attain only a fraction of the vision of its founders. And from the 1850s, in the northern reaches of New South Wales, the huge area that would become Queensland, the settled areas rapidly expanded with a moving front of bloody warfare. By taking this broader look at the continental spread of the Australian colonies in these early, formative stages, we can consider the varied nature of settler colonialism and the ways in which it subsumed what had been penal colonies.

At the same time, it is important to see these fledgling colonies not only as a connected continental network, but as part of the globally expanding British Empire. While the British in Australia were expanding their territorial grasp, so were British settler colonies in Canada, New Zealand, and South Africa, even as Britain maintained its Indian Ocean footholds. The British took Hong Kong as a prize of the Opium Wars with China in the early 1840s, and then with great difficulty suppressed the Indian Rebellion of 1857–58, before going to war with the Maori of the North Island in New Zealand in 1860. At the time British settlers saw these enterprises and fights as expanding their empire, which was why they occasionally moved from one colony to another, or in some instances volunteered to serve in an imperial battle elsewhere. As Chapter 7 will discuss, settlers in Australia understood that their own prosperity and security were linked to the fortunes of the British Empire in other colonies, and directly identified as Britons when imperial interests were attacked. This sense of colonial connectedness has often been overlooked in Australian history in recent decades, and is crucial to apprehending the settlers' world views at the time. Settlers' placing of the maturing Australian colonies within the imperial and global context casts light on their push for self-government and manhood (adult male) suffrage, as well as their claims to land and conceptions of warfare.

Recent work in imperial and world history has refocused attention on the category 'settlers', a term that has been reinvigorated through the imperative to better understand historical processes of colonialism. James Belich in his 2009 book on the Anglophone world uses the terms 'settlerism' and 'Settler Revolution' to encompass the massive territorial expansion of Britain and America combined in the nineteenth century, and the huge migrations of Anglophone populations to the newly conquered frontiers.[4] As Caroline Elkins and Susan Pedersen have argued, settler colonialism continued through the twentieth century, was conducted by a range of states (including, for example, Singapore and Israel) and ethnic groups, sparked continuing struggles over land, and has fundamentally structured the contemporary world.[5] Studying settlers and settler colonialism is a major component of modern world history. Settlers have been at the core of imperial expansion, the dispossession of indigenous peoples, and the establishment of new states and racially stratified societies.

From the 1820s onwards, the process of rapid settler expansion in the Australian colonies comprised one part of the vastly expanding British Empire and other empires around the globe. Lisa Ford argues that between the specific years of 1822 and 1847, settler colonies in the Anglophone world articulated their own sovereignty by asserting their jurisdiction over indigenous peoples. Ford demonstrates that in the US state of Georgia and in New South Wales, as well as in colonies ranging from Canada to New Zealand, settler courts defined indigenous violence as crime and asserted their right to punish it; in so doing, they conflated sovereignty, territory, and jurisdiction.[6] Ford's evidence suggests that settler colonialism expanded and changed in fundamental ways from the 1820s. This book contributes to the current interest in historicizing settler colonialism and in showing the significance of its massive expansion in the early to mid-nineteenth century. It seeks to do so by drawing connections between political, cultural, and social aspects of settler society in Australia.

This volume is concerned, amongst other topics, with the connections between rapidly expanding settler colonialism and the establishment of historically and geographically specific racially stratified societies. David Lambert's study of Barbados during the rise of the abolition movement from the 1780s to 1833 charts what he sees as a white creole identity shaped through the politics of resisting the abolition of slavery. In Lambert's view, whiteness in Barbados was shaped through contested political discourses, in a specific historical era when the British metropole and one of its successful colonies struggled over moral, political, and economic issues. A familiar term in Caribbean studies, the 'creolization' of colonizers refers to the process in which they developed a distinctive culture and polity, and the mutual articulation of difference between metropole and colony. Seeing white West Indian culture as 'creole' signifies its blending of various elements on Caribbean soil, a metropolitan view of the negative transformation of colonizers through the colonial encounter, the sense of difference white West Indians developed from their metropolitan counterparts, and the participation of non-white groups in defining white 'creole' characteristics.[7]

---

[4] James Belich, *Replenishing the Earth: The Settler Revolution and the Rise of the Anglo-world, 1783–1939* (New York: Oxford University Press, 2009).

[5] Caroline Elkins and Susan Pedersen (eds), *Settler Colonialism in the Twentieth Century: Projects, Practices, Legacies* (New York: Routledge, 2005).

[6] Lisa Ford, *Settler Sovereignty: Jurisdiction and Indigenous People in America and Australia, 1788–1836* (Cambridge, MA: Harvard University Press, 2010), pp. 1–3.

[7] David Lambert, *White Creole Culture, Politics and Identity during the Age of Abolition* (Cambridge: Cambridge University Press, 2005), esp. pp. 37–9.

The term 'creole' has not been applied to settler colonialism in Australia, yet several of the above elements were present in its establishment. Settlers in Australia quickly developed a culture based on land grants, the exploitation of convict labour, the dispossession of Indigenous people, and the establishment of the pastoral industry, as well as whaling and sealing; a culture shaped through adaptation to the Australian landscape, coastline, climate, and topography. The settler polity grew through dependence on and resistance to military rule, reliance on government for the supply of labour and the provision of buildings and roads, claims for land grants, the obfuscation of frontier violence, and demands for political representation that were fulfilled gradually in the 1840s and 1850s. As in Barbados, political claims were couched in terms of English liberties and rights. Australian settler identities and characteristics were shaped, in part, through the resistance of subordinated groups, particularly Aboriginal people, and the claims of ticket-of-leave and emancipated convicts.

The pivotal development of these decades and the political events that form the backbone of this story were the Australian colonies' gradual attainment of representative and then responsible government. Through a process of political struggle and negotiation in which Australians looked to the developments in Canada for their model of political progress, settlers slowly became self-governing. The first step was the principle of partially elected legislative councils to advise the governor, first achieved in New South Wales in 1842 with the other colonies following. Next the 1850 Australian Colonies Government Act gave South Australia, Tasmania, and Victoria legislative councils that were two-thirds elected, and lowered the property qualifications for voting in all the colonies.[8] Then in the 1850s, continuing colonial demands for self-government on the Canadian model resulted in new fully articulated constitutions for each colony: constitutions for New South Wales, Tasmania, and Victoria were enacted in 1855, for South Australia in 1856, and in 1859 for Queensland when it separated from New South Wales. For various reasons, Western Australia's evolution was slower; it would not achieve responsible government until 1890.

The events of the extended political drama that resulted in responsible government have been well covered by other historians.[9] Aspects of that story are integral to Chapters 4 and 5. Chapter 4 shows that this was an inherently imperial drama, one that cannot be seen as exclusively Australian, and that some of the leading proponents of self-government in the Australian colonies brought their advocacy and their experience from elsewhere in the British Empire. Moreover, we need to

---

[8] K. S. Inglis, *The Australian Colonists: An exploration of social history 1788–1870* (Carlton, Victoria: Melbourne University Press, 1974), p. 48.

[9] Recent work in this area has included Peter Cochrane, *Colonial Ambition: Foundations of Australian Democracy* (Carlton, Victoria: Melbourne University Press, 2006) and Terry Irving, *The Southern Tree of Liberty: The Democratic Movement in New South Wales before 1856* (Sydney: The Federation Press, 2006), while important earlier work includes John Hirst, *The Strange Birth of Colonial Democracy: New South Wales 1848–1884* (Crows Nest: Allen & Unwin, 1988), J. M. Ward, *Colonial Self-Government: The British Experience 1759–1856* (London: Macmillan, 1976), and A. G. L. Shaw (ed.), *Great Britain and the Colonies 1815–1865* (London: Methuen, 1970).

see the ways in which arguments for self-government and political manhood—
which were pioneered in the Australian colonies with their early achievement of
male suffrage—were tied to settler colonial conceptions of claims to land and the
dispossession of Indigenous inhabitants. The significance of the exclusion of
women from political rights and authority, women's challenges to that exclusion,
and the debates about gender that percolated through the Australian colonies and
beyond in consequence, form much of the subject of Chapter 5. While the term
'responsible government' refers primarily to the executive (the premier and cabinet
ministers) being responsible to the lower house of parliament, it had resonances for
all those who became voting political subjects in the new system, and for those
excluded. If, as David Denholm has suggested, the 'traditional proposition' was
that 'freedom was for free men, a self contained definition that variously excluded
servants, soldiers, convicts, and lesser subjects such as Irish peasants and Indians',
by implicitly dividing society into 'responsible and irresponsible men' on the basis
of the 'alleged capacity of a man to participate in the governance of freedom by free
men', male suffrage in the Australian colonies from the mid-1850s was a symbolic
development indeed.[10] It meant that significant numbers of men who had previously been held 'irresponsible' now became imbued with responsible manly authority that could be exercised and displayed as voting subjects. Manhood became a
political status as well as the benchmark of social independence, while womanhood
connoted its apolitical opposite. The Australian colonies acquired not only self-
government but international visibility as electoral pioneers.

Preceding settlers' claims to self-government were their aspirations and claims to
land. It was the promise of land that attracted settlers to the Australian colonies.
Land grants were made from the first founding of New South Wales. In the first
decades of the colonies' settlement, grants were predicated on turning emancipated
convicts into yeomen farmers, encouraging retired soldiers to stay in the same
capacity, and enticing some free settlers with lots of 130 acres. Between 1792 and
1795 civil and military officers also obtained the privilege of land grants of 100
acres.[11] In the 1820s the system of land grants changed at the same time that
convict transportation increased greatly in the wake of the Napoleonic Wars. The
number and size of land grants increased dramatically, as did the assignment of
convicts to private masters and mistresses, thus facilitating the rapid expansion of
large pastoral estates. In 1820 the lands beyond the Cumberland Plains of Sydney
were officially opened to pastoralism. Between 1822 and 1828, four times the area
of land was awarded in grants as had been awarded between 1788 and 1821.[12] In
Van Diemen's Land, which was established as a penal colony in 1803, land grants
were made on a similar basis to New South Wales. In the southern colony, too, the
1820s saw a dramatic expansion of grants. The watershed year was 1823 when a

---

[10] David Denholm, 'Some Aspects of Squatting in New South Wales and Queensland, 1847–1864', PhD thesis, Australian National University, 1972, pp. xviii–xix.
[11] Philip McMichael, *Settlers and the Agrarian Question: Foundations of Capitalism in Colonial Australia* (Cambridge: Cambridge University Press, 1984), p. 43.
[12] McMichael, *Settlers and the Agrarian Question*, p. 73.

total of 441,871 acres was allocated in 1,027 grants; by the early 1830s most of the island's land suited to agriculture and pastoralism had been granted or sold.[13] The halcyon days for military settlers—retired officers and those on half pay from the army—were the years from 1826 to 1831, when they were given land grants on superior terms to non-military settlers. In 1831, influenced by Wakefield and his supporters of systematic colonization, the Ripon Regulations sought to abolish land grants throughout the empire, creating systems of land sales in their place.[14] From 1831 even military officers had to purchase land, though they were given special reductions on the price of land correlating to their length of service.[15]

From the 1830s the occupation of land by squatters spread voraciously up and down eastern Australia. While squatting was at first frowned on, under Governor Bourke it was sanctioned through regulation, licensing, and the introduction of Commissioners for Crown Lands whose duties included monitoring squatters. Those who engaged in squatting were a diverse group, including established landowners who held mixed-farming estates in the more densely settled areas, and large pastoral runs further out. In the 1860s land reforms were enacted to redress the balance of land ownership and to open up more land to small farmers.[16]

The settlers' desire for land drove the slow and arduous processes of settlement. Often in small groups—sometimes several men cooperating, sometimes in families, and occasionally individual men alone—new arrivals moved inland with their bullock drays and horses to stake out land claims and begin to occupy them in rough shelters and huts. Commonly, the sparseness of the settler population meant that they were dependent on each other for assistance, such as routinely offering travellers the comfort of food and shelter in huts and homesteads, and even medical assistance, as they made their painstaking journeys from coastal towns inland and back again.

But it was not only other settlers with whom they developed relations of reliance and cooperation. The early settler frontiers were mixed places of violence and peaceful interaction with Aboriginal people, and the 'frontiers' were not just at the receding edges of settlement. As Penelope Edmonds has shown, we need to see the pervasiveness of these interracial interactions to recognize that: 'Colonial frontiers did not exist only in the bush, backwoods, or borderlands; they clearly sat at the heart of early town and city building'.[17] Aborigines who were displaced from their land, or forced to share it with these unwanted strangers, were often soon at least partly dependent on settlers for food and other goods, such as tobacco, which could be acquired through labour—though usually this labour was not properly compensated as that of white workers would have been. Thus interracial

---

[13] Sharon Morgan, *Land Settlement in Early Tasmania: Creating an Antipodean England* (Cambridge: Cambridge University Press, 1992), pp. 13, 22–3.

[14] McMichael, *Settlers and the Agrarian Question*, pp. 84–5.

[15] Christine Wright, *Wellington's Men in Australia: Peninsular War Veterans and the Making of Empire c.1820–40* (Basingstoke: Palgrave Macmillan, 2011), pp. 19–20.

[16] McMichael, *Settlers and the Agrarian Question*, pp. 91–3, 220.

[17] Penelope Edmonds, *Urbanizing Frontiers: Indigenous Peoples and Settlers in 19th-Century Pacific Rim Cities* (Vancouver: UBC Press, 2010), p. 5.

relations were often familiar, even intimate, as Aborigines and settlers lived and worked around and with each other.

Settlers learned Aboriginal people's names, or gave them names of their own attribution, often derogatory. They frequently learned a great deal from Aborigines, about the local topography and climate, and the plants and animals. Alice Hughes, in a memoir published much later, remembered life on her family's sheep station in the 1840s near the town of Wellington in South Australia, at the mouth of the River Murray. The family's interactions with local Aborigines were such that: 'We made great friends with the black fellows and were never tired of talking to them and seeing the strange things they did'. The Aborigines called her '"Alith" or "Big Man's piccaninny"'. Hughes readily criticized these Aboriginal 'friends' in her recollections, condemning them as 'very idle people', even though 'sometimes they would do a little work for tea or sugar or a stick of tobacco', and a 'black lubra [did] washing for us'. Despite their supposed laziness, Hughes recalled them as 'a good natured race, at least the half civilised ones we knew were' and admitted that 'we got a good many hints from them in general which gave us a taste for outdoor life'.[18] Other settler reminiscences and accounts similarly document frequent and familiar interracial relations in these decades. A particular challenge inherent to understanding the Australian settler colonies in this period is to comprehend the simultaneous cooperation and violence between Europeans and Aborigines. It was the settlers' drive to take and claim the land that spurred the violence, and it was often their need for labour that underpinned the cooperation; for Aborigines, there could be little choice.

The pervasive violence of the frontier was not only interracial. Relations between masters and mistresses on the one hand, and their convict labourers and servants on the other, could be fraught and at times involved appeals to magistrates and the punishment of convicts, which could include flogging. On larger pastoral estates and farms, in Van Diemen's Land at least, convicts were locked overnight in rudimentary cells. To some extent, labour relations overlapped with penal or custodial relations. Not surprisingly, it was widely understood that convicts resented their masters and mistresses. It was also understood that, typically, convicts would not come to the aid of their masters and mistresses in the event of an attack by bushrangers.

Lawlessness and violence in the early Australian colonies included not only frontier warfare but bushranging, which began as early as the late eighteenth century. The violence woven into the fabric of settler society in these decades was a merging of these different forms, which helped to justify harsh measures of control and to some extent blurred the categories of crime and warfare. As Chapter 6 will discuss, bushranging was linked to the convict system in that escaped convicts often turned to bushranging to survive. But bushrangers were a diverse group: the first person to be identified as a bushranger was 'Black Caesar', a convict of African descent who had arrived on the First Fleet in 1788, escaped into

---

[18] Mrs F. [Alice] Hughes, *My Childhood in Australia* (London: Digby, Long, and Co., 1892), pp. 19, 28, 44, 47.

the bush around Sydney in 1795, and was shot in 1796. There were also Aboriginal men identified as 'bushrangers', even though in their cases the crime of bushranging is difficult to distinguish from resistance to British invasion. Bushranging and the settlers' fear of it pervaded the eastern Australian colonies in their early decades, reaching highpoints in Van Diemen's Land in the 1820s, in New South Wales in the 1830s and again in the 1860s, and in Victoria in the 1850s. Fear of bushranging in New South Wales was such that from 1830 to 1842 (when New South Wales incorporated much of the eastern part of the continent) the Bushranging Act empowered any person to arrest someone found on the road with a firearm who looked like they might commit a robbery. This extraordinary legislating of citizen arrest reflects the degree to which bushranging had produced a colonial panic.

Settlers in the Australian colonies were a heterogeneous lot, dominantly Anglo-British but including people of other ethnic origins from the first. The 1850s gold rushes brought prospectors from China, America (including some African Americans), Germany, and elsewhere in Europe, some of whom stayed after gold fever subsided. And if they were mostly drawn from the middling classes, those with family backgrounds in military or civil service, commerce, professions, and the skilled trades, they also represented a wide range of levels of material affluence. At least some were attracted to the Australian colonies for reasons of freedom of worship; nonconformists sought to escape the dominance of the established Church of England, such that varieties of Protestantism flourished on Australian soil, while the Irish minority and other Europeans brought Roman Catholicism. While settlers were surprisingly mobile, typically they selected a particular Australian colony as their new home and identified with it such that they became divided by colonial loyalties. And political disagreements abounded. Yet there were factors of commonality and shared interests, even in these decades well before Federation appeared on the horizon.

The terms 'Australia' and 'Australians' were current in this period. Perhaps one common bond was the very fact of having made the journey from Britain, or elsewhere, or having been born into a family that had been transplanted, even if not fully voluntarily. Their shared enterprise of shaping these new colonies, with a profound sense of their rawness and innovation, also united settlers. From early on settlers and visitors described common attributes of colonial Australians—a range of qualities from the flattering to the less so. One resident of the 1840s and 1850s commented on 'the active, intelligent and go-ahead occupiers of Australia', perhaps reflecting a shared sense of the energy and resilience it took to make a life in a fledgling colony.[19]

This volume presents stories and incidents from the lives of scores of individual settlers in these decades, a few of them familiar historical figures, but many who are not so well known. One of the book's goals is to juxtapose these stories in such a way that the evidence they present forms overlapping layers, in the hope that the layers cohere as linked political, economic, social, and cultural aspects of these

---

[19] *A holograph memoir of Captain Charles Hervey Bagot*, p. 31.

evolving colonies. If the political maturation of self-government lies at its core, this history of the Australian colonies from the 1820s to the 1860s traces the development of a settler society based on speculative land ownership, and mixed systems of unfree, indentured, and wage labour that connected the dispersed and disparate Australian settlements. Paradoxically, British settlers relied partially on convict labour to build societies whose maturation depended on the ending of convict transportation. Displacing and criminalizing indigenous people, and the violence requisite to establish their pastoral holdings, farms, and towns, were justified by the settlers' belief in the superiority of Christian white Britishness, and buttressed by the knowledge that they were part of a global British ascendancy. The settlers' willingness to support and fight for British interests elsewhere, such as against the Maori in New Zealand, and their expressions of outraged righteousness over the Indian Rebellion in the 1850s, show that they understood their actions and their culture within not just a larger continental but an imperial context. Their lexicon of their own rights, and the moral certainties that underlay their frontier violence and social hierarchies, drew on global examples. But the societies they forged on this vast continent were unlike any elsewhere in their blending of extensive penal labour with other unfree and unpaid labour, and their interwoven aspirations to land tracts, pastoral and mining riches, and, for white men at least, democratic rights (a limitation against which some women protested).

1

Settler Family Networks, Imperial Connections

On 23 August 1851, writing from Adelaide to relatives in England, Caroline Clark revealed the detailed knowledge that settlers in the Australian colonies had of sea routes, cargoes, ports, and vessels, including the place of 'the East Indies' in the imperial mercantile economy:

> Your letter came by a direct ship from England and it is best to send 'by first ship direct from Plymouth' unless you know something of the vessels that are about to sail. Letters [come] to us by way of the East Indies. Though many that come here with a cargo go there to obtain a cargo for home again. There is such a great difference in the length of the voyages by different vessels that if any one had leisure to learn which are the best ships it would make a wonderful difference to us. Often not less than six weeks. Latterly Liverpool vessels have come far more quickly than any others, but it is not always the case that they carry mails . . . Newspaper intelligence is generally ten weeks in advance of information by letter so it is clear enough that our letters are much longer on their route tha[n] they need be.[1]

Caroline and Francis Clark had arrived only the year prior, in June 1850, with most of their eight surviving children and a servant, hoping for a healthier, more prosperous, and religiously freer life than they had led in Birmingham. Still in March 1867, Caroline Clark was obsessed with ships and the mail:

> The incoming of the English mail is the one event in the month that we colonists all regard with great interest, and its approach is signalled by the hoisting of a chequered flag, and also by the raising of a ball in town . . . We can see the flag and ball with the telescope from our garden, and we can see the smoke of the steamer as it passes along near the coast for four or five miles of its voyage.[2]

Mail to and from England was the settlers' source of contact and information with the world beyond the Australasian colonies. Ships carrying mail and newspapers were their lifeline to relatives and friends, and their conduit of knowledge about economic, political, cultural, social, and diplomatic affairs (see Fig. 1.1). But the knowledge brought and carried by ships extended beyond England: this imperial network had links in many directions, and the contact settlers so desired was to many global points.

---

[1] PRG 389/1, State Library of South Australia, letter from Caroline Clark to relatives in England, 23 August 1851.
[2] PRG 389/1, State Library of South Australia, letter from Caroline Clark to relatives in England, 26 March 1867, p. 10 'Arrival of the English mail'.

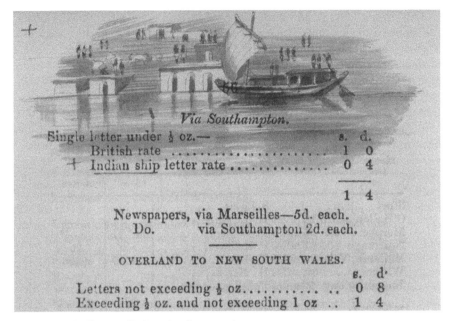

Fig. 1.1 J. M. Skipper, 'Indian ship letter rate'.
Courtesy of the State Library of South Australia, SLSA: PRG 72/13/2—*South Australian Almanack*, 1850 (J. M. Skipper, artist).

Settlers and residents in the Australian colonies had personal connections to and knowledge of many places around a rapidly globalizing world. Voyages to and from Australia involved calling at one or more ports, in regions ranging from Africa, to the Indian Ocean, South and South East Asia, and South America. Many settlers had themselves served in the British Army in India and elsewhere; sick or long-term officials, merchants, soldiers, and pensioners from India commonly sojourned in the Australian colonies and stayed. Settler families had members whose service in the British Army or Navy, ambitions, or trading interests had propelled them around the world; letters brought news from Calcutta, the West Indies, or Hong Kong. Flourishing colonial newspapers reprinted news from India, Canada, New Zealand, and elsewhere. Australian colonial newspapers assumed their readers were interested in a wide range of news items. On 24 September 1832, for instance, the *Sydney Herald*'s 'East India News' section included items about the danger of tigers around Singapore, calls for a law court in the Straits Settlements, a list of 'trades and occupations' carried on by 'Europeans and Indo-Britons' in Calcutta, the price fetched by New Zealand flax in Ceylon, and a report of an uprising by Parsis in Bombay.[3] Such news items reveal particular interest in other British colonies in the Asia-Pacific region and a wider curiosity about the world.

---

[3] 'East India News', *Sydney Herald*, 24 September 1832, p. 2.

This chapter looks at how settler connections and experience sprawled around the globe, using examples from the intermarried networks of the Dumaresq, Macleay, and Darling families of the 1820s to the 1850s—families who settled or sojourned in New South Wales and Van Diemen's Land and whose dynastic aspirations returned generations to the Australian colonies. In recent years historians have paid attention to the imperial careers and circulation of figures such as Edward John Eyre (1815–1901), the explorer and Protector of Aborigines in 1830s and 1840s South Australia who went on to higher posts, first in New Zealand, and became notorious for his harsh decisions in 1865 as Governor of Jamaica.[4] Governors in Australia, too, had come from other colonies, such as Sir Richard Bourke (1777–1855), the Governor of New South Wales from 1831 to 1837 who had held a previous post in southern Africa. However, historians have not yet fully explored the significance of this inter-colonial traffic: the circulation of officials, the connections of settlers, and the ideas they carried with them and adapted from place to place—ideas that included military conquest, unfree labour regimes, and racial hierarchies. Such backgrounds and transported ideas help us to understand settlers' willingness to take land grants and establish pastoral leases on land that had to be wrested forcibly from Indigenous inhabitants. This chapter argues that the settlers who, along with emancipated convicts, changed Australia from a set of penal stations into self-governing colonies, viewed those colonies as component parts of the wider, evolving British Empire.

A focus on settlers allows us to see the density and extent of connections between the Australian colonies and those elsewhere, through settler family networks. Life stories show the intimacy and pervasiveness of such connections, within and across families, and how family ties shaped imperial mobility. Several historians have used life stories heuristically to look at empire connections: David Lambert and Alan Lester's book on 'imperial careering' uses a series of mostly elite lives; and Zoe Laidlaw's book entitled *Colonial Connections 1815–1845* shows the role of patronage, war, and the colonial office in building personal networks around the empire.[5] Both of these as well as other valuable works reveal the extent to which colonial officials moved around the empire and exemplify its lateral connections, not just the direct channels between 'metropole' and 'colony'. Further, scholars have pointed to the significance of extended family networks in the East India Company's administration of Britain's Indian colonies in the early nineteenth century.[6] This chapter shows that the lives of settlers in the Australian colonies reflected the

---

[4] Catherine Hall, *Civilizing Subjects: Metropole and Colony in the English Imagination, 1830–1867* (Cambridge: Polity, 2002); Julie Evans, *Edward Eyre: Race and Colonial Governance* (Dunedin: University of Otago Press, 2005).

[5] David Lambert and Alan Lester (eds), *Colonial Lives Across the British Empire: Imperial Careering in the Long Nineteenth Century* (Cambridge: Cambridge University Press, 2006); Zoe Laidlaw, *Colonial Connections, 1815–45: Patronage, the Information Revolution and Colonial Government* (Manchester: Manchester University Press, 2005).

[6] For example, Malcolm Allbrook, *Henry Prinsep's Empire: Framing a Distant Colony* (Canberra: Australian National University Press, 2014).

density and reach of imperial connections, not only through their own mobility but through the compound connections embodied in family networks.

This chapter takes both a relatively confined and a wide-ranging look at how settlers in the eastern colonies of early to mid-nineteenth-century Australia maintained global connections. Lambert and Lester point out that we need to see the networks of empire not as fixed, but as creating imperial relationships in contingent and shifting ways. Moreover, we need to take seriously how geography and sense of place shaped the perception of colonies and the subjectivities of colonial inhabitants in relational and changing ways.[7] Settlers, along with the colonized, were key participants in shaping geographically based conceptions of colonial societies and regimes. Settlers actively created imperial knowledge of topography and geography, violently dispossessed indigenous inhabitants, forged new regimes of land 'ownership', and established colonial economies. They aspired to material comforts and a sense of belonging. In studying and claiming particular colonial landscapes, they articulated specific colonial characteristics, often through comparison or contrast with other colonial sites as well as the metropole. Some settler family networks spread through pastoralism and squatting within the Australian colonies even as they also connected those colonies to British trade networks in India and even China.[8] Settlers created their own new lives, at the same time as they discursively constructed the nature and place of their raw new societies within imperial networks and economies.

The massive surge in settlers to the Australian colonies from the 1820s occurred in the aftermath of the generation-long war between Britain and its cross-channel foe, starting in 1793 against revolutionary France, followed by the expansionist Napoleonic French Empire. British society and politics were thoroughly militarized by the vast and sustained war effort that lasted until 1815. The British Army expanded sixfold because of the wars, and in turn former and part-time soldiers and sailors came to dominate British politics and the professional and middle classes.[9]

In the 1820s, with the large-scale demobilization of peacetime, former military and naval officers constituted a significant proportion of settlers in the Australian colonies. Historian Christine Wright notes that from 1821 to 1825 the annual average number of settlers arriving in Van Diemen's Land and New South Wales was 650, which increased to 950 from 1826 to 1830, with army officers being a sizeable portion in the years from 1826.[10] In order to maintain a degree of military readiness, the British government retained significant numbers of army and naval officers on half-pay; for the officers themselves, half-pay presented challenges for the maintenance of both self and family. It was logical, then, that officers on half-pay were a natural constituency to settle the expanding colonies. They were regarded as desirable settlers because of their military training and understanding

[7] Lambert and Lester (eds), *Colonial Lives Across the British Empire*, pp. 8–15.

[8] David Denholm, 'Some Aspects of Squatting in New South Wales and Queensland, 1847–1864', PhD thesis, Australian National University, 1972, p. 18.

[9] Christine Wright, *Wellington's Men in Australia: Peninsular War Veterans and the Making of Empire c.1820–40* (Basingstoke, Hampshire: Palgrave Macmillan, 2011), p. 13.

[10] Wright, *Wellington's Men in Australia*, p. 28.

of conflict, skills such as surveying and engineering, and their experience of climates beyond the British Isles. Former officers who had previously had the command of soldiers and sailors would adapt well, it was thought, to being masters of convict labourers. Their own preparedness to consider migrating to remote colonies was purposefully enhanced by imperial schemes such as the land grants made to military officers in New South Wales from 1826, and in New South Wales, the availability of cheap convict labour was an added inducement. As Wright argues, this confluence of officers' demobilization, desire for greater income and opportunities, their perceived suitability as settlers, and the orchestrated frontier expansion of British settler colonies in Australasia and elsewhere resulted in a militarization of settlers. And as Wright further contends, the significance of this surge of military settlers for Australian colonial society has not been fully understood.[11]

Even as settlers and emancipated convicts shaped a creole society in the Antipodes, settlers saw their colonies as connected to and evolving in tandem with the rest of the empire and, indeed, a rapidly changing wider world. The reports they read in their flourishing press supplemented letters they received from relatives and friends, about events small and large elsewhere. Information from their various and scattered connections helped settlers to plan their pastoral and other landed ventures, to understand colonial rule in New South Wales (and other colonies) in comparative light, and to identify marriage prospects and other opportunities for family members. Their constant letter-writing (and in the case of the Dumaresq clan, the family journals they circulated) was a key form of imperial knowledge.

In her 2005 book *Kin*, Melanie Nolan uses New Zealand working-class biographies collectively to reflect patterns specific to nineteenth- and twentieth-century labouring class lives, and to raise questions of class-specific historical experience and variation therein.[12] My strategy here is to use the evidence that one extended family network provides about imperial connections radiating outwards from early colonial Australia, and about the motivations and perspectives of settlers, including their understanding of, for example, racial hierarchies and systems of labour. The Macleay, Dumaresq, and Darling network spanned a socio-economic range from the elite gentry to the lower middle-class; from those with close connections to power, to those who made a living from land granted and purchased, combined with holding mid-level jobs. Janet Doust's research on settler families in early to mid-nineteenth-century New South Wales and Victoria is also illuminating for my purposes. Doust has researched particular migrant families, especially the Booths and the Holloways, to examine settler ambitions and material success, family networks and intermarriage, gender, the role of government, racial attitudes, and the establishment of gentry society.[13] This chapter takes up an issue to which Doust alludes: the extent and significance of connections across colonies.

---

[11] Wright, *Wellington's Men in Australia*, p. 8.

[12] Melanie Nolan, *Kin: A Collective Biography of a Working-Class New Zealand Family* (Christchurch, NZ: Canterbury University Press, 2005).

[13] Janet L. Doust, 'Kinship and Accountability: The Diaries of a Pioneer Pastoralist Family, 1856 to 1898', *History Australia* Vol. 2, No. 1 (2004): 04.1–04.14; Janet L. Doust, 'Two English Immigrant Families in Australia in the 19th century', *The History of the Family* Vol. 13, No. 1 (2008): 2–25; Janet

The Mitchell Library (in the State Library of New South Wales) and the State Library of Tasmania between them hold an archive of correspondence of some of the interconnected network of the Macleay, Darling, and Dumaresq families. From the 1820s to the 1850s, this intermarried British clan not only ranged from the colonial elite to middle-ranking settlers, and spanned New South Wales and Van Diemen's Land, but had connections to India, Mauritius, Canada, and the Caribbean. Its initial lynchpin in Sydney was the 1824 appointment of Governor Sir Ralph Darling (1772–1858), whose wife Eliza (1798–1868) was a Dumaresq. Several of Eliza's brothers would migrate to Australia with them; her brother Henry Dumaresq had already served as her husband's private secretary during their previous imperial appointment in Mauritius. The new governor's powerful colonial secretary, who took up his appointment in 1825, was Alexander Macleay (1767–1848), who arrived with his wife (also Eliza) and six daughters. Several of their sons would arrive later.

IMPERIAL CONNECTIONS

In 1826 Rosa Macleay, a daughter of New South Wales Colonial Secretary Alexander Macleay, met Arthur Pooley Onslow, son of Lord Onslow and described as 'a writer', who arrived in Sydney as an invalid from India. In 1827 rather than returning to India, Onslow secured a job as Surveyor of Customs; later he turned to farming but failed. By 1829 when Onslow was forced to return to India to recover his finances through gainful employment, he and Rosa were engaged. The Macleays eventually agreed that Rosa might sail to India to marry Onslow. It was quite a process, not least because contemporary etiquette required a single woman travelling alone to be chaperoned. When Rosa finally sailed in March 1832 heading for Madras, her ship went first to Van Diemen's Land to pick up troops for India.[14] As things turned out, Rosa remained a resident of India for the rest of her life. In 1832, Onslow was appointed assistant judge at Cuddalore, and in 1835, Secretary to the Board of Revenue at Madras.[15] Over the years, Rosa and her husband returned to New South Wales on visits and sent their children for schooling and longer sojourns there.

The Macleays had other connections to India as well. In February 1831, for example, younger son George Macleay, who ran the family farm at Brownlow Hill south of Sydney and was appointed a magistrate for his local district, entertained 'the youngest son of Mr. Tom. Smith, who is an Officer in the Bengal Infantry and

L. Doust, 'Exploring Gentry Women on the New South Wales Frontier in the 1820s and 1830s', *Women's History Review* Vol. 18, No. 1 (Feb. 2009): 137–53.

[14] Letter from Fanny to William, 24 March 1832, ML A4301 [microfilm CY 1012] Papers of William Sharp Macleay, Macarthur Papers, Mitchell Library.

[15] Beverley Earnshaw and Joy Hughes (eds), *Fanny to William: The Letters of Frances Leonora Macleay 1812–1836* (Glebe, New South Wales: Historic Houses Trust of New South Wales and Macleay Museum, University of Sydney, 1993), pp. 155, 171.

at present upon leave of absence, on acct. of his want of health'.[16] But the family's regional and global connections spread further. In late 1830 James Macleay, a younger brother, was invited to sail on HMS *Comet* when it left Sydney for a voyage to New Zealand and Tahiti, including the task of transferring the inhabitants of Pitcairn Island to Tahiti. In April 1831 James wrote home to Sydney from the Bay of Islands on the New Zealand North Island, reporting that he was 'disappointed with the Country & its Inhabitants'.[17] When he returned to Sydney, he recounted to his family in detail the process of transferring the Pitcairn Islanders. Later in his life, James would work for the commission for the abolition of the slave trade in the Cape Colony. His eldest sister Fanny did not seem to share James's negative view of New Zealand; in late 1826, having conversed with French naturalists visiting Sydney, she declared that she must go to New Zealand before she dies.[18] In 1834, the Macleay family's set of imperial connections would expand to include South Africa when youngest daughter Barbara married Pieter Laurentz Campbell, an aide-de-camp to Governor Richard Bourke whose previous appointment had been as governor of the Cape Colony, where Campbell originated.[19]

The Macleays and the Dumaresqs had known each other a little in England, but became entwined through official and social networks as well as marriage, in New South Wales. The Dumaresqs, too, had a range of connections to points around the empire and in Europe. In January 1826, for example, the Dumaresq brothers seem to have engaged in a commercial venture of selling rice to Mauritius—though it is unclear if the scheme came to fruition; no doubt this must have involved Henry making use of his connections there, having left only a few months previously.[20]

CONNECTIONS TO OTHER GLOBAL SITES

From even before her arrival in Sydney in 1826 until her premature death in 1836 Fanny (Frances Leonora) Macleay, eldest daughter of New South Wales Colonial Secretary Alexander Macleay, maintained regular correspondence with her older brother William Sharp Macleay, who was stationed in Havana, Cuba, as British Commissioner of Arbitration to the Mixed British and Spanish Court for the Abolition of the Slave Trade. William took up this post at the same time as the Macleay parents and daughters sailed for Sydney; and in 1830 he would take another position in Havana as a judge. Eventually in 1839, William would settle in

[16] Letter from Fanny Macleay, 23 February 1831, ML A4301 [microfilm CY 1012] Papers of William Sharp Macleay, Macarthur Papers, Mitchell Library.

[17] Letter from Fanny to William 27 April 1831, ML A4301 [microfilm CY 1012] Papers of William Sharp Macleay, Macarthur Papers, Mitchell Library.

[18] Earnshaw and Hughes (eds), *Fanny to William*, p. 73.

[19] Elizabeth Windschuttle, *Taste and Science: The Women of the Macleay Family* (Glebe: Historic Houses Trust of New South Wales, 1988), p. 20.

[20] Govt. House 9th January 1826 [Letter addressed to Edward Dumaresq, Surveyor General, Van Diemen's Land] NS953/1/315 Letters to Edward Dumaresq from Henry Dumaresq between Jan. 1819 and Jan. 1838. Tasmanian Archives, Correspondence and Associated Papers of the Dumaresq, Darling, and Boissier Families.

Sydney—something Fanny had badly wanted, but which did not happen while she was alive. William would later acquire the imposing Elizabeth Bay House built by his parents through a financial settlement with his father (to whom he had lent money) and in Sydney would pursue his long-standing natural history research. Fanny's interest in Cuba, because of William, was gratified when the family first reached Sydney in January 1826: 'I am happy to find from many Persons that Cuba is a lovely Island because my beloved Brother will so much enjoy its richness'.[21] This cosmopolitan knowledge circulating in Sydney was confirmed in June 1826, when Fanny 'took tea with our next neighbour Mrs Forbes, the wife of our Chief Justice who gave me a most charming account of Cuba . . . Mrs Forbes is a native of Jamaica'.[22] Presumably Mrs Forbes was from the white colonial community of Jamaica, but it is unclear. She convinced Fanny that Havana was a fine place for William, not only a beautiful but a relatively healthy part of the Caribbean, and with a social 'gaiety . . . [that was] all but overwhelming'.[23]

Fanny's own exposure to the Americas had occurred when their ship stopped at Rio de Janeiro on its route to Australia. She liked Rio very much, repeatedly commenting on its natural beauty. She observed and commented on the system of slavery and the racial mix (noting that the ratio of black to white was nine to one), but was not at all offended by any of the subordination of the black population. The Macleays were lent the house of a local doctor for their stay; Fanny commented: 'We are here in ye midst of 40 slaves who speak no english— What scenes we have'. Despite noting the arrival of a slave ship, and the system in which even poor people would buy slaves and then rent them out as workers for their own profit, Fanny thought: 'the Slaves here seem as idle, as thoughtlessly happy, and as well fed as one could [sic] to see any persons'.[24] Such an acceptance of slavery and racial hierarchy was widely shared by other Europeans of her day, and in keeping with her own political conservatism, the political leanings of the Macleay family.

As well as her own observations on the voyage and her correspondence with William, Fanny had a well-established cosmopolitan sense of the world through her engagement with natural history. Her father Alexander Macleay was one of the eminent naturalists of his day, an entomologist and botanist, secretary of the Linnean Society, and a Fellow of the Royal Society in recognition of his scientific work. His eldest son William Sharp Macleay followed in his father's footsteps with his own research and publication in various fields of natural history, and also became a Fellow of the Royal Society. As a woman, Fanny was to some extent excluded from participation as a research scientist in her own right, but she, too, studied natural history, having access to her father's exceptional library and collection, and met and conversed with the leading scientists who regularly visited her

[21] Earnshaw and Hughes (eds), *Fanny to William*, p. 49.
[22] Letter from Fanny to William 12 June 1826. Earnshaw and Hughes (eds), *Fanny to William*, p. 57.
[23] Earnshaw and Hughes (eds), *Fanny to William*, p. 57.
[24] Earnshaw and Hughes (eds), *Fanny to William*, pp. 47–8.

Fig. 1.2 Robert M. Westmacott, 'From Sydney Cove, Government House with Harbour, New South Wales', 1840–46.
National Library of Australia, an3678265.

father. A long-term friend and correspondent of Fanny was Robert Brown (1773–1858), the botanist who made his name through his work on the voyages of Matthew Flinders (1774–1814), the naval officer who circumnavigated Australia and charted much of its coastline. In fact, in 1814 Brown wished to marry her, but she and her family declined the offer. Fanny assisted her father in the tasks of collecting, sorting, recording, drawing, displaying, and packaging specimens that were integral to his exchanges with scientific colleagues in Britain and around the world. Moreover, Fanny made her own significant contributions to the field, particularly through her illustrations. Fanny received training in drawing and painting as part of her education in London, and was sufficiently talented that several of her works were exhibited at the Royal Academy while she was in her twenties, before the family left for Australia. Her skill at scientific illustration was noticed by scientists beyond her father and brother, for some of whom she drew specimens.[25]

Fanny Macleay's global intellectual span, based on her natural history knowledge and circles, continued in Sydney. In December 1826, for example, she was delighted by the visit to Sydney of a group of French naturalists aboard the *Astrolabe*, which was on a lengthy voyage of discovery in the Pacific. (See Fig. 1.2.) This group included French naturalists Joseph Gaimard (1796–1858) and Louis de Freycinet (1779–1841); Gaimard lent Alexander Macleay his latest

---

[25] Windschuttle, *Taste and Science*, pp. 47–61.

book and Fanny read it too. By the time their ship embarked, Gaimard had given her some poetry books, and she had returned the favour with her drawing of a dolphin that he had evidently admired.[26] She apparently knew Italian and a little French. In Sydney she revealed some interest in Spanish, no doubt because of William's location in Cuba. She tells William that she can read the Spanish books he had given her, and had contemplated buying more; she notes that Henry Dumaresq speaks Spanish well, and that it had crossed her mind she could practise with him, but that she felt nervous about that idea—perhaps because of the seeming expectation of family members on both sides that something more might develop between them.[27]

In Sydney, Fanny maintained her connections with the world of natural historians, collecting and sending Australian specimens to England, receiving specimens from others as well as engaging in scientific discourse with William. From her correspondence with William, Fanny learned various things about the world, such as the frequency of shipwrecks, and the fact that all their mail passed through London. From their widely separated global locations, Fanny and William both read the English newspapers. In her letters Fanny mentions several news items, to which William replied a little snidely that he gets the papers too, so she need not bother—even though her letters included a great deal of detail on New South Wales politics. (Eliza Darling complained that in Mauritius, they got their news from India.) She must also have learnt miscellaneous matters of imperial politics, geography, and economics from the naval and military officers who regularly called at their house, and constituted much of the social world she and her sisters encountered at events such as parties at Government House. Soon after their arrival in Sydney, Fanny commented approvingly on the 'vast number of strangers visiting Sydney', which was at the time a significant port and entrepôt for the imperial and maritime worlds of the southern oceans, India, and South East Asia.[28]

She became acquainted with a Miss Wollstonecraft and her brother who were residents of Sydney's North Shore, and relations of Mary Wollstonecraft (1759–97); Fanny visited them and found Miss Wollstonecraft to be a 'very clever person' who had been brought up in France.[29] Fanny Macleay was an intellectual, very well educated by the standards of women's education in her day, and perhaps she was something of an intellectual snob. Certainly, she was privileged and part of Sydney's small elite. At the same time, her overtly privileged status was materially undercut by the realities of her daily life. Typically for the time, Fanny was financially dependent on her parents. As the eldest daughter of a family of ten surviving children, and even though her mother outlived her, Fanny's responsibilities included management of their constantly cash-strapped household. Alexander was continually in debt due to his incurable habit of buying natural history specimens he could not afford, as well as his desire to live life on a grand scale.

---

[26] Windschuttle, *Taste and Science*, pp. 62–63.
[27] Earnshaw and Hughes (eds), *Fanny to William*, p. 67.
[28] Windschuttle, *Taste and Science*, p. 12.
[29] Earnshaw and Hughes (eds), *Fanny to William*, pp. 70–1.

Fanny spent a great deal of her time nursing other family members, as well as, along with her sisters, sewing most of their own clothes. For years, she devoted a portion of her time to running and teaching at Sydney's Female School of Industry, a school for educating poor girls that was both a well-meaning charitable institution and a maternalistic training school for domestic servants, begun by Eliza Darling. At once an earnest Christian and a scientific illustrator, Fanny Macleay embodied many of the contradictions of her class and her times. One of those contradictions was that while she was bound to Sydney through her role as dutiful daughter, through Fanny Macleay we can see how settlers in 1820s and 1830s New South Wales understood themselves within the wider world, connected to diverse sites that were at once part of European imperial systems.

MILITARY MEN AS SETTLERS AND PASTORALISTS

The Dumaresq brothers exemplify the sizeable number of army and navy officers who became settlers in the Australian colonies, many of whom took advantage of an offer from the colonial government of converting their half-pay army retirement pension into a land grant. Not always automatic, this offer was at its peak from 1826 to 1831, after which time it involved the purchase of land with concessions depending on length of military service. Henry Dumaresq arrived in New South Wales directly from Mauritius, ahead of the rest of the Darling-Dumaresq family group; he overlapped for six weeks with the previous governor, Brisbane, whom he had known during his military service in Canada.[30] Henry and William Dumaresq had both served as officers in the Peninsular Wars against Napoleon, then in Canada against the Americans in the war of 1812, where William worked on the construction of the Ottawa canal. Henry was later badly wounded at Waterloo—an injury that would result in his premature death in 1838. The Dumaresqs' service in the Peninsular Wars placed them in the category of imperial official whom Zoe Laidlaw has discussed, those who forged tight networks during that difficult military campaign, networks that later expanded across the empire, and that helped to promote individual careers and opportunities.[31]

Even before Sir Ralph was appointed and the Darlings and Dumaresqs sailed to New South Wales in 1825, there seemed to be a family plan of settling there. In 1823 Eliza Darling in England wrote to Henry in Mauritius: 'Mother turns sick at the thoughts of Bottomhouse Bay & your turning wool merchant'.[32] The Dumaresq siblings hoped that they might all, including their mother, settle in New South Wales in some sort of family enclave. Eliza's fantasies stretched to imagining the siblings all having land grants in the same vicinity, living close to each other, and

---

[30] Brian H. Fletcher, *Ralph Darling—A Governor Maligned* (Melbourne: Oxford University Press, 1984), p. 79.

[31] Laidlaw, *Colonial Connections, 1815–45*.

[32] Letters from Eliza Darling to her brother Henry Dumaresq. NS953/31 Tasmanian Archives, Correspondence, and Associated Papers of the Dumaresq, Darling, and Boissier Families.

having their own handpicked Church of England pastor ministering to their religious needs—a veritable gentry pastoral vision transplanted onto a settler setting. But their mother never went; Eliza's hopes of returning to New South Wales and obtaining a land grant after her husband Ralph Darling was recalled to England were never fulfilled, though at least one of her sons returned. Several years after the Darlings returned to England, Ralph Darling continued to seek interviews with Lord Glenelg to ask him for the land grant in New South Wales which he supposedly had been promised. Eliza wrote in a letter that she was anxious about this land grant, 'looking forward as I have often said, to the probability of one if not all the Boys, wishing eventually to settle in Australia'.[33] But the Darlings never received such a grant.

Nevertheless, Eliza Darling's brothers all became long-term settlers. Henry received a land grant which Sir Ralph Darling helped to negotiate for him; as early as December 1825 he proudly announced to younger brother Edward: 'I am already the possessor of Blocks, and purpose to be the Proprietor of 10,000 Acres of land—this is a Noble Country'.[34] In 1829 brother William began to consider stepping down to half his army pay, in the hope that several years later he could, according to new regulations, retire from the army altogether, sell his commission, and obtain a land grant.[35] Both Henry and William Dumaresq became large landholders in the upper Hunter Valley (at Muswellbrook and Scone) and at Port Stephens. These two older Dumaresq brothers would also acquire large land holdings in New England, their big pastoral stock runs called Saumarez and Tilbuster; in fact, they were among the first settlers of the Armidale district in the mid-1830s, who, according to historian John Ferry, used brutal and lethal force against Aboriginal people.[36] Henry Dumaresq named his property Saumarez in honour of the Dumaresq family's ancestral estate on the island of Jersey in the English Channel, while William named his after Tilbuster Lodge, the Macleays' property in Surrey (his wife's family home).[37]

Henry Dumaresq was praised by John Dunmore Lang as a fair and progressive master of convict labourers. He was also praised on the same grounds by Edward John Eyre—in historical hindsight, perhaps a more dubious commendation. Yet the Dumaresq brothers' preparedness to use brute violence against Aboriginal people is telling. The brothers' long-term military service across multiple imperial sites provides significant background for this violence; their participation in multiple

[33] Letter from Eliza Darling to her brother Henry Dumaresq 2 October 1835. NS953/31 Tasmanian Archives, Correspondence, and Associated Papers of the Dumaresq, Darling, and Boissier Families.

[34] Letters to Edward Dumaresq from Henry Dumaresq between Jan. 1819 and Jan. 1838, NS953/1/315. Letter from Sydney 22 December 1825 to Edward in Hobart Town. Tasmanian Archives, Correspondence, and Associated Papers of the Dumaresq, Darling, and Boissier Families.

[35] Letter 12 February 1829 NS953/1/315 Letters to Edward Dumaresq from Henry Dumaresq between Jan. 1819 and Jan. 1838. Tasmanian Archives, Correspondence, and Associated Papers of the Dumaresq, Darling, and Boissier Families.

[36] John Ferry, *Colonial Armidale* (St Lucia, Queensland: University of Queensland Press, 1999), Ch. 2.

[37] Ferry, *Colonial Armidale*, pp. 2–3.

wars, exposure to the dispossession of indigenous people in North America, and in Henry's case, his administration of enslaved people in Mauritius, must all have helped to shape this willingness to use force in order to obtain the lands that might become the proximate estates of the envisioned extended family pastoral idyll.

The youngest Dumaresq brother, Edward, served in the East India Company Army for six years (from 1818 to 1824) in the Bombay Native Infantry, working on the topographical survey of Gujarat and learning Hindustani. In 1824 Edward took medical leave from India, sailing first to Van Diemen's Land and New South Wales, before returning to England. In 1825 he arrived in Australia with the family party, which stopped in Van Diemen's Land for Darling to oversee its administrative separation from New South Wales. Darling remained Governor of Van Diemen's Land and left Lieutenant Governor George Arthur in charge. Edward Dumaresq decided to stay and indeed lived there the rest of his long life (he lived until 1906)—he held official posts (including surveyor-general and later a justice of the peace) and became a settler, landowner, and master of convicts.

Soon after his arrival in Van Diemen's Land, Edward entered into negotiations with the East India Company to obtain half-pay retirement on the basis of his six years' service, and his having been forced to quit India due to ill health caused by the Indian climate and the nature of his work on the topographical survey. His case did not quite fit the rules, partly because his promotion to captain did not occur within twelve months of his three years' medical leave to England being granted. The Company wanted him to return to Bombay in order to assess his case. Edward based his argument for special consideration on the fact that the Australian colonies were within the East India Company's charter. Ironically, in March 1828 in correspondence to the East India Company making the case for his half-pay retirement, Edward claims: 'For the injury my health and constitution have thereby sustained has not only destroyed my very flattering prospects in the Company's service in India, but, has since prevented my obtaining other advantageous employment elsewhere that would have rendered me independent of the half pay of my rank'.[38] Such a claim about his reduced health is ironic in historical hindsight, given Edward's subsequent vigorous career as a surveyor, landowner, and pastoralist, and his living to the age of 104! But Edward's petition for his half-pay retirement, which appears from the record to have succeeded, is a pertinent illustration of the significance of army pensions in facilitating the settlement of Indian Army officers in Australia.

Fanny's sister Susan Macleay married William Dumaresq: in her letters to her brother, Fanny describes William as very sensible and honourable, if not very talented.[39] (Fanny herself may have had something of a flirtation with Henry.) William had served in the army and been trained as a military surveyor and engineer.

[38] Letter from Edward Dumaresq, Hobart, Van Diemen's Land, 31 March 1828, to the Adjutant General of the Bombay Army, Bombay. NS953/1/395 Tasmanian Archives, Correspondence, and Associated Papers of the Dumaresq, Darling, and Boissier Families.

[39] ML A4301 [microfilm CY 1012] Papers of William Sharp Macleay, Macarthur Papers, Mitchell Library.

He had hoped to be assigned to Mauritius when Henry (who had also been a military engineer) was there, but that did not happen. Nevertheless, he arrived in Sydney soon after Henry and the Darlings took up office. Governor Darling gave William a job as surveyor; in 1826 he was 'Inspector of Roads and Bridges'. Later Darling also employed Henry Dumaresq's new wife's [Sophie Butler-Danvers] cousin as military secretary—Charles Sturt, who would make his name in exploration.

It was not a coincidence that William and Edward Dumaresq were both employed as surveyors, William in New South Wales and Edward in Van Diemen's Land. Both men had military surveying experience and they arrived at a time when settlement was expanding rapidly in both colonies and the rules for land grants and sales were being codified. In April 1827 the Colonial Office issued from Downing Street a memorandum entitled 'Terms upon which Land is granted to Settlers in New South Wales and Van Diemen's Land'. Directed at 'persons proceeding to New South Wales and Van Diemen's Land, as Settlers', the memorandum noted that the land in both colonies was currently being divided into parishes and counties and being evaluated; an average price would be fixed and land put up for sale. Meanwhile, settlers wishing to purchase or obtain land by grant could choose the land they wished and apply for it; land could be purchased with a deposit of ten per cent with the rest to be paid half yearly by promissory notes under terms agreed on by the governor; land would generally be sold in lots of three square miles or 1,920 acres, and the largest sale would be 9,600 acres; anyone wishing a larger lot could apply to the Secretary of State in writing; and anyone wishing to obtain land by grant rather than purchase could apply to the Colonial Secretary. In this last kind of case, the applicant's character and respectability would be assessed, along with their capital, which was to include stock, 'implements of husbandry' and any half-pay or pension that the applicant received from the government—a direct reference to the case of army officers on half-pay pensions. It was expected that the applicant would have 'the power of expending in the cultivation of the Lands, a Capital equal to <u>one fourth</u> part of their estimated value at the least'. When the governor was satisfied with the applicant's character and capital, the applicant would be referred to the surveyor-general, who would authorize him to proceed in search of land. Once the settler had chosen the land he desired, he was to inform the surveyor-general, and await the governor's approval.

The smallest such grant to any 'fresh settler' would be 320 acres; the largest 2,560 acres. The rule of thumb was for the grant to be 'one Square Mile or 640 Acres, for every £500 Sterling of Capital which the applicant can immediately command'. Every settler receiving such a grant had to prove to the surveyor-general, within seven years, that he had expended one fourth of the land's value on its cultivation and improvement or forfeit the land. Moreover, settlers were required to reside on their land grants, or otherwise to employ 'on the spot . . . a free Man, of approved Character and respectability'.[40] This was the system in

---

[40] NS953/1/399 Edward Dumaresq—Indian Service—terms upon which land is granted to settlers in NSW and VDL. Tasmanian Archives, Correspondence, and Associated Papers of the Dumaresq, Darling, and Boissier Families.

which the Dumaresq brothers participated as surveyors, and from which they benefitted with land grants and purchases, all becoming major landholders. In April 1827, the month that the Colonial Office issued this memorandum, Edward told Henry he had just found a land grant for himself—presumably what would become his property at New Norfolk.

The expansion of pastoralism in the period from the 1820s was driven partly by settler family connections and cooperation, such as is evident within the Macleay family with younger son George Macleay taking responsibility for the family's first farm. David Denholm's research on squatting in this period reveals the ways in which familial relationships flowed into the nature of pastoralism:

> Beyond the boundaries [of settlement] was a land where owners, and owners' sons, and squatting partners, were forever in motion, taking over the superintendence here, giving it back there, helping, inspecting, overlanding, quarrelling over boundary disputes, building, and sometimes indulging in a little exploration of new country.[41]

The relatively easy cooperation among family members, as well as the dependence of sons on fathers, assisted the process in which pastoral holdings were expanded and thus the frontier extended. Family networks also helped settlers by facilitating the borrowing of money to buy land; land grants could be augmented with purchases, and profits made through land sales—though there were restrictions on how soon land grants could be sold.

The three Dumaresq brothers discussed strategies for land management—by correspondence with Edward, presumably in direct conversations between Henry and William. Their discussions canvassed financial strategies for purchasing land; when to give up their public employment, when and whether to attempt to sell their army commissions and pensions in order to settle full-time on their estates; how much land was optimal, when to lease it out, when and how much to spend on developing it, and how to use agents. Henry, as the eldest and the first to obtain land, often took the lead in doling out advice, yet admitting his mistakes, and hoping his brothers could learn from them.

Edward Dumaresq, as the youngest of the family, was the recipient of family favours, though also of copious advice. Henry, as the eldest brother (and perhaps because their father was dead), wrote to Edward frequently, dispensing advice on Edward's career, health, and proper manly behaviour. Such letters between New South Wales and Van Diemen's Land were a continuation of earlier brotherly correspondence. For example, in 1819 Henry, in Mauritius, wrote to Edward who had recently been sent by the army to Bombay. Henry advised Edward to keep up his Persian, to keep an eye on opportunities for promotion, to observe medical advice about living in the tropics, to behave in a respectable and moral fashion (he explicitly mentions drinking, and implicitly what it may lead to), and to be picky about the company he keeps—to which last injunction Henry added the name of

---

[41] Denholm, 'Some Aspects of Squatting', p. 61.

one officer Edward was specifically to avoid.[42] In later years, Henry advised Edward to keep up his writing (which Henry claimed 'would not have disgraced the Pen of Addison or Cowper'[43]), and praised his official reports as a surveyor. He also offered to send him sheep, lent him money, and repeatedly gave Edward advice on marriage, religion, and his career, including ambiguous advice about whether or not to return to India from Van Diemen's Land: on the one hand disparaging 'John Company', on the other suggesting that the promotion Edward would receive was desirable.[44]

Edward also turned to his brothers-in-law for assistance. In 1837, for instance, he wrote to both Sir Ralph Darling, now retired in England, and his other brother-in-law the Rev. Boissier, also in England. Only the return letters survive; it seems that Edward requested a loan of £2,000 in order to pay off a mortgage on some land; his Boissier brother-in-law agreed to lend it to him at an interest rate of six per cent. Not only the two brothers-in-law but also Edward's sisters Eliza and Marianne had participated in the family discussion; the sisters had agreed Edward should have the loan, but decided not to tell their mother. Ralph Darling, in conveying to Edward the news of the loan, took the opportunity also to chastise him for not managing his affairs better, commenting that he saw from the *Hobart Town Courier* that a certain Sir George had managed his estates much better than Edward, selling them for a good profit before being sent by the government to Upper Canada. Darling also offered advice to Edward on his farming practices, particularly that he should recover control of his own original farm rather than rent it out. He rubs this in with the further comment on appropriate manly behaviour:

> Whenever I am asked as to people going out as Settlers, I invariably say, it depends entirely on the Character of the Individual—and that one man would do more with one thousand pounds than another would with £5000—To succeed in Australia as a Settler, a man must put his Shoulder to the Wheel and make up his mind to rough it and be content with hard fare—but I need not tell you this.

Seemingly to leaven the dose of criticism and advice, Darling adds: 'Never mind, you are young enough to overcome all these mistakes'.[45]

---

[42] NS953/1/315 Letters to Edward Dumaresq from Henry Dumaresq between Jan. 1819 and Jan. 1838. Letter from Henry in Mauritius addressed to Edward in Bombay 25 August 1819. Tasmanian Archives, Correspondence, and Associated Papers of the Dumaresq, Darling, and Boissier Families.

[43] NS953/1/315 Letters to Edward Dumaresq from Henry Dumaresq between Jan. 1819 and Jan. 1838. Letter from Sydney 22 December 1825 to Edward in Hobart Town. Tasmanian Archives, Correspondence, and Associated Papers of the Dumaresq, Darling, and Boissier Families.

[44] Letter from Henry to Edward dated 18 Jan. 1826. NS953/1/315 Letters to Edward Dumaresq from Henry Dumaresq between Jan. 1819 and Jan. 1838. Tasmanian Archives, Correspondence, and Associated Papers of the Dumaresq, Darling, and Boissier Families.

[45] NS953/1/310 Letter to Edward Dumaresq [in VDL] from Sir Ralph Darling, Cheltenham, 7–8 December 1837. Tasmanian Archives, Correspondence, and Associated Papers of the Dumaresq, Darling, and Boissier Families.

RACIAL THINKING AND IMPERIAL CONNECTIONS

This interconnected network of settler families reflects the extensive experience and knowledge Australian settlers had of global systems of unfree labour and racial hierarchies—knowledge on which they drew in shaping settler society in the southern colonies. Henry Dumaresq, who served as Governor Ralph Darling's private secretary in Sydney in the 1820s, had previously served under Darling in Mauritius, where they ruled over a mixed-race workforce including slaves and convicts. Darling's own previous military career had included seventeen years in the West Indies (including Grenada, Barbados, and Martinique), and two years in India. In New South Wales, Darling's administration of soldiers and convicts included the infamous death of Private Sudds—one of the issues that provoked criticism of Darling as harsh and later led to calls for him to be dismissed. In 1826 Darling determined to stamp out the practice among some soldiers of the Sydney garrison to commit offences that would lead them to be discharged, even if by being sentenced as convicts. When the trial of Privates Joseph Sudds and Patrick Thompson for theft resulted in their sentencing to transportation for seven years, Darling commuted it to seven years of hard labour in chain-gangs—a commutation that proved illegal for him to enact. Then not only were Sudds and Thompson forced to parade publicly with iron collars around their necks attached to leg irons by chains, but a few days later Sudds died—probably of unrelated causes but it exacerbated the whole affair. The incident sparked much public criticism of Darling.[46]

Despite Henry Dumaresq's prior position in the slave colony of Mauritius, he expressed pity for the Indian sailors—*lascars*—who worked the Indian Ocean routes, particularly their physical hardship in adapting to cold weather:

> To see the poor Devil blowing into his frosty fists with an icicle hanging to his Nose and . . . to see him Buttoning himself up—and rounding his back and pushing up his shoulders to keep his neck warm—By G-d it is enough to melt the heart of a stone—& I do not know that I ever pitied poor Beggars more in my life than the wretched Lascars who manned our Ship coming from the Mauritius here—In fact, we stand their heat better than they stand our cold.[47]

Such pity, however, was not in evidence towards Aboriginal people in either New South Wales or Van Diemen's Land. While I have not yet found any trace in the Dumaresq family correspondence of the brothers' views on the frontier violence in which they engaged in the Armidale region, Henry was forthcoming in his advice to Edward on the Black War (as the war against Aboriginal people was called there) in Van Diemen's Land, in which Edward participated. On 4 December 1830 he wrote in response to a letter from Edward:

[46] 'Darling, Sir Ralph (1772–1858)', *Australian Dictionary of Biography*, Vol. 1 (Melbourne University Press, 1966), pp. 282–6.

[47] Letter dated 21 March 1826. NS953/1/315 Letters to Edward Dumaresq from Henry Dumaresq between Jan. 1819 and Jan. 1838. Tasmanian Archives, Correspondence, and Associated Papers of the Dumaresq, Darling, and Boissier Families.

I am quite sorry to learn that your operations against the Black Natives have been ineffectual.—It has been right however, to make the efforts which have been made, and the plan of operations seemed as far as I could judge of it, to have been very well conceived.—I never, however, had any opinion, that a Cordon drawn round certain Districts, wd. have the effect of enclosing its inhabitants one moment longer than they chose.—A similar proposition was made, in order to catch our Bushrangers, but I convinced the Govr. that it would be ineffectual.—But it is proper that whatever means were judged best, should have been adopted to lay hold of your Hostile Tribes, and activity, zeal and constancy seem to have been displayed in carrying Col. Arthur's projects into effect—Having done his best, and who can do more, I would now, endeavour to Extirpate the Enemy, or I do not see how people are to be found who will venture into the Country.[48]

Perhaps this commentary on Van Diemen's Land casts oblique light on Henry Dumaresq's own behaviour in New South Wales.

These same family networks, though, belie any simple assumptions about settlers' racial views and social hierarchies. In 1836, only six weeks before her premature death, Fanny Macleay, daughter of New South Wales Colonial Secretary Alexander Macleay, married Thomas Cudbert Harington, her father's long-term valued assistant—a marriage of which at least one of her brothers, George, disapproved because Harington was 'a half-caste Indian'.[49] In his letter to William, seemingly to break the news of Fanny's marriage, George gave Harington a decidedly mixed assessment:

Harington is a clever honourable and most agreeable person respected by all who know him—a sincere [Christian?] & trustworthy man—yet as a half-caste Indian person—of little common sense—and a visionary—not qualified to make his way in the world or to possess [. . . ?]—he is moreover in debt & not too scrupulous and peculiar in his notions [. . . ?] to be any other than a poor man—Fanny who has lived the best part of her life in the enjoyment of all kinds of comforts—is not the person in my opinion to submit to the inconvenience of poverty in a 'Cottage'—and yet retain 'Love' or content. However it cannot be helped—at least I cannot help them further or prevent it—It perhaps may be all for the best.[50]

Perhaps the most patronizing part of George's brotherly disapproval towards Fanny's marriage was the comment that: 'There is one thing that I am very certain of—that women should marry young—if they can—for they can't expect good matches when old'.[51] Fanny was forty-two years old when she married Harington. George's concession that it 'perhaps may be all for the best' would remain untried, given the tragic brevity of the marriage. (See Fig. 1.3.)

---

[48] Letter dated 4 December 1830. NS953/1/315 Letters to Edward Dumaresq from Henry Dumaresq between Jan. 1819 and Jan. 1838. Tasmanian Archives, Correspondence, and Associated Papers of the Dumaresq, Darling, and Boissier Families.
[49] Windschuttle, *Taste and Science*, p. 22.
[50] Letter from George Macleay to William Sharp Macleay, 1836. ML A4303, Macleay Family Letters 1834–40, Macarthur Family Papers [CY2388], Mitchell Library.
[51] Letter from George Macleay to William Sharp Macleay, 1836.

Fig. 1.3 Colonial Secretary's House, Bridge Street, Sydney, 1826–1830. Artists Frances Leonora Macleay and Gerard Krefft.

State Library of New South Wales, PXA 707/2 Digital a965001.

The fact that Fanny herself and other family members did not comment on Harington being mixed-race raises an interesting question about how common non-white and mixed-race people were in the Australian colonies in these decades. It is well known, for example, that Colonel William Light who successfully surveyed the city of Adelaide during the foundation of South Australia had been born in Malaya to an English father and Eurasian mother who was probably part-Portuguese.[52] (Light was yet another of the Peninsular War veterans to come to the Australian colonies.) In her last letter to William before both her marriage and her terminal illness, Fanny does raise the issue of race in an elliptical way, in the context of commenting on remarks William seems to have made comparing Spanish, English, and Australian women. In her wandering and humorous response to these comparisons and William's views, Fanny alludes to the possibility that William might choose to marry a Spanish woman of colour:

> I fancy you must wait until you see *our Dames* ere you become quite *charmed*—unless, which is not improbable, some Spanish—I was going to write *fair*—what a mistake!— *brown* may have taught you to say 'Te Amo'—Well, I will love her for *Your* sake—if so it be—but you must bring her here with you . . . Come-Come-Come!![53]

---

[52] See, for example, Thomas Gill, *A Biographical Sketch of Colonel William Light, The Founder of Adelaide and the First Surveyor-General of the Province of South Australia* (Adelaide: Royal Geographical Society of Australia, SA Branch, 1911), Ch. 1.

[53] Earnshaw and Hughes (eds), *Fanny to William*, p. 176.

It is as though Fanny was indirectly telling William that her own fiancé was 'brown', and asking William to love him anyway for Fanny's sake. Indeed, in a postscript to the letter, Fanny exhorted William on exactly this point: 'I wish that you *knew* and *loved my Husband*—that is to be I hope! You must love him, my dearest Brother, already he feels affection for you—if he did not I would say nothing to him'.[54]

There is corroborating evidence that Thomas Cudbert Harington was of mixed English and Indian parentage. He was born in India in 1798, son of John Herbert Harington, an Orientalist scholar and translator from Persian, who worked for the East India Company and served on both the Supreme Court of Calcutta and the Supreme Council of Bengal. The senior Harington's only recorded marriage was in 1808 to Amelia Johnston, with whom he had five children.[55] His son Thomas seems therefore to have been born out of wedlock, a not uncommon aspect of British colonial society in India, yet he received an education that fitted him for the legal profession. Perhaps it was the awkwardness of his being extraneous to his father's legitimate family that led him to decide to migrate from Calcutta to Sydney in 1820 at the age of twenty-two. There is no evidence either that he returned to India or that his father visited Sydney. When Harington arrived in Sydney he received a land grant from Governor Macquarie and in 1822 became a clerk in the Commissariat Department. In 1825 he was appointed as a magistrate and worked for the new and expanding Australian Agricultural Company (with which Henry Dumaresq would later be involved).[56] In 1826 he was appointed as Assistant Colonial Secretary to Alexander Macleay, in which capacity Fanny met him. When she first encountered Harington in 1826, she described him as 'a person of great abilities and excellent principle'.[57] Perhaps, in 1830s Sydney, it took a woman of such determination, moral conviction, and self-possession as Fanny seems to have been, to marry a man of mixed English and Indian parentage.

If she may have been relatively open-minded on questions of race, Fanny was not a radical. Her elitism was clear enough in comments she made in 1831 about assigned convicts on her brother-in-law William Dumaresq's pastoral property, where she spent some months to keep her sister company. She objected to a new tax on assigned convicts, saying that their 'masters' would not be able to afford sufficient labour. Referring to the convicts, she wrote to her brother William in Cuba: 'the animals are so little interested in their work having nothing to gain or lose by industry or the lack of it that they would sicken you to see them at their work—They just perform enough to escape the lash and no more—I should

---

[54] Earnshaw and Hughes (eds), *Fanny to William*, pp. 176–7.

[55] 'Harington, John Herbert (1764/5–1828)', entry in *Oxford Dictionary of National Biography* (Oxford University Press, 2004–13) http://www.oxforddnb.com.virtual.anu.edu.au/view/article/12329, accessed 4 October 2013.

[56] Arthur McMartin, 'Harington, Thomas Cudbert (1798–1863)', *Australian Dictionary of Biography*, National Centre of Biography, Australian National University, http://adb.anu.edu.au/biography/harington-thomas-cudbert-2155/text2753, accessed 4 October 2013.

[57] Earnshaw and Hughes (eds), *Fanny to William*, p. 56.

suppose that your Negroes are as active as these fallen sons of Great Britain'.[58] Earlier, she had complained bitterly about the convict workers assigned to renovate the Macleay residence; some had used the opportunity to steal some of the family silverware. Theft, she contended, was a common occurrence when convict workers were around the house.

Fanny Macleay's exposure to convicts had begun on the voyage to Sydney: the *Marquis of Hastings* on which the Macleay family had departed Portsmouth in August 1825 had 152 male convicts on board.[59] Her condescension was not restricted to convicts. In May 1826 she commented in a letter to William: 'The lower orders of the community make money very quickly they do not therefore know the value of money and are inclined to squander it away to please any idle fancy which may arise in their pates'.[60] Emancipated convicts she found particularly challenging, calling them 'the most impudent independent creatures you can imagine—quite Yankies & as idle as Negroes'.[61] Yet her views on frontier violence were relatively humane for her day. Reporting in September 1826 that there had been 'sad accounts' of several 'Settlers' killed by 'Natives' on 'Hunter's River', she observed: 'Poor wretches they are really forced to commit these crimes tho' [sic] hunger & shameful treatment from the up country settlers who are anxious (from sordid motives) that they (the Blacks) should be all exterminated'.[62]

Eliza Darling's letters also provide insight into contemporary racial views, rather less sympathetically. In Mauritius, Darling complains that her infant daughter's complexion has deteriorated: 'She is as yellow "almost not quite," as the Mulatto Children'.[63] On the point of returning to England in 1823, Eliza refers to 'the introduction of her little Creoles to a northern atmosphere'—an interesting application of the word 'creole' often associated with the Caribbean, reflecting a pragmatic view of colonial difference.[64] In 1823 letters after she returned to England, back to her brother Henry still in Mauritius, Eliza refers to Mauritius as a 'barbarous place' and complains bitterly about a servant (probably non-white) whom she had brought back to England, who had been 'one of the best' she had in Mauritius, but fell far short of her standards. She tells Henry that she has developed a plan for education of the children of the government slaves at Mauritius that she can send him: she thinks the boys should be employed breaking stones for MacAdam roads; reading should be absolutely forbidden except perhaps for a privileged few. Thus Darling enacted the role of lady philanthropist through her

[58] Letter from Fanny to William 21 July 1831, ML A4301 [microfilm CY 1012] Papers of William Sharp Macleay, Macarthur Papers, Mitchell Library.

[59] Earnshaw and Hughes (eds), *Fanny to William*, p. 41.

[60] Earnshaw and Hughes (eds), *Fanny to William*, p. 55.

[61] Earnshaw and Hughes (eds), *Fanny to William*, p. 70.

[62] Earnshaw and Hughes (eds), *Fanny to William*, p. 63.

[63] Letter from Eliza Darling to her brother Edward Dumaresq, 3 May 1821, NS953/1/30, Tasmanian Archives, Correspondence, and Associated Papers of the Dumaresq, Darling, and Boissier Families.

[64] NS953/1/315 Letters to Edward Dumaresq from Henry Dumaresq between Jan. 1819 and Jan. 1838. Tasmanian Archives, Correspondence, and Associated Papers of the Dumaresq, Darling, and Boissier Families.

expressed concern for the lower orders, laying out a social scheme in which the children of slaves would be firmly limited in their education and opportunities and restricted to hard manual labour. Eliza Darling's support for slavery is clear in her abhorrence of what she calls the frightful scenes in the West Indies and the talk of freeing the slaves. She says they are sending more troops in 'menofwars' to the West Indies; freeing the slaves can never be safely done except in such a manner as it is being done at the Cape.[65] The Darlings were avowed political conservatives, so such views are unsurprising, yet they show that some residents in 1820s and 1830s New South Wales openly supported slavery and systems of unfree labour elsewhere in the empire, views that would sit easily with the convict system and Aboriginal dispossession.

THE ROMANCE OF BEING A SETTLER

The correspondence among family members speaks to romantic contemporary understandings of being a settler: the dreams and visions of possessing these new territories, settlers' fantasies of placing their stamp on the new landscape, and the new lives such land ownership would enable. In 1826 Henry Dumaresq waxed lyrical in a letter to his youngest brother:

> I will . . . take some Line of unknown Country—in order that I may give it names according to my own fancy—I will connect it with scenes of other days, and baptize it after those I love; thus enlisting the local recollections . . . [of] our Homes, or other places where we have been happy, into the recesses of our adopted Country—You must know that this is rather a favourite vagary of mine—and Philosophers would certainly give it the preference over my first endeavours at fame—viz. "Cutting Foreign throats".[66]

Dumaresq's comparison between his violent actions in imperial wars and the supposedly more innocuous acts of naming his prospective new estate in New South Wales seemingly serves to sanitize the latter. Yet the very juxtaposition of the two, the possessing and naming of land he imagines as his, and the violence of his military past, at once raises the spectre he seeks to obscure, the violence necessary for such land to become his.

Henry's desires soon focused on particular sites, with him changing his preferences several times in the process of selecting his land grant and consulting both an agent and the surveyor-general. He also daydreamed about flocks of merino sheep in which he would invest any spare cash, and the bales of wool they would produce. Eventually he settled on a site on the Hunter River, the property he would call

---

[65] NS953/31 Letter from Eliza Darling to her brother Henry Dumaresq, 30 October 1823. Tasmanian Archives, Correspondence, and Associated Papers of the Dumaresq, Darling, and Boissier Families.

[66] Govt. House 9 January 1826, Letter addressed to Edward Dumaresq, Surveyor-General, Van Diemen's Land. NS953/1/315 Letters to Edward Dumaresq from Henry Dumaresq between Jan. 1819 and Jan. 1838. Tasmanian Archives, Correspondence, and Associated Papers of the Dumaresq, Darling, and Boissier Families.

St Heliers, which also commemorated the Dumaresq family connection to Jersey. In 1829, soon after his marriage and before he moved full-time to St Heliers, Henry's visit there gave rise to a highly romantic fantasy in which religion, the patriarchal family, and the prospects of being a settler all merged:

> I could not but remember with pleasure, the feelings of <u>happiness real happiness</u>, which attended my first tour to the Lands, destined for my children's children, as I thought, and some little of this joyous leaven was traceable, as I followed the beautiful Valley of St Heliers, & viewed my <u>Territory</u> from the Rocky Heights which bound it— I fancied myself as living there, and followed by my children, on little excursions of pleasure, to the [sensual?] romantic spots in the Neighbourhood; and I pictured to myself, the lasting and advantageous impressions which I might make on their Youthful minds by the lessons to be drawn from the scenes around us—I thought of the plan, embellished and arranged by the tasteful fingers or under the guidance of my dearest Wife, and I could fancy us, living for each other, for our Children and for our Merciful and bounteous Creator, more thoroughly and more acceptably, than 'in the busy haunts of Men'—and, if the World looks darkly on us, we will try what resources we have in the above means of Consolation and happiness.[67]

This was a vision of land ownership and financial independence on a scale well beyond Henry Dumaresq's reach in England, and which suggests the desires, ambitions, and fantasies at the heart of settler colonialism.

CONCLUSION: IMPERIAL CONNECTIONS, GENERATIONAL TIES, AND SETTLER COLONIALISM

This extended network of settler families spanned generations as well as continents. Henry and William Dumaresq had served in the army in the Peninsular and later wars against Napoleon, exemplifying the imperial networks of veterans from those wars, as well as in Canada. In 1838 Henry died at the relatively young age of forty-six, from effects of wounds he received at Waterloo. William outlived him by thirty years, and would acquire, as well as his large pastoral and agricultural estates, a house called Tivoli on Sydney Harbour at Rose Bay. William and his wife Susan sent two of their sons from New South Wales back to Britain to school, in Guernsey—from where they corresponded with their grandmother, and presumably visited relatives. Edward Dumaresq, whose military career had been in Bombay and Gujarat and thus differed from those of his older brothers, remained based in Tasmania for the rest of his remarkably long life. Following his early appointments as surveyor-general, and then police magistrate at New Norfolk, he turned to land speculation and farming; his growing investments in land came to include

---

[67] Letter 27 November 1829. NS953/1/315 Letters to Edward Dumaresq from Henry Dumaresq between Jan. 1819 and Jan. 1838. Tasmanian Archives, Correspondence, and Associated Papers of the Dumaresq, Darling, and Boissier Families.

property in Victoria and Queensland. Edward married twice; with his first wife Frances Legge he had four daughters and four sons.

The children of Sir Ralph and Lady Eliza Darling continued the pattern of imperial connections: their daughter Cornelia married Sir Francis Ford. Ford was a captain in the Bombay Regiment, which went to India in 1845; in October 1846 Cornelia and Sir Francis were married by Cornelia's brother the Rev. Frederick Darling. Cornelia sailed to India with Sir Francis after their marriage, but he died suddenly in November 1850. Cornelia returned to England with her six-month-old son. The family papers note that 'Augustus joined the Bengal Artillery and fought in the Punjab [sic] campaign of 1848, retiring on 1 August 1872 as an Honorary Lieutenant-Colonel. Sydney joined the 51st Regiment, then the 9th Regiment, serving in Malta, Van Diemen's Land, the Crimea and the West Indies, eventually rising to the rank of Major-General'.[68] At one point in his life Frederick, who chose the church rather than the military, visited relatives in the West Indies—returning to the setting of a large portion of his father's early military career. Additional to the imperial careers of Ralph and Eliza Darling's children were those of Sir Ralph's nephews, Charles and William, who were both officers in the army before first arriving in the Australian colonies in the 1820s.[69] In the 1860s Sir Charles Darling would become governor of Victoria, though in the meantime his career in imperial administration had taken him to the West Indies, Cape Colony, and Newfoundland.

Spanning several generations from the late eighteenth to the mid-nineteenth century, the Dumaresq, Darling, and Macleay network of settler families embodied connections between the Australian colonies, metropolitan Britain, India, Mauritius, the West Indies, Canada, the Iberian Peninsula, Malta, and Crimea, and first-hand knowledge of yet other locations. Their surviving correspondence reflects the large number of former British Army officers from India and elsewhere who settled in Australia, and the role of army and navy pensions and land grants in encouraging their settlement. From this family archive, we can see evidence of networking between army officers and its role in promoting settlement and colonial expansion, and thus glean a sense of military culture as a pervasive influence. Family records reveal the knowledge of other colonies and places around the globe that settlers in Australia acquired through their own experience, as well as connections and correspondence. Even the limited range of issues discussed in this chapter suggests the ways in which looking at the entwined life stories of an extended set of settler families reveals connections between colonialism in Australia and that in other imperial sites.

The intimate correspondence between individual members of the Macleay, Darling, and Dumaresq families, sharing their fantasies and ambitions as well as their quotidian observations, provides some insight into contemporary settler thinking. It is possible to discern some settlers' preparedness to countenance the violent dispossession of Indigenous people, violence that was integral to their claiming of the desired land grants and purchases that would underpin their

---

[68] Fletcher, *Ralph Darling*, pp. 342–4.   [69] Fletcher, *Ralph Darling*, p. 212.

financial security. At the same time, their casual comments on workers such as convicts, slaves, and *lascars* reveal their familiarity with systems of unfree and colonized labour—even as Fanny Macleay's marriage to Thomas Harington shows that class and social status could outweigh worries about racial intermixing. Settler society in the Australian colonies in its formative decades was shaped by wider imperial culture, as racial thinking, class hierarchies, and ideas of manhood and womanhood all circulated with the settlers themselves, as well as with colonial officials, and a variety of free and unfree labourers.

2

Systematic Colonization: From South Australia to Australind

If some settler family networks were joined by military imperial service, the availability of land grants, and the desire for pastoral estates, at least one family network was spurred on by an idealistic vision of a new form of settler colonization. Among the extended settler families with multiple members who helped to establish the Australasian colonies in disparate but connected ways were the Wakefields. Emigration and colonization theorist Edward Gibbon Wakefield, whose plan for 'systematic colonization' was integral to various Australian and New Zealand settlements in the 1830s and 1840s, is a major historical figure. Yet his brothers, who actively participated in the founding of several of these colonies, are less well known. Wakefield was aided in his bold schemes by four of his brothers and his son. Like the Dumaresq, Darling, and Macleay clans, the Wakefield family shows that we need to see how extended family networks could be integral to 'imperial careering'.[1] Families relied on motivation, support, duty, persuasion, and indebtedness to involve members in imperial projects. In the case of the Wakefields, Edward Gibbon Wakefield's grand schemes, and his personal moral and political investment in them, were factors in inveigling his brothers and son.

Wakefield's brother Arthur had a long and successful global career in the Royal Navy in which he rose to the rank of commander; his naval experience and prominence made him an extremely valuable participant in the older Wakefield's schemes. Arthur was involved in the formation of the New Zealand Association, and in 1841 led the association's first expedition to New Zealand as well as the establishment of Nelson on the South Island, only to be killed by Maori in 1843.[2]

---

[1] David Lambert and Alan Lester (eds), *Colonial Lives Across the British Empire: Imperial Careering in the Long Nineteenth Century* (Cambridge: Cambridge University Press, 2006).

[2] Wakefield family detail is all from the admirably extensive biographical information in Philip Temple, *A Sort of Conscience: The Wakefields* (Auckland: Auckland University Press, 2002). Arthur Wakefield (1799–1843) joined the navy at age ten; his career took him to Cape Colony, Java, India, Brazil, America (the war of 1812), Bermuda, France, Algiers, and Canada. Daniel Wakefield (1798–1858) spent time with his brother Edward in Italy and emulated his older brother with his first marriage by elopement. Many commentators (including Henry Chapman) were a bit scathing about Daniel's abilities and character; his second marriage temporarily failed because he gave his wife an unmentionable disease, but his wife and children migrated to New Zealand to join him in 1848. In his early years Felix Wakefield (1807–75) worked in his father's estate management business. He lived in France in 1830 and learnt about irrigation, married a Frenchwoman, and had a daughter. His marriage failed in Van Diemen's Land due to his inability to support the family and his erratic behaviour. His wife Marie sailed to Adelaide in October 1857 with baby Percy; three of her sons

Daniel Wakefield was two years younger than brother Edward. He, too, became a lawyer, and incurred his own share of scandal, including having to leave England due to bad racing debts. Edward sent Daniel to Plymouth in New Zealand under an assumed name; Daniel then moved to Wellington under his own name where he was appointed a crown solicitor and public prosecutor in September 1847, becoming Attorney General in 1850. Younger brother Felix Wakefield trained as a surveyor and civil engineer with the Ordinance Survey. In 1832 he migrated to Van Diemen's Land where he worked as a surveyor on the roads; he moved from Hobart to Launceston, but in 1839 was struck off the list of surveyors due to errors. Felix became embroiled in a fight with the surveyor-general; he also became, curiously, both a temperance advocate and a gambler. In 1847 he abandoned his wife and his youngest child in Van Diemen's Land, returning to England with his other eight children, for whom he seems to have handed temporary responsibility over to his father Edward and brother Edward Gibbon. In 1851 Felix and six of his children arrived in Lyttelton, New Zealand, thence moving to Wellington.

In 1826 William Wakefield helped his older brother Edward to abduct the heiress Ellen Turner and was imprisoned along with Edward for his efforts. After serving as a mercenary soldier in Portugal, William led the New Zealand Company expedition as its principal agent on its first ship, the *Tory*, in 1839 and settled in Wellington. William was involved in land purchases and settlements of the New Zealand Company. Edward Jerningham Wakefield was Edward Gibbon Wakefield's son from his first marriage, his mother Eliza Pattle Wakefield having died in giving birth to him in 1820. At age seventeen, Jerningham, as the family called him, went to Canada as his father's private secretary when Edward Gibbon Wakefield was part of Lord Durham's mission. In 1839 Jerningham sailed on the first New Zealand Company expedition with his uncle William, living in both Wanganui and Nelson. When his father arrived in New Zealand in 1853, Jerningham again became his private secretary and representative. He remained in New Zealand, his career included serving as the elected member of the colony's House of Representatives for Christchurch, and later in 1871 he was elected to the Assembly.

These disparate stories of the Wakefield clan reflect the organic possibilities of settler colonialism in this period, and the extent of the Wakefields' involvement with the Australian and New Zealand 'systematic' colonies. They show, too, how a prominent figure such as Wakefield did not work alone, but within a network that included friends, supporters, and, crucially, family members. In tracing the lineaments of Wakefield's theory—including his embrace of Pacific Islander, Indian,

---

arrived in South Australia 1853–54, two of whom later went to New Zealand, but the other two stayed and son Salvator became successful in business. After his first sojourn in New Zealand, Felix went back to England in 1852; volunteered for the Crimean War in 1855 where he worked as an engineer; travelled to Russia, Turkey, Syria, and Egypt, and perhaps to India during the Rebellion; went back to England in 1859; and returned to New Zealand in 1864. William Wakefield (1801–48) as a young man travelled to Austria, Russia, and Lapland; in 1832 he went to Portugal; in New Zealand his own shortcomings were implicated in his brother Arthur's death. Edward Jerningham Wakefield's (1820–79) chequered career in New Zealand included journalism, being active in local theatre, and writing a comedy. His alcoholism made him an unreliable breadwinner; his wife Ellen opened a boarding house to keep herself and her daughters alive, and he died destitute in March 1879.

and Chinese labourers in his visions—and briefly surveying key aspects of the establishment of South Australia and Australind, this chapter suggests that both the novel and the common elements of 'systematic' colonization added to the broader picture of Australian settler colonialism.

Edward Gibbon Wakefield (1796–1862) was one of the most important advocates and theorists of settler colonialism during its nineteenth-century ascendancy. Historians' assessments of Wakefield's significance and influence have been mixed over the years, with many pointing out the inconsistencies in his schemes and writings as these evolved,[3] and yet some assessments continue to argue for the originality and impact of his writings.[4] Most discussion of Wakefield has centred on his scheme for the sale of colonial 'waste lands' to fund the emigration of poor British labourers, and his notions of when labourers should be enabled to buy their own land, not least in relation to the vexed issue of the 'sufficient price' of colonial lands on which Wakefield was so evasive.

Wakefield laid out his ideas in his writings, including *A Letter from Sydney* (1829) which, as is well known, would have been more accurately entitled a 'Letter from Newgate Gaol'. Wakefield believed that in Canada and Australia so much Crown land had been given away or sold cheaply that virtually everyone could own their own land. Therefore, the population was scattered too widely, and labour was too scarce to attract 'gentlemen' landowners who preferred not to have to do their own work. While a radical on some issues of political representation, Wakefield wanted colonial societies with class distinctions. He thought that if a 'sufficient price' were placed on all colonial lands, labourers would be forced to concentrate in the vicinity of employment. Capitalist employers would then be willing to purchase land and settle in the colonies. Having never been to New South Wales, Wakefield imagined an English kind of stratified agricultural society, with landowning squires and yeomen labourers who would till the soil. He seemingly did not realize that pastoralism based on sheep- and cattle-grazing was becoming the dominant rural pursuit in the Australian colonies.

In Wakefield's utopia, land policy would limit the expansion of the frontier and regulate class relationships. There would be higher wages than in England, which would induce respectable and skilled workers to migrate and would, in time, enable the 'industrious and thrifty' among them to become 'masters of servants'. There would be a leisured and wealthy class of landowners—'persons of cultivation and refinement'. Colonization would thus be 'systematic'. Free settlers would replace

---

[3] Tai-Sook Lee, 'Edward Gibbon Wakefield and the Movement for Systematic Colonization, 1829–1850' ((PhD thesis, University of California, Berkeley, 1986), (University Dissertation Information Service Xerox, 1988).

[4] Eric Richards has argued for Wakefield's impact and significance. Eric Richards, 'Wakefield and Australia', in Friends of the Turnbull Library Symposium, *Edward Gibbon Wakefield and the Colonial Dream: A Reconsideration* (Wellington: GP Publications, 1997). James Belich, on the other hand, contends that Wakefield was riding the wave of public opinion rather than shaping it, and that the emergence of the 'settler revolution' from 1815 was due to a mass shift in attitudes towards emigration, not just the effects of the writing of Wakefield, Selkirk, or Horton. Belich, *Replenishing the Earth: The Settler Revolution and the Rise of the Anglo-World, 1739–1939* (Oxford: Oxford University Press, 2009), pp. 147–8.

the undesirable transportation of convicts, which would enable the Australian colonies to raise their standards of civilization. While colonial society would consist of a range of classes from English society, it would not have the lowest stratum. It would retain the best of England but eliminate the poverty and overcrowding. Moreover, Wakefield envisioned that settlers would have a voice in the framing of their own laws.

These aspects of Wakefield's schemes have been thoroughly rehearsed by historians, but Wakefield's and his followers' enthusiasm to include Indian, Chinese, and Pacific Island labourers in their visions of 'systematic colonization' has been overlooked. The evidence of their inclusion in Wakefield's schemes allows new interpretations of the labouring class within the Wakefieldian vision. To begin with Wakefield's comments on slavery: Wakefield was opposed to convict transportation, and opposed to 'negro slavery'.[5] In his 1829 *Letter from Sydney* he condemned the two systems: 'Convict labour being a kind of slavery, the employer of convicts is a species of slave driver, and his children are little slave drivers'.[6] His scheme for systematic colonization was intended in part to make the convict system redundant.

Wakefield drew direct comparisons among slavery, convict transportation, and indentured labour:

> every colony . . . has enjoyed in some measure what I have termed combination and constancy of labour . . . They enjoyed it by means of some kind of slavery . . .
>
> In the greater part of the English colonies in North America, negro slavery counteracted the scarcity of labour for hire. In New South Wales and Van Dieman's Land, there has been convict slavery. In the colonies of North America, where negro slavery was not at all, or not largely, established, there has been a virtual slavery in the forms of servants kidnapped in Europe, and 'indented' in America . . . a contract bound to their masters for a term of years.[7]

It is not surprising that Wakefield should have commented on slavery and its wrongs: slavery was, of course, the overriding moral and political issue animating British reform circles of the 1820s and 1830s, Wakefield's milieu. Moreover, Wakefield had been born into a family of Quakers with strong reform traditions and proclivities for contributing to public discussion. One of Wakefield's cousins was prison reformer Elizabeth Fry, and another married Thomas Fowell Buxton, the great anti-slavery activist.[8]

---

[5] M. F. Lloyd Prichard (ed.), *The Collected Works of Edward Gibbon Wakefield* (Glasgow: Collins, 1968), p. 166.

[6] Lloyd Prichard (ed.), *The Collected Works*, p. 136.

[7] Edward Gibbon Wakefield, 'The Art of Colonization', in M. F. Lloyd Prichard (ed.), *The Collected Works of Edward Gibbon Wakefield* (Glasgow: Collins, 1968), pp. 849–50. In his 1833 discussion of the evils of the growing market in the United States for slaves bred in America, Wakefield points to the scarcity of other forms of labour and draws parallels with the Australian colonies: 'In New South Wales and Van Diemen's Land, prosperous colonies, capitalists are supplied with slave labour in the shape of convicts. That they set the highest value on this labour, is proved by the extreme fear lest the system of transportation should be discontinued; although the evils it produces are too many to be counted'. Wakefield, 'England and America', in Lloyd Prichard (ed.), *The Collected Works*, pp. 479–80.

[8] Paul Bloomfield, *Edward Gibbon Wakefield—Builder of the British Commonwealth* (London: Longmans, Green and Co., 1961), p. 16.

While Wakefield was influenced by Adam Smith, it seems that he genuinely intended his 'systematic colonization' to benefit the working classes of Britain. Part of his motivation was a reform impulse, a desire to solve social problems, and to help improve the lot of labourers. Among his multiple trips to Canada (where in 1842 he was elected to the Canadian General Assembly), his 1841 trip involved a plan for migrant Irish labourers to be employed on public works schemes funded from land revenues.[9]

It is clear, too, from his various writings that he had a vision of the ideal British labourers to be assisted by the emigration funds raised by his scheme's controlled sale of lands. In *The Art of Colonization* he articulates who these ideal labourers would be:

> the poor immigrants brought to the colony by the purchase-money of waste land, ought to be men and women in equal numbers; and if married, so much the better... they ought to be young people, whose powers of labour would last as long as possible, and who would readily turn their hands to new kinds of work... [and who] would be of a class fit to produce the most rapid increase of people in the colony...
>
> Every pair of immigrants would have the strongest motives for industry, steadiness and thrift.[10]

Throughout his writings, Wakefield continually stresses the significance of equal numbers of women among the desired emigrants, arguing that they will raise the social standards of the colonies. It is tempting here to note that among the illustrious members of his extended Nonconformist family, his grandmother Priscilla Wakefield published a feminist tract in 1798. Interestingly, in light of Edward Gibbon Wakefield's own artifice in his *Letter from Sydney*, Priscilla Wakefield's multiple publications included her *Excursions in North America*, a work that she had proffered despite not having travelled outside Britain.[11]

While Wakefield's life work held the interests of British labourers as a core principle, yet he and his followers embraced the possibility of Pacific Islander, Indian, and Chinese labourers in their visions of new British settlements in the southern oceans. In a *Postscript* to his 1829 *Letter from Sydney*, Wakefield opined that:

> Many of the islands of the Pacific Ocean have a superabundant population, who, constantly exposed to the want of food, would rejoice to emigrate to this country and to supply our urgent want of labourers, if we did but offer them a free passage and plenty to eat. The British Dominions in India might afford us a much larger supply; for though, hitherto, the Hindoos have been disinclined to emigrate, the most careless observer must see that a great moral revolution has commenced in British India, that the obstinate prejudices of the ages are there beginning to disappear, and that but little management would be required to induce the poorest class of Hindoos to labour and

---

[9] Graeme L. Pretty, 'Wakefield, Edward Gibbon (1796–1862)', *Australian Dictionary of Biography Online*.

[10] Wakefield, 'The Art of Colonization', in Lloyd Prichard (ed.), *The Collected Works*, pp. 563–7.

[11] Bloomfield, *Edward Gibbon Wakefield*, pp. 21–2.

enjoy in Australasia, rather than drown their children in the sacred stream, or die of misery near their own temples. But the Chinese, especially, who, with a population of 300,000,000, feel the pressure of people upon territory more than any other nation whatsoever,—who are greatly disposed to emigrate—and who are by far the most industrious and skilful of Asiatics—might, not only supply the wants of labourers now felt in the British Australasian settlements, but they might in the course of the century, perhaps, convert the whole of this enormous wilderness into a fruitful garden . . .

The labouring classes . . . [in China], I am credibly informed, frequently make offers to the masters of English ships to bind themselves to labour, without wages, during three days in the week, for a term of years, in return for a free passage to any British settlement . . . there might be a constant immigration of Chinese labourers at every settlement in Australasia . . .[12]

In October 1852 when the New Zealand colonies were struggling to receive enough labourers, especially because of the attractions of gold across the Tasman, Wakefield wrote to the New Zealand *Spectator* urging large-scale migration of labourers from China. Pointing to California's reliance on Chinese labourers and lauding California's political independence, Wakefield argued that the Australasian colonies were too dependent on the imperial government and lacked the 'self-managing strength enough for setting on foot a large and systematic Chinese immigration'.[13] Ironically, in view of the large-scale arrival of hopeful Chinese prospectors in Australia, Wakefield's argument depended on his contention that the Chinese labourers 'would cordially engage before embarking to keep away from the gold fields'.[14] Wakefield's 1852 letter was followed the next year by an advertisement published between June and August 1853 in several New Zealand papers, which Muriel Lloyd Prichard, editor of Wakefield's collected works, attributes to his followers.[15] Signed by four men in Wellington and two in Lyttelton, the advertised scheme proposed to bring labourers from Shanghai under five or seven years of bonded indenture, to work in New Zealand as 'shepherds and stock-keepers, mechanics of every description, workers in the dairy, sawyers, fishermen, gardeners, cooks, grooms, footmen, &c.'.[16]

One of Wakefield's key colleagues in advocating his carefully planned settlements was Henry Chapman—lawyer, judge, and politician—who features in Chapter 4 and whose career would span Canada, New Zealand, and Australia, and who would become one of the leading proponents of responsible government in Australia—which Wakefield also supported. In 1841 Chapman was a propagandist for the new Wakefieldian settlement called Australind being launched in Western Australia. Just as Wakefield had hoped South Australia would avoid the

[12] Wakefield, 'A Letter from Sydney, the Principal Town of Australasia', in Lloyd Prichard (ed.), *The Collected Works*, pp. 170, 176.

[13] E. G. Wakefield, 'Dangerous Condition of the Australias and New Zealand. To the Editor of the "Spectator"', *New Zealand Spectator and Cook's Strait Guardian*, 23 October 1852, p. 4.

[14] E. G. Wakefield, 'Dangerous Condition of the Australias and New Zealand'.

[15] Lloyd Prichard (ed.), *The Collected Works*, p. 68. Apparently the advertisement appeared in the *Spectator* on 18 August 1853 and in the same issue the *Spectator*'s editorial simultaneously condemned the scheme.

[16] 'Immigration of Chinese Labourers & Servants', *Wellington Independent*, 15 June 1853, p. 2.

failures of the Swan River settlement, it was hoped that Australind, like the New Zealand colonies, would avoid the problems of both Swan River and South Australia by achieving the lauded 'sufficient price' for land. But the Wakefieldians were not relying totally on British labourers in their plans for Australind either, citing the possibility of procuring labourers 'from Hindostan, or the neighbouring islands of the Malay archipelago'.[17] Thus from 1829 to 1853, Wakefield and his associates who actively pushed systematic colonization included non-white labourers in their vision of these burgeoning British settlements.

SOUTH AUSTRALIA OR 'FELICITANIA'

South Australia was a key colonial experiment of the 1830s, often seen as a successful implementation of Wakefield's systematic colonization. This carefully planned new settlement, designed to attract free settlers who would raise the Australian colonies from their low and disreputable status as Britain's distant gaols, was the object of the philosophical radicals' enthusiasm. Even Jeremy Bentham (1748–1832), the doyen of philosophical radicals, took a keen interest before he died, suggesting that South Australia might be called 'Felicitania', 'Felicia', or 'Liberia' to signal its promise. In 1865 John Stuart Mill (1806–73) claimed that he had worked behind the scenes to facilitate the founding of South Australia as a Wakefieldian settlement that would bring the benefits of systematic colonization to Australia.[18] Utopian socialist Robert Owen (1771–1858) was also a supporter, stating in 1834 that the proposed colony was the best emigration plan to date.[19] The social planning embodied in the South Australian Association's vision gained added lustre when it was bolstered by urban planning principles for the new town, including open spaces and parklands that would allow Adelaide's inhabitants to enjoy health-giving exercise.[20] When the plans for South Australia finally received parliamentary approval and the first expedition was dispatched in 1836, it was surrounded by lofty ideals and great hopes.

Success and exceptionalism were foundational to South Australia's story from its inception. As historian Douglas Pike has detailed, in the mid-1830s the first commissioners for South Australia printed innumerable tracts extolling its promise in the effort to raise investment funds. South Australia was touted as a province where respectable members of the middling classes would have no sneering aristocracy above them, where there would be free institutions, especially free churches without tithe, and where land was to be sold outright with freehold ownership. The climate was described as salubrious and the potential for agriculture great (a view evidently not based on familiarity with the region's relatively low rainfall).

---

[17] Henry S. Chapman, *The New Settlement of Australind* (London: Harvey and Darton, 1841), pp. 85–6.

[18] Kelly Henderson, 'Adelaide: The ideal city of the philosophic radicals, and the great experiment in the art of colonization', *South Australian Geographical Journal* Vol. 105 (2006), p. 138.

[19] Henderson, 'Adelaide', pp. 140–1.   [20] Henderson, 'Adelaide', pp. 141–3.

There would be no convicts and a representative system of government would be developed. Planners, investors, and emigrants came to believe that 'South Australia was to be a model province, rid of every fault of the mother country and of previous colonial systems'.[21]

The idea of South Australian difference or distinctiveness has been perpetuated by its citizens, politicians, and historians. As Robert Foster and Paul Sendziuk have recently summarized it, 'the narrative is that South Australia was established independently of the earlier Australian colonies, outlawed the importation of convicts, was based on rational economic principles, and was a pioneer of social and political reform'.[22] In the nineteenth century particularly, South Australia's founding mythology and sense of difference were continually recreated by annual celebrations of its 'national' day, the anniversary of the reading of Governor John Hindmarsh's proclamation of the province at Glenelg on 28 December 1836.[23]

Despite the long-lived stories of South Australian exceptionalism, historical evidence shows the ways in which its early development overlapped with that of the eastern colonies. Prior to the founding of the South Australian Association's settlement at Adelaide, from very early on in the nineteenth century a creole community developed on Kangaroo Island with the arrival of European and American men sealers. In these decades sealing and whaling ships plied their bloody business along the southern coastlines of Australia, as well as other parts of the southern oceans. Camp-like communities proliferated in Van Diemen's Land, on islands in the Bass Strait, and on Kangaroo Island off the coast of South Australia, founded on unions between white men and Aboriginal women. Many of the women were abducted from their own clans and violently forced into service, yet, as Lynette Russell argues, we need to recognize the limited agency of Aboriginal women, who at least in Van Diemen's Land had traditionally hunted and killed seals themselves. Creole cultures developed with blended languages, rough dwellings comprised of Aboriginal and European elements, and methods of hunting, trading, and cooking that drew on skills of both the colonizers and the colonized. Mixed-race children grew up, and the white men who founded these camps were occasionally described by European observers as having become Aboriginal in their ways and appearance. The Kangaroo Island sealing communities shared features with those in Bass Strait and Van Diemen's Land, not least the fact that some of the women abducted from one place were taken to another along this stretch of coastlines inhabited by seals.[24]

Even the British settlers who arrived after the founding of the much-vaunted colony were not always particularly different in their behaviour from the supposedly

---

[21] Douglas Pike, *Paradise of Dissent: South Australia 1829–1857* (Carlton, Victoria: Melbourne University Press, 1967), p. 147.

[22] Robert Foster and Paul Sendziuk (eds), *Turning Points: Chapters in South Australian History* (Kent Town, South Australia: Wakefield Press, 2012), p. 2.

[23] Robert Foster and Amanda Nettelbeck, 'Proclamation Day and the Rise and Fall of South Australian Nationalism', in Foster and Sendziuk (eds), *Turning Points*, p. 49.

[24] Lynette Russell, *Roving Mariners: Australian Aboriginal Whalers and Sealers in the Southern Oceans, 1790–1870* (Albany: State University of New York Press, 2012), pp. 14–15, 125–7.

inferior convict-ridden stock of the eastern colonies. We know about one contingent of early settlers from the journal of a young emigrant, James Bell, who in November 1838 at the age of twenty-one left London on the *Planter* bound for South Australia with around 120 other passengers. In his daily journal entries recorded during the voyage, Bell noted that the other passengers included 'a number of poor people with their families who, induced by poverty at home and a belief that there is more of this worlds goods to be acquired in the far distant colony of S. Australia, have clung to it as a last hope', and that the 'Steerage passengers . . . are a motley group'.[25] James Bell's diary shows him to be a sober and religious young man, who repeatedly evinces homesickness for Scotland. But his sobriety and piety do not fully account for his jaundiced views of his fellow passengers. On 17 February 1839, not long after the ship had left Rio de Janeiro, Bell recorded:

> An unfortunate female fell down the main hatchway last evening and broke her leg. She is one of the 16 young women we have on board (though not young). She may be about 40 and has been no doubt a balladsinger. By her loose conduct among the sailors, and noisy, coarse and disgusting talk, joined to a very unprepossessing personal appearance, she had become obnoxious to almost every one, and went under the soubriquet of 'Old Gallows'.
>
> Her real name is Lizzy Taylor and it was with a kind of triumph that some heard of her misfortune, that appeared in my eyes no less than savage. She had no friends nor acquaintances on board, and it wd be difficult to say what object she can have in going to S. Australia, but still more so what object the Comrs can have in granting such a creature a free passage.[26]

But it was not only the other passengers whom Bell found morally lacking. On 23 February 1839 he recorded:

> We have on board an old man who was called a Dr at the beginning of our voyage. It seems however he has been licensed to preach, but has always taught a school at Liverpool, from which place he is, and goes out to S. Australia having got a free passage with 11 daughters and 2 Sons. His name is McGowan . . . Well our Capt of course could not want a mistress till he returned to his own in England, but made love to 2 of McGowans daughters. They, silly enough, listened to him and, instead of being corrected by their father, were rather encouraged, as the whole family found their profit in it, in the way of sundry presents of wine, brandy, fresh provisions &c. &3. The Capt was allowed to keep the daughters company at all hours and, during the whole time of our being in warm weather, one bed on deck sufficed for all three, while at Rio he took them ashore and had the audacity to exhibit them there. The stupid old father winked at such ongoings—altho' in the opinion of every one on board the honour of his daughters was sacrificed to his neglect of his duty as their father, while his wife was equally deficient in hers.[27]

[25] Richard Walsh (ed.), *A Voyage to Australia 1838–39: Private Journal of James Bell* (Sydney: Allen & Unwin, 2011), pp. 7–8.
[26] Walsh (ed.), *A Voyage to Australia*, p. 97.
[27] Walsh (ed.), *A Voyage to Australia*, pp. 103–4.

Travelling himself in the 'intermediate' deck, lower in status and comfort than the cabin passengers, Bell found those travelling in steerage like the McGowans frequently confronting, but, as is clear from this passage, far from alone in conduct of which he did not approve.

If James Bell imagined that the behaviour of some of his fellow passengers befitted the convicts who populated the eastern colonies rather than ideal free settlers, we know that some actual former convicts made their way to the supposedly moral colony of South Australia. Eliza Mahoney, for example, in her 1898 memoirs recalled that in the early years of South Australia, around 1840 when she was a teenager, her father employed some 'time-expired and ticket-of-leave men' from the eastern colonies. She describes these men as skilled at hut-building, better workers than the free labourers, and than whom 'we never had more honest and more industrious servants'.[28] While Mahoney defends these former convicts, her testimony belies the mythology of South Australia as free of the convict taint. Clearly, there was little to stop ticket-of-leave workers or emancipated convicts from journeying to South Australia if they wished.

In 1862 one jaundiced commentator published his scathing views of South Australia, based on having lived there from 1856 to 1861. Robert Harrison condemned the colony's every aspect, from the climate that he found suffocating in summer, to the paltry scale of its water courses, including the River Torrens. Specifically, he judged the whole Wakefield scheme to have failed in South Australia:

> [I]n 1842, the total debts of a colony which it was to have been *an illustration of self-supporting colonization*, were £400,000, besides the large capital sunk and lost by unfortunate and enterprising colonists, and all the fine fictions about concentration, hired labour price, and balance of capital and labour, and the relations between the Employers and Employed, were remembered by 'curses, not loud but deep,' by unhappy people brought to poverty by the delusion.[29]

While Harrison's depiction of South Australia is exaggerated in some respects, the colony was economically fragile in its early decades and was at first financially dependent on the British government to stabilize it. It was the case, too, that some early arrivals endured difficult conditions. One settler who arrived in 1839 recalled not only the hard work of obtaining water in barrels from the River Torrens, but the rough shelters to which others had to resort: 'in fact many lived in tents, mud huts, reed huts, caves and holes cut in the river banks'.[30]

Despite South Australia's initial failure to be economically self-supporting, its early instability and challenges, the colony survived and eventually throve. Moreover, it did achieve some distinction, not least in disestablishing the Church of

---

[28] Eliza Sarah Mahoney, 'The First Settlers at Gawler' [Ms. dated 1898], *Proceedings of the Royal Geographical Society of Australasia, South Australian Branch* Vol. 28 (1926–27), p. 56.

[29] Robert Harrison, *Colonial Sketches: or Five Years in South Australia, with hints to capitalists and emigrants* (first published 1862; Hampstead Gardens, South Australia: Austaprint, 1978), p. 7.

[30] Geoffrey H. Manning (ed.), *Memoirs of Thomas Frost 1825–1910* (Adelaide: Gillingham Printers, 1985), p. 27.

England. Many who migrated to South Australia were attracted by its promise of freedom of worship. The Rev. Ridgeway Newland, a Congregationalist from England's Potteries district, migrated in 1838 because he was 'determined to be free of the disabilities existing in England for non-conformists, and South Australia offered the opportunity for the foundation of an ideal settlement'.[31] Newland brought with him a group of skilled artisans, farm labourers, and their families, presumably from his congregation. After years of debate, in 1851 the newly reformed Legislative Council passed a measure entrenching voluntary support for religion, under which churches were to be supported through voluntary gifts of their adherents rather than being reliant on state aid, and which removed the privilege of the Church of England. Thus South Australia achieved its reputation as a 'paradise of dissent' in which a plethora of mostly Protestant sects flourished.[32]

Because of the principle of religious freedom integral to the planned colony from its inception, early settlers included labouring Germans who sought freedom of worship and were brought under the auspices of colonial investor George Fife Angas (1789–1879). These impoverished German settlers founded several of their own villages, including Klemzig and Hahndorf, and participated in the establishment of the Barossa Valley wine industry. They were renowned for their physical strength and their work ethic, especially the women. Contemporary observers recorded that the German women were to be seen ploughing their fields yoked to a bullock; they would plough under contract to other farmers including by digging with spades, and were in demand as shearers because they were as competent as men yet 'were not so rough in handling the shears, thereby causing less pain to the poor patient animals who are often horribly cut about by "green hands"'.[33]

Contemporary observers also commented on the ubiquitous presence of Aborigines, and the relations of mutual curiosity and codependence that quickly evolved between Indigenous people and the settlers. (See Fig. 2.1.) H. Hussey recorded the common practice of Aborigines in Adelaide's early years to present 'themselves at the doors and windows of the early settlers with some such application as this . . . "Me cut wood; you give me . . . bit of baccy"'.[34] Around 1850, one young would-be pastoralist, who had been in the colony for two years, leased a parcel of land east of the Murray River. When he first reached his new estate:

> I was told there were in the neighbourhood some *tame blacks* who could run up a couple of bark huts, weather tight and quite large enough for our purpose in three or four days, and that a messenger should be sent off at once to a creek at some distance where a large party of sawyers were located to bring up a couple or three to set to work on our stockyard . . .

[31] *Memoirs of Simpson Newland CMG* (Adelaide: F.W. Preece and Sons, 1926), p. 1.
[32] Pike, *Paradise of Dissent*, esp. pp. 434–7.
[33] H. Hussey, *More than Half a Century of Colonial Life and Christian Experience* (Adelaide: Hussey and Gillingham, 1897), p. 64; Anthony Stuart (ed.), *A Miller's Tale: The Memoirs of John Dunn of Mt Barker* (Kingswood, Southern Australia: Waterwheel Books, 1991), p. 30; Jane Isabella Watts, *Family Life in South Australia* (Adelaide: W. K. Thomas and Co., 1890), pp. 98–9.
[34] Hussey, *More than Half a Century of Colonial Life*, p. 29.

Fig. 2.1 S. T. Gill (1818–1880) Australia. *Captain Davison's house 'Blakiston' near Mount Barker* (1848), Adelaide (Watercolour on paper 21.3 cm × 33.8 cm).
South Australian Government Grant 1979. Art Gallery of South Australia, Adelaide.

Sure enough the next morning brought blacks and whites . . . The 'blackies' we left in the hands of the overseers of the neighbouring flocks, who saw our huts run up and paid the natives in various goods, the total value of which was under a couple of pounds . . .

These same blacks are queer looking fellows, straight and tall, with *rather* intelligent features, certainly much more so than my reading had induced me to conceive . . . They are useful too from their skill in tracking footsteps; seldom failing to track and recover any stray cattle or sheep . . . and if well treated, I fully believe are equal to a white man as a shepherd in the bush.[35]

This account reveals at once the settlers' dependence on Aboriginal people for labour, the fact that they paid them with minimal quantities of goods and not wages, and instances of white labourers and Aborigines working together.

Interestingly, in at least one account of early interaction, settler boys became intrigued by Aboriginal weapons and hunting skills. Jane Sanders kept a journal of her family's experience of settling in South Australia from 1839. Sanders' father and stepmother took up a land selection at Echunga Creek, in the hills not far to the southeast of Adelaide. When they arrived on the land they found an Aboriginal clan there, who would camp close to their vegetable garden and with whom they had peaceful relations, perhaps due to her father being a Quaker. Sanders recorded that her 'brothers often visited the natives in their wurlies, and my younger brothers

---

[35] G. B. Earp (ed.), *What we did in Australia: being the practical experiences of three clerks* (London: George Routledge and Co., 1853), pp. 81–5.

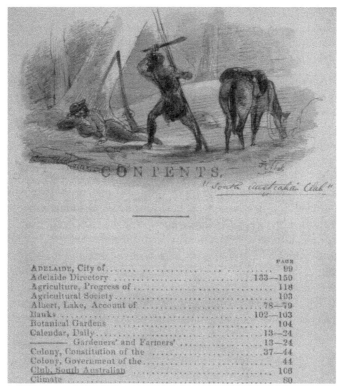

Fig. 2.2 J. M. Skipper, 'South Australian Club'.
Courtesy of the State Library of South Australia, SLSA: PRG 72/13/1—*South Australian Almanack*, 1841 (J. M. Skipper, artist).

copied their weapons, spears, waddies etc. And they became quite expert in using the weapons, accompanying the native men and boys on their hunting expeditions'.[36]

For all of this peaceful interaction, pervasive cooperation and codependence, in South Australia as elsewhere early frontier relations easily turned violent. (See Fig. 2.2.) The overland stock route along the Murrumbidgee, Darling, and Murray rivers from New South Wales to South Australia became notorious for violent conflicts between Aborigines and drovers, with serious fighting occurring on the Rufus River near Lake Victoria in New South Wales close to the border with South Australia. A South Australian settler who participated in one 1841 expedition to punish the Aborigines in that area recalled that the subsequent expedition engaged in greater violence, when the Aborigines were caught between a police party on the west bank of the Rufus River and the overland party of Mr William Robinson on the east bank:

[36] C. S. Sanders (ed.), *The Settlement of George Sanders and his Family at Echunga Creek from the Journal of Jane Sanders* (Adelaide: Pioneers Association of South Australia, 1955), p. 16.

The firing lasted about fifteen minutes, 30 natives were killed, 10 wounded and 4 taken prisoner . . . This was the Protector's report but in after years when I was residing on the Murray and had learnt the language of the natives, I ascertained that a much larger number had been killed, for Mr Robinson's men were all picked marksmen.[37]

Attacks by Aborigines on outstations, sheep, and settlers occurred in various parts of South Australia, from Eyre Peninsula in the west to the regions of the north, and included one in 1844 at Mount Schank in the southeast, where, as commonly occurred, the attacks were followed by violent reprisal.[38] Robert Foster, Rick Hosking, and Amanda Nettelbeck, who have documented and discussed this frontier warfare in South Australia, call it 'an undeclared war' that was 'clothed in euphemisms'.[39] Indeed, Foster, Hosking, and Nettelbeck argue that in South Australia racial violence was made more covert because of the colony's pretence of being founded as a free settlement based on racial harmony. Governor Hindmarsh's Proclamation Speech in December 1836 had declared that 'the Native Populations' would receive protection by lawful means, and that he the governor would 'punish with exemplary severity, all acts of violence and injustice which may in any manner be practised or attempted against the Natives, who are to be considered as much under the safeguard of the law as the Colonists themselves, and equally entitled to the privileges of British subjects'.[40] These lofty sentiments were contravened soon enough by the realities of race relations like those elsewhere.

AUSTRALIND

South Australians soon learned that they were not the only participants in the experiment of systematic colonization, even if they had pride of place as the first. They were followed by the later systematic colonies in New Zealand, also based on Wakefieldian principles, including from 1840 the settlement in the Wellington area, and later those at Wanganui, New Plymouth, Nelson, Otago, and Canterbury. In Australia, there would be just two. Regarded as the less successful version of Wakefield's idea, and perhaps for that reason largely overlooked in Australian history, was the settlement of Australind in Western Australia.

Australind was established in 1840 by the Western Australian Company, just north of Port Leschenault or Bunbury (see Fig. 2.3). The very name of 'Australind' was significant: it was called Australind to signify its location on the Australian coast, in a situation that was hoped would foster a relationship between Australia

---

[37] James C. Hawker, *Early Experiences in South Australia* (Adelaide: E. S. Wigg and Son, 1899; facsimile ed. 1975), p. 79.

[38] Edward Arthur, *A Journal of Events from Melbourne, Port Phillip, to Mount Schank in the District of Adelaide, New Holland, a distance of 400 miles undertaken in 1843 by Messrs Edward and Fortesque Arthur, sons of Captain Arthur, RN, with a Flock of 4000* (first published Sheerness, *c.*1844; Hobart: Sullivan's Cove, 1975), pp. 39–45.

[39] Robert Foster, Rick Hosking, and Amanda Nettelbeck, *Fatal Collisions: The South Australian Frontier and the violence of memory* (Adelaide: Wakefield Press, 2001), p. 8.

[40] Foster, Hosking, and Nettelbeck, *Fatal Collisions*, p. 3.

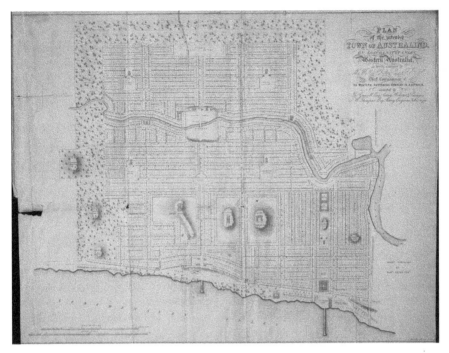

Fig. 2.3 'Plan of the intended town of Australind on Leschenault Inlet'.
State Library of Western Australia, Acc 336A/28.

and India. Australind—the name of a contraction of Australia and India—would represent the possibilities of trade and exchange between these two parts of the British Empire on the periphery of the Indian Ocean. These hoped-for possibilities belie assumptions that the white-settler colonies such as in Canada, New Zealand, and Australia were seen as categorically different from the mercantile colonies in India, at least in the early to mid-nineteenth century.

Just like South Australia, Australind was founded on the careful plans and schemes of a group of men in London. Maps were drawn up, plans made for a supposedly ideal town, a prospectus compiled, and much effort put into advertising the colony. The company's prospectus showed the town as the planners intended it to be laid out, with formal streets, public squares, wharves, market places, even colleges, a hospital, a theatre, a town hall, and six churches. Hundred-acre farms were sold in London ahead of the settlement being established: off the plan, as it were. As in South Australia, the proceeds of land sales were to be used to pay for the passage of labourers as well as improvements to the town; the settlers who sailed were thus a mix of the more affluent elite of the colony and those intended to do the labour. Australind's chief commissioner, Marshall Waller Clifton, even used different terms in his journal for these two classes: 'settlers' were those who purchased land before departure, while those whose passages were paid as the would-be labourers were called 'emigrants'. It was a community that would have clear class

lines, as well as developing racial divisions—including the employment and criminalization of the local Aborigines, and the presence nearby of some labourers
brought from India. Australind survived, despite setbacks and defectors, and is
today a dormitory suburb of Bunbury. But it did not fulfil its founders' dreams, and
as an Australian example of systematic colonization was always overshadowed by
South Australia.

The Swan River Colony, which became Perth, was established in Western
Australia in 1829 as a free settlement. Its first governor, James Stirling, had
extensive connections to India, and saw Western Australia's proximity to India as
a major advantage. At the time of its founding it was the first settlement established
for free settlers, although it too eventually became a penal colony—yet another of
the string of penal colonies scattered around the perimeter of the Australian
continent, this time a trajectory from free to penal colony. It also had the advantage
of being a port at which ships from Britain could call as soon as they reached
Australia. Other settlements on the southwestern corner of Western Australia
followed. King George Sound had actually begun earlier as a military base in
1826 and then was established as a settlement in 1832; it would become the
town of Albany. The town now known as Bunbury was first established as a
military camp in 1830, then as a town in 1836; it was first called Port Leschenault.

A few settlers showed early interest in the Bunbury or Leschenault area, not least
the first governor of Western Australia himself, Sir James Stirling, who claimed a
large land grant there and in late 1837 to early 1838 established a manager in
residence to supervise his estate.[41] A Colonel Latour was first given a grant of land
at Australind itself in 1829. He sent out an agent and some settlers but in fact did
not use the land that had been granted to him on this extensive site. In 1837 a
group of investors in Calcutta met to establish a joint-stock company called the
Australian Association, to develop trade between India and the Australian colonies.
Brothers William and Charles Prinsep were among the investors. While Charles
Prinsep also bought land near Australind that same year, the Australian Association
was but one of many companies and ventures founded in this period to profit from
rapid British settler colonial expansion. In these years plans for new settlements
bound up schemes for migration, trade, and indentured labour together. In 1838
the Calcutta newspaper *The Englishman* argued that British investors in India
should take note of the Australian Association, because the Australian colonies
were a possible destination for Britons on Indian service as well as an investment
opportunity, including 'the man of small income—to the retiring officer,—to the
children of the present generation—to the penniless adventurer, and to the parent
who cannot afford to send his offspring to England'.[42] Australind's planners took
up this last point, including in their scheme the idea that it would have 'Schools of a

---

[41] A. C. Staples, 'The Prinsep Estate in Western Australia', *The Western Australian Historical
Society: Journal and Proceedings* Vol. V, Part 1 (1955): 16–19.
[42] Malcolm Allbrook, '"A Triple Empire...United Under One Dominion": Charles Prinsep's
Schemes for Exporting Indian Labour to Australia', *South Asia: Journal of South Asian Studies* 14
August 2012, DOI: 10.1080/00856401.2011.649676, p. 13.

superior order, for the youth of both sexes', which would attract students not only from settler families but also the children of officers in the East India Company, and the British military and civil service in India, Ceylon, and Mauritius.[43]

In 1840 the Australind land grant was purchased in London by the Western Australian Company, which was formed to establish a new colony on the scheme of systematic colonization developed by Wakefield. The July 1840 prospectus for Australind compiled by the company claimed that, while the Swan River Colony had 'almost remained stationary', Australind would be based on the superior method of colonization proven by South Australia: 'South Australia has risen into a degree of importance, and attained a state of prosperity not less astonishing than advantageous to those who embarked in the formation of that settlement'.[44]

The site for Australind was the subject of considerable confusion. The original, and what would be the final, site was that south of Perth and just north of Bunbury—a place chosen because of the conjunction of the Collie and Preston rivers. In 1840 the first boat was sent out with a medical officer and nine surveyors whose job it would be to begin laying out the settlement. A second boat, the *Parkfield*, was soon to follow, carrying around ninety settlers and workers. But just before the *Parkfield* was to embark in October 1840, the explorer Lieutenant Grey (who later became Sir George Grey and governor of both South Australia and New Zealand) arrived in London announcing that the colonial governor was about to resume the land grant on which the settlement was based (the original grant to Latour). Moreover, Grey strongly advised that there was a more promising site for the Australind settlement to the north of Perth—a location that was to be named Port Grey after him, near the current town of Geraldton. In fact, Govenor Hutt had just cancelled his decision to resume the land grant and was willing to let the Western Australian Association have it. But Grey's twin announcements destabilized the Australind plans to the extent that many investors withdrew their money, the number of settlers dropped, and the sailing of the *Parkfield* was delayed.[45]

One of the main proponents of the Wakefield scheme, Henry Samuel Chapman, a lawyer who had lived in Canada, quickly wrote a new treatise extolling the land at Port Grey as the best possible and most felicitous location for Australind. Quoting at great length from Grey's journal of his discovery of the area, as well as other reports, Chapman drew a picture of exceptional climate and fecundity:

> there are two facts to be taken into account which render the climate of Australind peculiarly favourable to animal and vegetable life, and especially to the human constitution—we mean the general elevation of the country, and the equability of climate . . . From excessive [temperature] fluctuation, Australind is necessarily free—a circumstance which is much in favour of its salubrity . . . The abundance of moisture, the luxuriance of the vegetation, the number of kangaroos and emus with which

[43] 'The Australind Prospectus', Phyllis Barnes et al. (eds), *The Australind Journals of Marshall Waller Clifton 1840–1861* (Victoria Park, WA: Hesperian Press, 2010), p. 685 [Appendix 4].

[44] Barnes et al. (eds), *The Australind Journals of Marshall Waller Clifton*, p. 684 [Appendix 4].

[45] E. L. Burgess, 'The Settlement at Australind', *Western Australian Historical Society: Journal and Proceedings* New Series Vol. 11 (Oct. 1939): 24.

[Grey's party] met, and the constant recurrence of warran grounds [areas where Aboriginal people cultivated yams and fern roots], at once proclaim the superiority of the soil at Australind to that of the other colonies.[46]

Combined with what he asserted were well-flowing rivers, rich valleys, and 'a harbour, which, according to our present information, has no equal on the western coast of Australia', the site was all that could be desired.[47]

A central figure in the whole project was Marshall Waller Clifton, who had been secretary of the Victualling Board of the Admiralty. An expert on horticulture, Clifton's work in natural science had resulted in his being elected a Fellow of the Royal Society—a distinguished honour. Clifton had retired from the Admiralty Board at the age of forty-five and was supporting his wife and family of fourteen children on his pension. Even moving to France for a while did not help his financial situation sufficiently. He became a supporter of Wakefield's colonization scheme, perhaps in part because his wife Elinor was related to Wakefield. Indeed Clifton was appointed as Australind's salaried resident commissioner, to be in charge of the first settlement party embarking on the *Parkfield*. When the plans for the colony were thrown into disarray with Grey's arrival and announcements in London, Waller Clifton kept things on an even keel despite some investors withdrawing their money. The boat embarked with instructions to go first to the original site, to pick up the surveyors, and sail to Perth so that Clifton could see the governor about the change of plans, then head north to Port Grey and settle there. Before the *Parkfield* left England, on 5 December 1840, the eve of its departure from Gravesend, the deputy chairman of the Western Australian Company addressed 'the Emigrants & Settlers in a most feeling manner' by way of farewell.[48]

The *Parkfield* finally arrived in Western Australia in March 1841, and went straight to the originally planned site near Port Leschenault. Those already there were distressed that the plans and site had been changed. The surveyors especially objected: they said the southern site was perfect. The arriving settlers on the boat also liked what they saw, so Clifton rode on horseback to Perth and persuaded the governor to agree that they could stay there rather than move north to Port Grey. Things seemingly settled down, but, not surprisingly, clearing the land and starting the whole settlement from scratch was a huge undertaking. There were various emotional vicissitudes. One of the original surveyors, a Mr Gaudin, had become insane even before the *Parkfield* arrived; his wife, arriving in the second ship, had to look after a deranged husband. A servant woman also seemingly lost her mind, wandering off into the bush, and was lucky to be found two days later. Australind's beginnings were a far cry from a town with formal streets, public squares, wharves, market places, colleges, a hospital, a theatre, a town hall, and six churches. Some of the settlers became disillusioned with the challenges, and decamped to places further afield. Despite a few more ships arriving with settlers, Australind foundered;

---

[46] Chapman, *The New Settlement of Australind*, pp. 72, 74–5.
[47] Chapman, *The New Settlement of Australind*, p. 64.
[48] Barnes et al. (eds), *The Australind Journals of Marshall Waller Clifton*, p. 1.

it did not collapse completely, but it became only a fraction of what had been intended.

The desertion of some of the labourers may have been related to factors besides the back-breaking work of clearing the trees and building every structure from the ground up. Tensions between the settlement leader Waller Clifton and the British labourers in his group had developed quickly on the *Parkfield*'s voyage, and may have prevented the possibility of good working relations after arrival. As early in the voyage as 23 December 1840, when they called briefly at Tenerife, Clifton recorded in his journal his disappointment that the 'Emigrants' became very drunk. On 10 January 1841 he lectured a Mr Williams for his indecent behaviour with his wife in public spaces on board; and on 24 January he prohibited card-playing among the emigrant men and confiscated the cards.[49] Perhaps these repeated assertions of his authority undermined goodwill among this closely confined community. Tensions certainly continued after arrival and during the founding of the settlement, with Clifton repeatedly facing challenges from insubordinate underlings or from those whose work he considered inadequate. Even one of Clifton's descendants would later call him 'a strict disciplinarian'.[50]

Of particular interest is the racial mix at Australind, just who the workers were. And on this point Chapman is suggestive. In his 1841 book extolling the land at Port Grey as the ideal location for Australind—entitled *The New Settlement of Australind with a map of the district, and a full description of the colony, and of the principles on which it is settled. Compiled for the use of colonists*—Chapman emphasized its agricultural potential. Based on the observations of Grey and others about the region, he predicted that it would grow olives, grapes for wine, and fruit ranging from oranges and other citrus, to figs and mulberries (for silk); that almond and other nut trees would grow; that cotton, rice, and tobacco were all possible crops; and that the wool industry would flourish there. It could also provide a base for the whaling industry which he thinks would enable British whalers to overtake the dominant American whaling boats. Chapman acknowledges that labour will be an issue for Australind, and notes that Sir James Stirling, the former governor of Western Australia, advocated that sugar and cotton could be grown in the northern section of the colony 'by means of free labour to be procured from Hindostan, or the neighbouring islands of the Malay archipelago'.[51]

Chapman does not expand on this, yet we know that labourers were brought to Western Australia from various parts of South and South East Asia. Historian F. K. Crowley says that some settlers in Western Australia in these years brought with them a 'small number of Indian and Chinese coolies'.[52] J. S. Battye, in his history of the state, mentions a failed 1833 attempt to establish 'an Anglo-Indian settlement [from Calcutta] at King George's Sound'; the 1836–37 arrival of 'a few

---

[49] Barnes et al. (eds), *The Australind Journals of Marshall Waller Clifton*, pp. 6, 12 and 14.

[50] E. Clifton, 'Australind: The Founding of Australind', *The Western Australian Historical Society: Journal and Proceedings* Vol. 1, Part 1 (1927): 40.

[51] Chapman, *The New Settlement of Australind*, pp. 85–6.

[52] F. K. Crowley, *Australia's Western Third: A History of Western Australia from the first settlements to modern times* (Melbourne: Heinemann, 1960) p. 17.

Indian settlers with native servants' at Albany; and the 1847 procurement by the government of a few Chinese indentured workers from Singapore.[53] According to James Jupp, the 1847 group consisted of twenty Chinese workers from Singapore, who were taken to Perth, Albany, and York where they worked as agricultural labourers, carpenters, and domestic servants. They were followed the next year by a group of thirty-one, and in total in the nineteenth century about a thousand Chinese people arrived in Western Australia as indentured labourers.[54] We know that in 1842 the Agricultural and Horticultural Society of Western Australia wrote to Governor Hutt asserting: 'while we feel it to be imperatively necessary again to call your Excellency's attention to the distressing condition of the colonists for the want of labour, we feel assured that the well-meant efforts to procure servants from India and elsewhere, will be successfully persevered in'.[55] Thus the actual number of Indian and Chinese workers in the colony in the 1830s and 1840s was relatively small. But it did include some Indian labourers in the Australind vicinity because of the estate established by Charles Prinsep, Advocate General to the East India Company, in the late 1830s.

The Prinseps were a Calcutta merchant and official family, members of whom had first joined the East India Company service in the eighteenth century and who had since made money in indigo, among other pursuits. They formed yet another of the extended British settler families who found multiple opportunities in the Australian colonies, though their main imperial involvement was in India from where their family network moved to and from England. The Prinseps established properties in Van Diemen's Land and Western Australia in these years, at both of which they employed indentured Indian labourers. In 1829 Charles and Augustus Prinsep visited Van Diemen's Land. The consumptive Augustus sailed there from Calcutta and stayed for six months. In some respects, Augustus Prinsep found Van Diemen's Land disturbing, from the Aboriginal people whom he considered frightening and primitive, to the convicts who were the only available servants. Prinsep commented in a letter that because 'our own blackies [servants brought from India], though three in number, could not undertake the household', they too had to rely on convicts: 'if the histories of every house were made public, you would shudder. Even in our small ménage, our cook has committed murder, our footman burglary, and the housemaid bigamy!'[56] Yet despite these distressing aspects, Augustus Prinsep found Van Diemen's Land surprisingly attractive and civilized: 'You have never supposed that it has a beautiful harbour, a fine metropolis, with towns, streets, shops, and pretty shopkeepers, like some of the larger towns of

[53] J. S. Battye, *Western Australia: A History from its Discovery to the Inauguration of the Commonwealth* (Oxford: Clarendon Press, 1924), pp. 124, 142, and 186.

[54] James Jupp (ed.), *The Australian People: An Encyclopaedia of the Nation, Its People and Their Origins* (Cambridge: Cambridge University Press, 2001), p. 214.

[55] Alfred Gill, *Western Australia, containing a Statement of the Condition and Prospects of that Colony, and some account of the Western Australian Company's Settlement at Australind . . . Compiled for the use of settlers* (London: Smith, Elder, & Co., 65 Cornhill, 1842), p. 66.

[56] Mrs A. Prinsep (ed.), *The Journal of a Voyage from Calcutta to Van Diemen's Land: comprising a Description of that Colony during a Six Months' Residence, from original letters* (London: Smith, Elder, & Co., 65 Cornhill, 1833), p. 52.

Devonshire or Sussex'. Moreover, he noted, there were counties and farms, the shops were well supplied with goods at reasonable prices, and there were not only several chapels but a number of schools, even a well-regarded girls' boarding school. Tasmania, in Prinsep's view, had wonderful prospects, so much so that he contemplated returning in a couple of years, and even concluded that 'I could willingly change India for Tasmania, and fall from diplomacy to farming with content'.[57] But Augustus Prinsep would not have the chance to return to Van Diemen's Land, dying in 1830 at age twenty-seven of the tuberculosis that was the reason for his visit, on a voyage home to England. From 1832 to 1834 his older brother Henry Thoby Prinsep also visited Van Diemen's Land for a recuperative break from India, suffering from dysentery and fever.[58]

In 1829 brother Charles Prinsep not only visited Van Diemen's Land but decided to invest in land there, buying an estate called 'The Adelphi' near Launceston in order to breed horses for the Indian market.[59] Later he would acquire his estate in Western Australia, as well as establishing a nutmeg plantation in Singapore. Augustus had noted the presence of Chinese labourers in Van Diemen's Land, which may also have spurred Charles's thinking: 'Chinese labourers, to the amount of two or three hundred, have lately been taken to Van Diemen's Land, and are likely to prove a most useful addition to the working classes there. They are the most ingenious artisans in the world'.[60] The Prinsep estate at Australind employed a group of labourers who arrived from Calcutta with Prinsep's chief overseer Thomas Little in February 1838.[61] This first shipload of animals, cargo, and labourers for the Prinsep venture included thirty-seven Indian '*lascars*' as well as one 'Chinaman', and thirteen British workers. They formed the first contingent to establish the Prinsep estate on land along the Leschenault estuary. Named 'Belvidere' after Charles Prinsep's Calcutta home, the estate would expand to over 23,000 acres by 1850.[62] Its main commercial activity, like the Prinsep estate in Van Diemen's Land, was as a stud to breed horses for the Indian market, particularly the Bengal and Madras Presidencies, but it was also the base for trade in hardwoods, and was a working farm.[63] Due to the presence of 'hill coolies' among the workers, one observer found it 'a droll sort of East India establishment'.[64]

---

[57] Mrs A. Prinsep (ed.), *The Journal of a Voyage from Calcutta to Van Diemen's Land*, pp. 55, 78, 89, and 107.

[58] Sir Henry Thoby Prinsep, 'Three Generations in India, 1771–1904', Vol. II, Mss Eur C97/2, British Library.

[59] Staples, 'The Prinsep Estate in Western Australia', p. 17.

[60] Mrs A. Prinsep (ed.), *The Journal of a Voyage from Calcutta to Van Diemen's Land*, p. 116.

[61] Joyce Westrip and Peggy Holroyde, *Colonial Cousins: A Surprising History of Connections Between India and Australia* (Adelaide: Wakefield Press, 2010), pp. 6, 75, 77, 81; Pamela Statham Drew, *James Stirling: Admiral and Founding Governor of Western Australia* (Crawley: University of Western Australia Press, 2003), pp. 348–9.

[62] Malcolm Allbrook, *Henry Prinsep's Empire: Framing a Distant Colony* (Canberra: Australian National University Press, 2014), p. 122.

[63] Edward Wilson Landor, *The Bushman: Life in a New Country* (1847; republished Twickenham, UK: Senate, 1998), p. 374; Allbrook, *Henry Prinsep's Empire*, p. 123.

[64] Drew, *James Stirling*, p. 349.

Nevertheless, Aboriginal labour was perhaps a more significant issue. Waller Clifton turned to the local Aboriginal people for assistance from the moment the *Parkfield* arrived on 18 March 1841. Within three days of arrival, Clifton headed to Perth to consult the governor on Australind's site. His small party included 'a Native Guide' who went 'on Horse back with Us'; such reliance on Aboriginal guides was typical for both settlers and explorers.[65] Interaction between the Australind community and local Aborigines continued. On 27 April 1841, Clifton noted in his journal amid the welter of other details, 'Natives forboded Rain, but there was no indication of it'.[66] [The rain arrived two days later.] Seemingly, Waller Clifton often took one or two Aborigines with him on his early short explorations of the Australind vicinity. Soon after noting in his journal that, on 6 May 1841, he had named a beautiful park-like area 'Wakefield Plain' after 'my Friend our Director' Edward Gibbon Wakefield, he vents his disgust towards the Aboriginal man Jugan who accompanied him on this trip. Jugan and his wife camped close by Clifton's party:

> Jugan & his wife pigged together close with us & I was entirely disgusted with the savage brutality of this Native. In fact they are all Murderers & fellows who are a disgrace to human Nature and have not one redeeming quality. The selfishness of the Man & his brutal unkindness to his Wife & refusing her almost anything we offered her made me detest this Race more than ever.[67]

Despite Clifton's vitriolic condemnation, Aborigines were employed to perform labour at Australind, such as clearing roads, for which they were paid in flour.

In late June, though, a spate of thefts of flour and pork from the community's storehouses caused much turmoil. Interaction between the settlers and the Aborigines in the area was such that the latter were known to settlers individually, though with a cultural mix of names. Clifton and other officials between Bunbury and Australind quickly had warrants for the arrest of eight specific Aboriginal men, including Ninda, Yourga, 'Morechap called Troublehouse', and 'Deerbuck called Chapman'. Clifton sent a party of men in pursuit. The Aboriginal men held responsible escaped, but the party 'seiz[ed] 3 or 4 Women & [broke] about 50 Spears'.[68] On 2 July, 'Chapman the Native' surrendered to settler authorities, soon after which 'Troublehouse & Ninda' were also apprehended. Clifton played a role in the three Aboriginal men being remanded and committed for punishment, which involved sending them to Bunbury, during which journey Chapman escaped. Troublehouse and Ninda were less fortunate: they were sent by ship to Fremantle.[69] This was one small incident in the larger process in which many Western Australian Aborigines were deemed criminals and made convicts.

By 10 September 1841, perhaps because of the settlement's continuing dependence on Aboriginal assistance, Clifton decided on a path of negotiation. He 'called

---

[65] Barnes et al. (eds), *The Australind Journals of Marshall Waller Clifton*, p. 26.

[66] Barnes et al. (eds), *The Australind Journals of Marshall Waller Clifton*, p. 32.

[67] Barnes et al. (eds), *The Australind Journals of Marshall Waller Clifton*, p. 35.

[68] Barnes et al. (eds), *The Australind Journals of Marshall Waller Clifton*, pp. 46–8.

[69] Barnes et al. (eds), *The Australind Journals of Marshall Waller Clifton*, p. 50.

[the] Natives together and passed a Bill of Amnesty on Na[s]ting & all of them on condition of good behavior. If they commit any improper act, then Nasting(?) is to be given up for the Flour Robbery'.[70] Relations between the Australind settlers and 'their Natives' were sufficiently congenial that on 13 September, when the resident Aborigines held a corroboree 'at Tea Time by the Store', the settlers 'all attended'. Waller Clifton, however, found the event 'degrading to Human Nature to see Men in such a state of Monkeish action'.[71] Clifton's journal shows his continuing struggle between racial vilification and dependence on the Aboriginal people for their labour. For the Aborigines, working for the settlers was a survival strategy in a world where, since around 1830, the coastal groups of the southwest had suffered deaths from frontier conflicts, dispossession, and loss of their food sources.[72]

Penelope Hetherington has argued that the twenty or so years, from the first establishment of the Swan River Colony in 1829 until the importation of convict labour in 1850, constituted a distinct period in which British settlers sought control of the land, but, rather than wanting to be rid of the indigenous people, viewed them as a potential labour source. The 1848 census of the colony showed 541 Aborigines employed by the settlers, 418 men and 123 women. Hetherington points out that Aboriginal people lost their livelihood when they lost their land, so it is unsurprising that they were willing to turn to farm and domestic labour as a means of survival. In 1841 Governor Hutt reported to London that 'owing to the scarcity of European labourers, many are employed in different parts of the colony as menial servants in the houses, or on the farms'.[73] There was no need to separate Aboriginal people onto reserves, Hutt contended, because they should be encouraged 'to mingle among us, and to frequent our dwellings . . . to receive the wages and rewards of hire'. Hutt's views were supported by the Protector of Natives, who in 1841 considered that: 'in the present dearth of white labour, their usefulness to the settler, either in domestic drudgery, or in the rural occupations of the farms, is daily becoming more apparent'.[74] Aboriginal children were part of this labour force. The expectations that Aboriginal children would become workers for the settlers were such that in 1840 a Wesleyan Missionary School for Aboriginal Children was established in Perth, funded partly by the colonial government and partly by local donations. At the school, indigenous children received a little education as well as Christian evangelizing, and were sent out to Perth settlers to work for several hours each day. A similar school was established at Guildford. In return for their labour, Aboriginal children were clothed and fed. Despite initially

---

[70] Barnes et al. (eds), *The Australind Journals of Marshall Waller Clifton*, p. 69.

[71] Barnes et al. (eds), *The Australind Journals of Marshall Waller Clifton*, p. 71.

[72] E. S. Ilbery, 'The Battle of Pinjarra, 1834: I. The Passing of the Bibbulmun', *The Western Australian Historical Society: Journal and Proceedings* Vol. 1, Part 1 (1927): 24–30.

[73] Penelope Hetherington, 'Aboriginal Children as a Potential Labour Force in Swan River Colony, 1829–1850', *Journal of Australian Studies* No. 33 (June, 1992), p. 47. See also Penelope Hetherington, *Settlers, Servants and Slaves: Aboriginal and European Children in the Nineteenth-Century in Western Australia* (Crawley: University of Western Australia Press, 2002).

[74] Hetherington, 'Aboriginal Children as a Potential Labour Force', p. 47.

positive reports on these schools, by the late 1840s not only difficulties at the schools but other aspects of black–white relations made the settlers uneasy.[75]

Chapman devotes a whole chapter of his 147-page Australind treatise to 'The Natives and their Civilization', crediting a friend for help with the chapter—though he does not give the name of the friend, or the extent of the help, other than implying that readers would be impressed if they knew who it was. Conceivably, it may have been George Grey. The chapter argues that 'the natives of New Holland' have been maligned and overlooked by colonizers and observers in Australia, and that:

> the natives of Western Australia, as a body, form a superior class of New Hollanders ... [who] seem, on the whole, to be an inoffensive people, and to have exhibited considerable aptitude for European habits, and have not unfrequently been taken in some small degree into the employ of the settlers.[76]

Chapman continues:

> In every new colony labour is one of the most expensive requisites, and imperfectly as the experiment has hitherto been made, ample proofs have been obtained that there are various occupations to which the powers of the natives might be very advantageously directed, and in which they might be readily engaged, if adequate inducements were held out.[77]

He further suggests that Aboriginal people are known to be skilled at crafts, they engage in trade, and also show inclination towards cultivation of the land. In a pastiche of quotations by unknown observers, recurrent points include that the Aborigines around Perth have become accustomed to working for the settlers: 'They cut wood, draw water, go errands for the settlers', but instead of being paid proper wages, they receive only 'flour and broken bread'. The settlers should instead work towards 'the civilization and settlement of the native population' by 'rewarding them proportionately to the white labourers for the work they perform', and thus bring them 'into the state of an industrious peasantry'.[78] Chapman indicates that the Western Australian Company has worked with the Aborigines Protection Society, and submitted a petition to the Secretary of State for the Colonies asking that, in connection to Australind, the Aborigines be given some land adequate to their needs in return for the 'extinction of their title to the crown lands of the colony'. The petition requests some legal protection of Aboriginal life and property, measures to promote their advancement, and their 'enjoyment of equal civil rights with the other inhabitants of the colony'.[79] The settlers at Australind, then, according to Chapman, should employ the local Aborigines, and turn them into a peasant class who work for wages, in order to save and civilize

[75] Hetherington, 'Aboriginal Children as a Potential Labour Force', pp. 41–55.
[76] Chapman, *The New Settlement of Australind*, p. 95.
[77] Chapman, *The New Settlement of Australind*, pp. 97–8.
[78] Chapman, *The New Settlement of Australind*, p. 112.
[79] Chapman, *The New Settlement of Australind*, pp. 102–3.

Fig. 2.4 T. C. Dibdin, 'A View of Koombana Bay, or Port Leschenault' from a sketch by Louisa Clifton *c.*1840 (London: Smith, Elder, & Co. for the Western Australian Company). National Library of Australia, an6016139-V.

them. Sadly, however, rather than becoming an employed peasant class, Aborigines around Australind faced dispossession and criminalization.

One of the rich sources we have about Australind is the journal of Louisa Clifton, the eldest daughter of Waller and Elinor Clifton (see Fig. 2.4). We can see in Louisa's private record perhaps a more mixed reaction to Aborigines than her father's. At first, she was repelled, commenting on two Aborigines who came aboard the *Parkfield* two days after its arrival:

> They were both covered, but I was more shocked than I can express at their appearance. I never witnessed so affecting a sight as this display of the degradation of humanity. They do not look like human beings, so thin, so hideous, so filthy; oiled and painted, red faces and hair, and pieces of rush passed through their hair. They danced and distressed us still more; in fact I feel distressed at the idea of living among such a people, so low, so degraded a race.[80]

---

[80] Lucy Frost (ed.), *No Place for a Nervous Lady: Voices from the Australian Bush* (Melbourne: McPhee Gribble Publishers, 1984), p. 46.

Louisa Clifton continues to refer to the 'natives' who were around the settlement, and who were used in various ways as servants and messengers. Soon after the *Parkfield* arrived, Mr Eliot, the Resident Magistrate for Port Leschenault, came on board one evening with other settlers and officials. He brought 'his two little native boys' with him, who, though frightened by the group, 'behaved extremely well': 'Guanga hung round Mr Eliot with a sweet confiding manner and then read the English alphabet clearly and boldly'.[81]

At one point Louisa refers to the 'Coombanah Road which Papa had set some Indians to clear'.[82] By 'Indians', did she mean the Aborigines, as in the British usage common, for example, in the first few years of settlement in Sydney? Or, did she actually mean Indian workers, such as those employed at the nearby Prinsep estate? Her mixed usage leads to some ambiguity, such as her journal entry for 21 June 1841, when she refers to 'the store which a native informs Papa has been broken up by some Indians, and 3 casks of flour stolen'. Are the 'native' and the 'Indians' from the same group, or not? The fact that by 'Indians' she means Aborigines is clear when she refers to 'the delinquents, Troublehouse, Chapman and Wemar' and later describes the sequel:

> Houblehouse and another Indian were brought up here, Chapman having turned King's evidence and given up his accomplices in stealing flour out of the store. William Hooper brought the poor creatures to Papa. Their distress and terror appeared great... Some of them will be sent, I fear, to Rottnest; a dreadful punishment, it is; their heads are shaved and they become convicts in fact; but being deprived of liberty and independence so dear to wild man, they soon die of broken hearts... When will justice appear on earth? Not I fear while white man who professes Christianity falls so far short of acting up to its first principles. I cannot help liking these poor people, especially the children.[83]

This allusion to convicts on Rottnest Island confirms that the 'Indians' to whom she refers were Aborigines, for whose incarceration a prison had been established on the island in 1839. Louisa Clifton seems to have developed more sympathy for Aborigines, but the ambiguity in her terminology suggests a conceptual blurring of types of non-white labourers—as well as vagueness with their assigned names.[84] Perhaps it is not surprising then, given this blurred classification in at least one settler's mind, that, according to a contemporary observer, Aborigines and Indian labourers in the Australind area seemed to understand each other much sooner than the white settlers understood the Aborigines.[85] Waller Clifton's racial categorization is not always entirely clear either: was the 'Black Tom' who became his household servant on 22 September an Aboriginal man or Indian?[86]

The extended Clifton family stayed on at Australind. Louisa married Mr Eliot, the Resident Magistrate, with whom she had eight children; they remained near

[81] Frost (ed.), *No Place for a Nervous Lady*, p. 52.
[82] Frost (ed.), *No Place for a Nervous Lady*, p. 61.
[83] Frost (ed.), *No Place for a Nervous Lady*, pp. 76, 81–2.
[84] Drew, *James Stirling*, p. 325 and following.   [85] Landor, *The Bushman*, p. 55.
[86] Barnes et al. (eds), *The Australind Journals of Marshall Waller Clifton*, p. 72.

Australind until 1870 when he was appointed magistrate at Geraldton. This was a fortuitous outcome for Louisa, who had left behind a sweetheart in England when her mother had made it clear that Louisa was needed to help care for the younger children, and Louisa put her duty ahead of self-interest. When they arrived in Western Australia, Louisa was twenty-six; her sister Ellen was twenty; Mary eighteen; Lucy eleven; Rachel seven; and Caroline five years old. Louisa and her sisters have left us a pictorial record of the early stages of Australind, which shows the colony as more bucolic than harsh. We know from the journals that much was uncertain about Australind, with its rocky start compounded by the physical challenges and discomforts of life under canvas and with few amenities. Louisa, Ellen, and Mary's artwork of Australind demonstrates the respectability and gentility they seemingly strove to maintain in their novel and difficult circumstances. But the challenges thrown up by expansionist colonialism were considerable. Ellen became engaged to one of the surveyors at Australind, but her fiancé left to work for the British Colonial Survey department in Ceylon, and died two years later in Singapore when he was returning to marry her. Mary's husband Harley Johnston died in 1853, on his way back home after having taken off for the Victorian goldfields; she was left with four children.[87] These stories of the young Clifton women at Australind illuminate the physical discomforts and emotional trials inherent to white settler colonialism.

While the Cliftons seem to have entrenched their status as Australind's first family, the settlement lost many of the workers they had counted on for labour. To redress this, they sought other kinds of workers. From 1842 onwards, the Western Australian colonial government took 'Government Juvenile Immigrants' from Parkhurst Prison on the Isle of Wight—that is, boy convicts and apprentices—a few of whom escaped on American whaling ships that frequented the area. By 1850 Australind and other parts of Western Australia had become so desperate for labourers that they decided to accept adult convicts—even as the eastern colonies either had or were trying hard to have convict transportation ended. Also, Aboriginal labour continued to be used.[88] We know about the Aboriginal mailmen used in the Bunbury region from 1848 to 1852. As early as August 1841 Waller Clifton first suggested the establishment of such a postal service,[89] and later in 1848 suggested a plan for Aboriginal mail carriers between Fremantle and Bunbury. The scheme was indeed implemented, with Aboriginal convicts being released from Rottnest Island, the Perth road gang, and elsewhere, to serve out their sentences by carrying the mail on these southern routes; it was also extended to other routes. The Aboriginal mailmen were given rations of flour and meat, sometimes tobacco; sometimes they wore government-supplied uniforms. It was arduous physical labour, as various commentators observed.[90]

---

[87] Barnes et al. (eds), *The Australind Journals of Marshall Waller Clifton*, pp. 2, 661–3.

[88] Penelope Hetherington has written about the extensive use of child labour in nineteenth-century Western Australia, both white and Aboriginal, in *Settlers, Servants and Slaves*.

[89] Barnes et al. (eds), *The Australind Journals of Marshall Waller Clifton*, p. 55.

[90] Brian Pope, 'Aboriginal Message and Mail Carriers in South Western Australia in the Early and Mid-Nineteenth Century', in B. K. de Garis (ed.), *Portraits of the South West: Aborigines, Women and*

Perhaps because of the serious setback in England prior to the *Parkfield*'s departure, Australind struggled severely in its first years. Whereas in December 1842 its population was about 350, by October 1846 it had dropped to only 76. In June 1843 the directors of the Western Australian Company dismissed Waller Clifton, though they employed his son Pearce at a lower rate for the next few years. In 1846 the shareholders of the company decided to dissolve it, although it continued to exist legally until the 1870s.[91] Despite its own difficulties and Western Australia's wider struggle to attract settlers, Australind did stay afloat, though it did not become the Wakefieldian utopia its planners had envisaged. The 1848 census in Western Australia showed Australind rebounding with a population of 4,622, of whom 413 were landed proprietors, professional men, or merchants, and 1,157 were workmen. By 1850 the population had risen to 5,886. Australind still exists as a holiday town and dormitory suburb of Bunbury.

According to Edward Landor, who visited Australind in December 1842 as a companion of the colony's governor, the reason that the settlement failed to fulfil its founders' hopes was clear: the land allotments were too small for profitable farming. Landor reported that Australind seemed promising at the time of his visit, indeed that it was 'alive with well-dressed young men and women' who had just arrived as settlers, and that the Clifton family provided him and the governor with hospitality. But, writing in 1847, he noted that 'the town has long since been deserted, except by half a dozen families; and the newly arrived settlers are dispersed over the colony'. The hundred acres allotted to each settler was too small, he contended: 'far too small for the wants of the settler who found that he might probably be able to supply his table with vegetables, [but] he had small prospects of ever applying his capers to boiled mutton or [beef]'. Instead, most settlers abandoned Australind to look for 'a grant of three or four thousand acres'.[92] It was not an outcome that Edward Gibbon Wakefield had envisioned, though to some extent it underscored his reasoning for seeking to concentrate settlement.

CONCLUSION

In the last two decades, work in imperial and colonial history has produced new perspectives on Wakefield. Studies of settler colonialism have begun to incorporate the perspectives of the indigenous people who were dispossessed by it, though there is still much work to be done. For example, Ngata Love's 1997 assessment of the significance of Wakefield's work in establishing the New Zealand Association and the New Zealand Company was as follows:

the Environment (Nedlands, Western Australia: University of Western Australia Press, 1993), pp. 63–73.

[91] Burgess, 'The Settlement at Australind', pp. 26–7.

[92] Landor, *The Bushman*, pp. 403–30.

[Maori] lost their lands, their laws, their language, their livelihood, their very reason for being. It was total devastation... The people could not even protest peacefully to protect their land ownership, their way of life. Without committing violence, they were brutally taken, imprisoned without trial, and some died.[93]

Rebecca Durrer's doctoral thesis completed at the University of Houston in 2000, on Wakefield and the settlement of New Zealand, makes a related point about the strength of Maori resistance and Wakefield's shortcomings in overlooking 'the realities of colonizing an occupied land in his theoretical foundation', and thus not anticipating the need for a British military presence and the expense of maintaining it.[94]

As Tracey Banivanua Mar and Penelope Edmonds contend, 'settler colonialism's political economies have always pivoted on relations of race'.[95] Given that insight, perhaps we should not be surprised by the inclusion of Asian labourers in the planners' visions for systematic colonies; perhaps, rather, we should be more surprised about their absence from earlier discussions of Wakefieldian settlements. The historiographical shift towards the transnational and the global is also relevant here. Even a cursory glance at the decades of historical work on Wakefield shows the extent to which it has been contained within colonial or national borders. Wakefield's work on 'systematic colonization' shaped several of the Australian colonies, was quite significant in Canada, and foundational for multiple settlements in New Zealand, yet his involvement in these disparate places has often been studied discretely. Looking across colonial boundaries helps us to see broader patterns in Wakefield's visions, and points to their significance.

The earlier scholarly focus on Wakefield's core scheme of land sales and an emigration fund for British labourers excluded attention to his interest in Pacific and Asian labourers, and their significance for his planned colonies. We now know that there *were* indentured Asian labourers in Wakefieldian settlements from early on, not only those nearby Australind. Heather Foster's research has given us a picture of the seventeen or eighteen indentured Indian labourers brought to South Australia from Chota Nagpur in Bihar state by Joseph Bruce as early as 1838 who were employed by Bruce and others in the Adelaide region. Foster further notes the twenty-four Indian labourers brought to Adelaide by E. B. Gleeson from Calcutta in the same year, many of whom were taken by Gleeson to labour for him in the Clare Valley, along with some of the surviving labourers from the group imported by Bruce.[96]

---

[93] Ngata Love, 'Edward Gibbon Wakefield: A Maori Perspective', in Friends of the Turnbull Library Symposium, *Edward Gibbon Wakefield and the Colonial Dream: A Reconsideration* (Wellington: GP Publications, 1997), p. 5.

[94] Rebecca Durrer, 'Changing British Imperial Ideology: Edward Gibbon Wakefield and the Colonization of New Zealand', PhD thesis, University of Houston, 2000 (Proquest, Ann Arbor, MI, microform), pp. 179–80.

[95] Tracey Banivanua Mar and Penelope Edmonds (eds), *Making Settler Colonial Space: Perspectives on Race, Place and Identity* (Houndmills, Basingstoke: Palgrave Macmillan, 2010), p. 4.

[96] Heather Foster, 'The First Indians: The Bruce and Gleeson Indentured Labourers in Nineteenth-Century South Australia', *Journal of the Historical Society of South Australia* no. 39 (2011): 21–30.

As Chapter 3 will discuss in detail, settlers in the Australian colonies rapidly came to depend on Aboriginal labour. As white settlers dominated more and more land in the Australian colonies from the 1820s, and Aboriginal people were increasingly dispossessed, in frontier and rural areas settlers turned to Aboriginal people for labour—though they did not compensate them as they would have European labourers. Various historians have documented this widespread exploitation of Aboriginal labour, such as Hetherington's study of the schemes under which Aboriginal children were used for labour in southern Western Australia in the early to mid-nineteenth century.[97] And it is worth noting that, in relation to New Zealand, Wakefield argued that Maori below the rank of chief 'should be encouraged to work for wages'.[98]

One conclusion we can draw, of course, is that Wakefield spread himself rather widely in his discursive wanderings as well as his travels. But perhaps there is more at stake than that easy conclusion would allow. Wakefield's 'systematic colonies' were integral to the founding of New Zealand, and a key factor in the continental spread of British colonization in Australia. Wakefield and his followers, who included four of his brothers and his son, spurred settler colonialism in Australasia, as well as contributing to the movement for representative and responsible government. Historians have long connected Wakefield's work to the migration of British settlers and labourers, and have been preoccupied with the class implications of Wakefield's schemes—though some have condemned Wakefield as a conservative seeking to replicate English class structures in the southern colonies, while others have hailed him as a radical and reformer. But the Wakefieldian vision was of British settler colonies that had racial as well as class divisions. It has long been acknowledged that Wakefield's visions were not fully realized; and perhaps were so contradictory that they could not have been. Yet it has not been recognized that Wakefield's vision was not of purely British settler colonies; rather, it was of British settler colonies that depended on a racially mixed variety of labourers, including Indian and Chinese indentured workers as well as indigenous peoples. Wakefield's systematic colonization, integral as it was to rapidly spreading settler colonialism, contained key features of plantation societies and mercantile and crown colonies, suggesting that colonialism in this period was both broad and blurred. For all of Wakefield's condemnation of slavery and convict transportation, unfree labour and the exploitation of non-white workers were both factors in his scheme.

---

[97] Hetherington, *Settlers, Servants and Slaves.*
[98] Bloomfield, *Edward Gibbon Wakefield*, p. 221.

3

Settler Men as Masters of Labour: Convicts and Non-white Workers

From the 1820s to the 1860s as white settlement expanded, Indigenous people lost their land, their livelihoods, and their lives in an unequal struggle. Settlers pushed across Van Diemen's Land, in and around the Swan River Colony, into and extending from the Port Phillip District, in and across South Australia, and south, westward, and north from the Sydney region up into what became Queensland. Knowledge of frontier violence, often tacit, was integral to white settler society in these decades, but the establishment of a racial system that benefitted white settlers involved more than dispossession and violence. It also involved the exploitation and employment of Aboriginal and other non-white labourers. The employment of Aboriginal people by settlers has usually been studied separately from the importing of indentured labourers. When we put both forms of non-white labour together, we see how widespread it was in the decades of rapid settler expansion. Moreover, the employment of Aboriginal, Indian, Chinese, and Pacific Islander workers around the Australian colonies occurred alongside the extensive system of convict assignment to private masters and mistresses in New South Wales and Van Diemen's Land. Thus settlers in the Australian colonies from the 1820s to the 1860s had access to an extraordinary range of labourers, in combinations that varied by time and place.

Key to Australian history in the mid-nineteenth century are the connections between the struggle for political rights and representation, settler definitions of manhood, and the status of master of non-white labour. Looking at the broader imperial frame, these connections occurred in the period when, after a long and intense campaign, the British parliament legislated to end slavery (1833–34), indentured labour subsequently grew dramatically as an imperial system, and the Australian colonies curtailed their dependence on the recently expanded system of convict labour in staggered steps from 1840 to 1868. Labour systems based on divisions of race, and/or categories of free and unfree, were evolving in ways connected to changing political structures.

The scholarship to date on the mid-nineteenth-century evolution of self-government in the Australian colonies has not focused on the significance of gender—in surprising contrast to work on federation, where gender has long been recognized as a central issue. At the same time, work on masculinity in Australia has focused not on this period so much as on the later nineteenth and the twentieth centuries, so there is much we do not yet know about changing race- and class-contingent ideas of manliness in the early to mid-nineteenth century. When we look beyond Australia's shores, connections between gender and legal and political changes abound. Liberal revolutionary movements around the world in the 1840s were tied to evolving conceptions of (racially restricted) individual male rights, while the gradual nineteenth-century abolition of slave systems also had gendered impacts. Slavery and plantation societies were especially patriarchal in their legal arrangements and cultural practices, compounding early modern patriarchal household structures with racial subordination and the supreme role of the master in slave codes. In his evocation of the complex social world of eighteenth-century Virginia, Rhys Isaac contended that 'the domination of masters over slaves was the fullest manifestation of social power'. Masters of slaves had few constraints on their power over them, and indeed in 'a land of plenty, slaves were kept on short rations by masters relentlessly bent on collecting the surplus needed to sustain their own proud display'.[1] Widows or single women slave owners could be 'female masters', but as wives they were 'in an intermediate situation—as subordinate junior partners to the master'.[2]

The emancipation of slaves led to profoundly gendered cultural as well as economic changes in South Africa, the Americas, and elsewhere, as, for example, freed people created family and community life previously denied them.[3] Like post-slavery societies, in Australia ideas of gender, especially manhood, were at the heart of political struggles: over the social status of emancipated convicts, access to land, class relations, and, ultimately, claims for self-government. Kirsty Reid has drawn connections between the model of patriarchal familial authority in the system of convict assignment, and evolving colonial political authority in Van Diemen's Land in the first half of the nineteenth century. Settler men developed 'a moralised masculinity' as fatherly heads of colonial households, each of which became a 'miniature "panopticon"' for the reform and social integration of convicts, thus becoming the virtuous 'fathers of a new race'.[4]

Claims that they were spreading the nobler aspects of British civilization formed a central plank in colonial men's campaign platforms for political representation, alongside assertions of their inheritance of rights to English liberty. Yet evidence from the colonial master and servant laws suggests that control of labour was so crucial to settlers that rights to English liberty were not equally available to all. White settlers, both men and women, shared the status of employing non-white labour across the Australian colonies in this period. Yet I contend that the status of master of non-white labour was especially key to evolving patriarchal conceptions of white settler manhood, and integral to the ideas of such manly independence

---

[1] Rhys Isaac, *The Transformation of Virginia 1740–1790* (Chapel Hill: University of North Carolina Press, 1982), pp. 132–3.

[2] Rhys Isaac, *Landon Carter's Uneasy Kingdom: Revolution and Rebellion on a Virginia Plantation* (New York: Oxford University Press, 2004), p. 181.

[3] Pamela Scully and Diana Paton (eds), *Gender and Slave Emancipation in the Atlantic World* (Durham: Duke University Press, 2005).

[4] Kirsty Reid, *Gender, Crime and Empire: Convicts, settlers and the state in early colonial Australia* (Manchester: Manchester University Press, 2007), pp. 11, 21, 95, 125, 257.

deployed to argue for responsible government in the Australian colonies. Masters outnumbered mistresses, and the magistrates and police constables who oversaw the labour system were all men. And as the restriction of rations was one way in which slave masters exercised their power, in judging how different categories of labourers should be treated and compensated, white settler men asserted their moral authority in legal and material ways.

CONVICT ASSIGNMENT

In the 1820s and 1830s, and continuing up to the last convict shipment to Western Australia in 1868, tens of thousands of convicts were transported by the British imperial government to the Australian colonies. Like the numbers of free settlers, the numbers of convicts transported escalated sharply after the 1815 end of the Napoleonic Wars. Whereas 510 convicts had arrived in 1810, the figure for 1820 was 2,579.[5] Between 1816 and 1840, on average 3,737 convicts arrived each year in New South Wales and Van Diemen's Land, around seven times the annual arrivals in the first decades.[6] While colonial governments continued to use convicts for their own purposes such as constructing public buildings, roads, and bridges, from the 1820s to the 1840s convicts formed the great majority of servants and labourers employed by settlers and constituted the largest part of the colonial population, especially in the eastern parts of Australia. For example, in New South Wales in 1828 assigned convicts outnumbered free settlers by four to one.[7]

Despite the familiar discourse that labelled convicts as worthless reprobates, many employers of assigned convicts not only benefitted economically from the free labour but found convicts to be valuable workers. Annie Baxter, for example, whose husband sold his army commission to become a squatter at Port Macquarie in New South Wales, noted in her memoir, referring to the early 1840s: 'Our farm servants were prisoners but we had only two black sheep out of ten . . . As to my female servants I must say that in Australia I have found the prisoners undoubtedly the best'.[8] In 1820 it was widely thought in New South Wales that justice of the peace William Cox of Richmond benefitted from his close association with Governor Macquarie and the governor's influence in the assignment of convicts to private masters. On Cox's estate, Clarendon, he was master of assigned convicts who included 'a pair of sawyers, a carpenter, a painter and glazier, two blacksmiths, a butcher, a tanner, a harnessmaker, three cobblers and a tailor' as well as those

---

[5] Barrie Dyster, 'Public Employment and Assignment to Private Masters, 1788–1821', in Stephen Nicholas (ed.), *Convict Workers: Reinterpreting Australia's Past* (Cambridge: Cambridge University Press, 1988), p. 134.

[6] Reid, *Gender, Crime and Empire*, p. 123.

[7] David Neal, *The Rule of Law in a Penal Colony: Law and Power in Early New South Wales* (Cambridge: Cambridge University Press, 1991), p. 133.

[8] Annie Baxter, *Memories of Tasmania and of the Macleay River and New England districts of New South Wales and the Western District of Port Phillip, 1834–1838* (Adelaide: Griffin Press Ltd, 1980), p. 13.

employed in his own private textile manufactory.[9] The system of private assignment was a key aspect of settlers' ability to improve their social and economic status in the colonies compared with their standing in Britain.

The assignment of convict workers to private masters began soon after the arrival of the First Fleet in 1788 and evolved in the changing, hybrid system of colonial labour. Governor Phillip began assigning convict labourers to work for discharged soldiers to whom he granted farming land, and those receiving assigned convicts expanded. Convicts' hours of forced labour were regulated, and a system evolved in which convicts could perform additional labour for pay after 3 p.m. or otherwise in their own time. By 1800 masters could choose to command the after-hours paid labour time of their convict workers, for an annual wage of £10. The ticket-of-leave system developed, in which convicts with records of good behaviour were free to work on their own accord for wages, though they remained under the control of the magistrates and could not return to Britain. There is some evidence that small landowners in particular, who only needed much labour at times such as harvest, worked out flexible arrangements with their assigned convicts such that the convicts could hire themselves out even during normal working hours and the masters received a share of the earnings.[10]

In Van Diemen's Land the private assignment of convicts began early on. When Lieutenant Governor George Arthur arrived in 1824 he introduced a tightly regulated and organized system in which private assignment was considered preferable to government work. In Arthur's system of rewards and punishments, consistent work and respectful demeanour led to a ticket-of-leave, or with further good behaviour, a conditional pardon; free pardons were sometimes awarded though with less frequency. Failure to work, misbehaviour, and offences, on the other hand, were punished by flogging, assignment to government gangs including road work, hard labour in chains, banishment to one of the penal stations such as Macquarie Harbour and Port Arthur, or even execution for serious crimes. This assignment system stayed in place until 1840 for men convicts and 1844 for women, when it was replaced by a different system of probation. Assignment was a system in which convicts with labour skills did well, as could those who chose to abide by the rules and reap the rewards. For the government, private assignment meant a reduced financial burden to maintain the convicts; for settlers, the advantages of free labour were obvious and it was one of the great attractions of Van Diemen's Land in these decades.[11]

Masters and mistresses, not surprisingly, varied a great deal in their treatment of and behaviour towards assigned convicts, as surviving records testify. Some were kind and developed good relationships with their convict servants. Others relied on the system of punishment overseen by magistrates to compel their convicts to work. Relations between masters and mistresses and their convict workers were shaped by

---

    [9] Dyster, 'Public Employment and Assignment to Private Masters', p. 146.
    [10] Dyster, 'Public Employment and Assignment to Private Masters', pp. 128–31.
    [11] Alison Alexander, *Tasmania's Convicts: How Felons Built a Free Society* (Crows Nest: Allen & Unwin, 2010), Ch. 3.

multiple factors, including the location or isolation of the property. Van Diemen's Land farmer George Hobler insisted that his convicts remain clearly subordinate to his authority and believed that flogging was essential to this: 'It is very painful for me to be obliged to flog in this manner, but if I give way to them at all, they at once become my masters'.[12] In this view, the relationship between master and convict was a contest of wills, in which it was necessary for the master to assert and demonstrate his authority in order not to be subordinated.

MASTER AND SERVANT LAW

Magistrates, whose powers were based on those of their counterparts in England but were greater, administered both the convict assignment system and master and servant law. Given the spread of magistrates' districts in Australia, and the autonomy they enjoyed in their local areas, it is not surprising that there is much evidence of abuse of their powers. David Neal, in his authoritative study of the rule of law in early Australia, contends that magistrates enjoyed a 'creative confusion' between the convict code and master and servant law, that overreaching their powers in relation to free labourers was widespread particularly in the 1820s, and that this tendency was helped by the fact that many magistrates had naval and military backgrounds.[13] Magistrates, who also supervised the police, oversaw the daily functioning of the convict assignment system in their districts, such as the keeping of musters, assignment to particular masters and mistresses, decisions on tickets-of-leave, hearing of cases brought by employers against convicts, and punishment. Punishments they could inflict included imprisonment, further transportation, the treadmill, and floggings. Flogging was more widely inflicted in New South Wales in the early nineteenth century than it was in England; the colony had a higher ratio of police to population than in England and higher levels of surveillance and corporal punishment.[14] Governor Bourke introduced the 1832 *Summary Jurisdiction Act* to regulate magistrates' powers, yet even the new act allowed them to impose such a wide array of corporal punishments that Bourke, who was familiar with slavery from his time in South Africa, thought it not unlike what might be stipulated in a slave code; he was not alone in drawing such comparisons.[15]

New South Wales enacted the first Australian master and servant law in 1828; from 1828 to 1868 law in this area was passed and revised in multiple instances and in the various colonies. Michael Quinlan has studied the Australian colonies' enactment of master and servant legislation in the early to mid-nineteenth century, starting with New South Wales in 1828, then Van Diemen's Land and South Australia in 1837, and finally Queensland in 1861. Most colonies had a succession of such laws, and retained them far longer than Britain, which repealed its law in 1875. Quinlan suggests that colonial master and servant legislation was harsher in general than its metropolitan counterpart, calling it 'an overtly interventionist

[12] Quoted in Alexander, *Tasmania's Convicts*, p. 38.   [13] Neal, *The Rule of Law*, p. 134.
[14] Neal, *The Rule of Law*, pp. 139, 165.   [15] Neal, *The Rule of Law*, pp. 136–7.

reshaping of employment relations'.[16] Initial colonial laws 'granted sweeping powers to aggrieved employers and scant redress to servants'; later versions were somewhat more moderate, but still tougher than British law.[17] One notable colonial innovation was the compulsory discharge certificate system, requiring workers to receive a written discharge from an employer at the end of a contract term, which they then had to present to a new employer.[18] Quinlan characterizes the Australian colonial laws as 'more one-sided' and 'more coercive' than the British version, with 'expectations of worker deference'.[19] Further, he posits reasons for colonial severity in this area: that labour regulation in the colonies was at first shaped by the convict system; labour was scarce in the colonies, which gave workers more advantage; the population was thin and widely scattered, which meant workers could threaten the property and even the lives of employers; and in the early 1850s the gold rush made all this worse.[20] The severity of colonial master and servant law shows how important their powers as employers were to settlers, and underscores the significance of settler demand for non-white labour. As Alan Atkinson and Marian Aveling have put it, 'the dream of a cheap, reliable, non-British workforce scattered through the Australian countryside was a common one'.[21]

In the nineteenth century, both British and colonial master and servant law changed. Christopher Frank's work on the law in Britain shows how it was renegotiated through mid-century stand-offs between employers and unions.[22] In Australia, master and servant law evolved in the mid-century too. Colonial law evolved to supplement British law, and to cover situations particular to the colonial context, such as workers absconding from pastoral stations after they arrived, and evading their pre-arranged contracts when they found wages elsewhere higher than their contracts stipulated.[23] Other provisions developed to cover situations specific to the colonies included those pertaining to injury to and loss of livestock by shepherds, harbouring absconders, hiring servants indentured to another, and the certificates of discharge intended to prevent such poaching of labourers.[24] Adrian

---

[16] Michael Quinlan, 'Pre-arbitral Labour Legislation in Australia' in Stuart Macintyre and Richard Mitchell (eds), *Foundations of Arbitration: The Origins and Effects of State Compulsory Arbitration 1890–1914* (Melbourne: Oxford University Press, 1989), p. 29.

[17] Michael Quinlan, 'Australia, 1788–1902: Workingman's Paradise?', in Douglas Hay and Paul Craven (eds), *Masters, Servants, and Magistrates in Britain and the Empire, 1562–1955* (Chapel Hill: University of North Carolina Press, 2004), pp. 223–5.

[18] Quinlan, 'Pre-arbitral Labour Legislation in Australia', p. 31.

[19] Quinlan, 'Australia, 1788–1902', pp. 224, 225, and 247. Also relevant here are Kay Saunders, *Workers in Bondage: The Origins and Bases of Unfree Labour in Queensland 1824–1916* (St Lucia: University of Queensland Press, 1982) and David Denholm, 'Some Aspects of Squatting in New South Wales and Queensland, 1847–1854', PhD thesis, Australian National University, 1972.

[20] Quinlan, 'Australia, 1788–1902', pp. 224–7.

[21] Alan Atkinson and Marian Aveling (eds), *Australians 1838* (Sydney: Fairfax, Syme & Weldon Associates, 1987), p. 122.

[22] Christopher Frank, *Master and Servant Law: Chartists, Trade Unions, Radical Lawyers and the Magistracy in England, 1840–1865* (Farnham, Surrey: Ashgate, 2010).

[23] Adrian Suzanne Merritt, 'The Development and Application of Masters and Servants Legislation in New South Wales—1845 to 1930', PhD thesis, Australian National University, 1981, pp. 40–2.

[24] Merritt, 'The Development and Application of Masters and Servants Legislation in New South Wales', pp. 50–2.

Merritt has shown that, particularly prior to 1860, Australian master and servant laws discriminated against employees by applying criminal penalties (gaol terms), whereas employers faced only civil penalties such as being forced to pay outstanding wages.[25] Over the course of the nineteenth century, the weighting of the system against employees shifted. In the early to mid-century, New South Wales court cases under master and servant law were predominantly those brought by employers against employees, with, for example, absconding charges constituting 39.7 per cent of cases between 1845 and 1860. Later in the century workers increasingly used the law to claim their rights: employee-initiated cases rose steadily from the 1860s, with wages cases being 69.3 per cent of those brought between 1861 and 1880.[26]

The settlers who were masters of labour benefitted from this system created by the legislators among them and overseen by the magistrates. Merritt contends that employees saw the system as operating in the employers' and magistrates' favour, with magistrates commonly descending from the bench to act as complainant or defendant in a case, before returning to the bench.[27] The conflict of interest between settler men as masters of labour on the one hand, and as magistrates and supposed arbiters in the employment system on the other, produced some egregious instances. David Denholm discovered that:

> at Tenterfield in northern New England [New South Wales], between November 1847 and December 1850, the magistrate Dr Rowland John Traill summonsed a total of 22 of his station servants; his brother-in-law Edward Irby presiding over seven of the cases. Six of the 22 were awarded the maximum gaol sentence of three months, and another six were awarded the maximum gaol sentence in default of monetary fines which themselves varied.[28]

While magistrates were legally prohibited from punishing their own assigned convict workers, the practice of magistrates doing favours for each other in sentencing each other's convict workers, or turning a blind eye to irregularities, was widespread.[29]

The Australian colonial labour system was built on the peculiarities of the convict system, which was its backbone, and sought to overcome the common shortage of labour—perceived by settlers as a serious problem especially after 1840 with the gradual winding down of convict transportation—as well as the isolation of pastoral properties. It was a hybrid system that incorporated not only ticket-of-leave and free workers, but also the numerous, scattered groups of Indian and Chinese indentured labourers (and indeed Pacific Islanders even before 1850), and

[25] Adrian Merritt, 'The Historical Role of Law in the Regulation of Employment—Abstentionist or Interventionist?', *Australian Journal of Law & Society* Vol. 1 No. 1 (1982): 68–9.

[26] Merritt, 'The Historical Role of Law in the Regulation of Employment': 62; Merritt, 'The Development and Application of Masters and Servants Legislation in New South Wales', p. 208.

[27] Merritt, 'The Development and Application of Masters and Servants Legislation in New South Wales', p. 99.

[28] Denholm, 'Some Aspects of Squatting in New South Wales and Queensland', p. 140.

[29] Neal, *The Rule of Law*, p. 134.

Aboriginal workers pulled into the system in casual, often improperly compensated and unregulated ways.

EXPLOITING ABORIGINAL LABOUR

Mrs J. Fairfax Conigrave, who arrived with her parents in 1853, and whose father purchased land on Hindmarsh Island in South Australia, recalled: 'Papa used to employ a number of [Aborigines] at harvest time, as the wheat had to be reaped with the sickle ... The consequence was we often had a whole tribe of blacks, with their lubras and piccaninnies camped a few hundred yards below our house ... Some of the women made excellent servants and we became very attached to them ... We had a washerwoman who was really a fine character'.[30] Many and varied accounts from the mid-century decades reflect the extent to which Aboriginal people were employed in pastoral, agricultural, and household labour. One writer, commenting on several parts of New South Wales in the 1830s and 1840s, observed an Aboriginal girl working as a shepherd, other Aborigines mustering cattle on horseback and working as stock keepers; but it was 'in tracking that they excel most', being invaluable 'for finding horses and cattle'.[31] A New South Wales sheep station manager in the late 1860s reported that, during shearing: 'I found the blacks, especially the gins, splendid hands at rolling the fleeces and picking up [the wool] on the floor'.[32]

Richard Broome has shown that, while in South Australia from 1836 Aboriginal people worked as servants, messengers, seamen, blacksmiths, and gatherers of wood and water, in southern New South Wales and the Port Phillip District from 1830 they worked in similar capacities as well as clearing ground, ferrying sheep across rivers, as native police troopers and guides, in fishing, sealing, whaling, and gardening, and in the pastoral industry as shepherds, stockmen, bullock drivers, and in sheep washing.[33] Similarly, Henry Reynolds, in documenting and paying tribute to the Aboriginal people who worked as 'stockworkers, shepherds, trackers, troopers, pearl-divers or servants' across the Australian frontier, contends that they 'were in a very real sense Australia's black pioneers'.[34] (See Fig. 3.1.)

Evidence of the employment of Aboriginal servants and labourers is to be found in records from across the Australian colonies. As mentioned in the introduction to this volume, Mrs Alice Hughes wrote in her memoir of her 1840s childhood in Wellington, South Australia, about 'a black lubra who [did] washing for us' and other Aboriginal people who 'would do a little work for tea or sugar or a stick of

---

[30] Mrs J. Fairfax Conigrave, *My Reminiscences of the Early Days* (Perth: Brokensha and Shaw Ltd, 1938), p. 21.

[31] John Henderson, *Excursions and Adventures in New South Wales* (London: W. Stroberl, 1851), pp. 122–3, 194.

[32] Robert D. Barton, *Reminiscences of an Australian Pioneer* (Sydney: Tyrrell's Ltd, 1917), p. 157.

[33] Richard Broome, 'Aboriginal Workers on South-Eastern Frontiers', *Australian Historical Studies* No. 103 (1994): 202–20.

[34] Henry Reynolds, *Black Pioneers* (Ringwood, Victoria: Penguin Books, 2000), pp. 15, 16.

Fig. 3.1 Robert Dowling, *Mrs Adolphus Sceales with Black Jimmie on Merrang Station* (1856). (Oil on canvas mounted on plywood, 76 cm × 101.5 cm).

National Gallery of Australia, Canberra. Purchased from the Founding Donors Fund 1984.

tobacco'.[35] Lady Denison noted in her journal in December 1847, in relation to Van Diemen's Land, a small number of Aboriginal people having been 'brought up . . . in the service of English people'.[36] Kathleen Lambert, in her 1890 memoir, recalled Aboriginal servants in 1850s New South Wales: 'A friend of mine had a woman, Emma, an excellent laundress; her husband Harry was groom and handy-man, and Fanny was nurse to my friend's first child'.[37] The careful training of Aboriginal people to work as servants occurred in instances around the colonies. In her memoir of her childhood in Port Fairy, western Victoria, in the 1850s, Margaret Brown recalled that a Mrs Dunlop and her two sons 'had a pretty house and garden in a hollow between two hills and were served entirely by aboriginal [sic] servants, men and women whom Mrs Dunlop had trained'.[38] (See Fig. 3.2.)

[35] Mrs F. [Alice] Hughes, *My Childhood in Australia* (London: Digby, Long and Co., 1892), pp. 28, 47.

[36] Sir William Denison, *Varieties of Vice-regal Life* (London: Longman Green and Co., 1870), p. 67.

[37] Kathleen Lambert ('Lyth'), *The Golden South: Memories of Australian Home Life, 1843–1888* (London: Ward and Downey, 1890), p. 62.

[38] Margaret Emily Brown, *A Port Fairy Childhood 1849/60* (Port Fairy, Victoria: Port Fairy Historical Society, 1990), p. 26.

BUSH MAILMAN

Fig. 3.2 S. T. Gill, 'Bush Mailman', from *Australian Sketchbook* (Melbourne: Hamel & Ferguson, 1865).

National Library of Australia, an7149190.

Some settlers claimed to have affectionate patronage relationships with individual Aboriginal children, such as Thomas Browne [Rolf Boldrewood] who noted in his memoirs, referring to the western districts of Victoria in the 1840s: 'I had adopted a small black boy [named] Tommy... He was a good deal spoiled and, though occasionally useful with the cattle, did pretty much as he liked'.[39] Yet such supposedly benign relationships were often coercive.

Shirleene Robinson's research has revealed the pervasive exploitation of Aboriginal child labour in Queensland from 1842 to 1902, when some regulation was finally introduced. Robinson contends that Aboriginal child workers were commonly kidnapped and taken from their families (often by the Native Police Force), received no wages, and were often treated with harsh physical violence and emotional abuse. Aboriginal girls were mostly used as domestic servants, and Aboriginal boys in the pastoral, pearling, and *bêche-de-mer* (trepang or sea cucumber) industries; smaller numbers were employed as companions and guides for explorers and settlers, as labourers, interpreters, and even as circus performers.[40]

[39] Rolf Boldrewood [Thomas Alexander Browne], *Old Melbourne Memories* (first pub. 1884; republished Melbourne: William Heinemann, 1969), p. 59.

[40] Shirleene Robinson, 'The Unregulated Employment of Aboriginal Children in Queensland, 1842–1902', *Labour History* No. 82 (May 2002): 5–6.

It was a brutal system in which Aboriginal children suffered even more than European child workers or Aboriginal adults; colonial officials usually ignored their suffering, and even when black children ran away they were typically forced to return to their 'employers'.[41] Meanwhile, across the continent in the Swan River Colony, in 1840 the Wesleyan Missionary School for Aboriginal Children was established in Perth to train Aboriginal children to be servants and labourers for settlers, a scheme considered to be of such value that it received public funding.[42]

In some circumstances, records reveal a mutual interdependence of settlers and displaced Aboriginal people for whom casual employment was their livelihood, an unequal reciprocity forged through mutual needs. Margaret Menzies, from Perth, Scotland, arrived in New South Wales in 1839 and settled with her husband in the small coastal town of Kiama, south of Sydney. She recorded in her diary her interactions with local Aboriginal people:

> Some of the natives are useful for sending from place to place and deliver their message distinctly. One brought me a lb of lard from Mick Thrace's wife at Jamberoo the other day . . . This morning two or three women came with some crayfish and got sugar from Mrs Smith and Roberts [an Aborigine] gave her 2/- for ½ lb tea and 2 lb sugar and understood perfectly the quantity he should get . . . it is astonishing how fond they are of tea and sugar.[43]

But it is clear, too, that Aboriginal people, as far as they could, engaged in these relations on their own terms. Eliza Sarah Mahoney, for example, whose family arrived from Ireland in 1839, recalled in her memoir of her parents' farm north of Adelaide in the Gawler area: 'The blacks we were very much afraid of at first, though they were very quiet. There were about 250 in the Para tribe. We tried to get them to work for us and to wear clothes. After a time they did some work for us, but would never wear the clothes we gave them'.[44]

MIXING CATEGORIES OF LABOURER

As early as 1838 the Western Australian government began a system of criminalizing Aboriginal men, punishing with imprisonment any act that could be interpreted as resistance to settlers or infringement of settlers' property, as well as inter-Aboriginal conflict. In order to establish this system, they took advantage of geography to turn Rottnest Island, off the coast not far from the Swan River, into an Aboriginal prison. Between 1838 and 1904, more than 5,000 Aboriginal men were imprisoned on the island, in a system that made convicts of Aborigines (a fusing of two categories usually considered quite separate in Australian history) and removed

---

[41] Robinson, 'The Unregulated Employment of Aboriginal Children in Queensland': 1–15.
[42] Penelope Hetherington, 'Aboriginal Children as a Potential Labour Force in Swan River Colony, 1829–1850', *Journal of Australian Studies* No. 33 (June 1992): 47–8.
[43] Diary of Margaret Menzies, MS 3261, National Library of Australia.
[44] Eliza Sarah Mahoney, 'The First Settlers at Gawler', in *Proceedings of the Royal Geographical Society of Australasia, South Australian Branch*, XXVIII, 1926–27, from manuscript dated 1898, p. 70.

them from their traditional lands during the period when British invasion of this vast colony was at its most rampant. Aboriginal prisoners were compelled to work at jobs including constructing prison buildings and a lighthouse, on the prison's farm and salt works, and further afield such as in road-work gangs and pearl diving. As Anita King has demonstrated, Rottnest Island exemplifies how the modern evolution of the prison was tied to settler colonialism and the dispossession of indigenous people.[45]

When Edward Landor visited Rottnest in August 1841, he observed 'about twenty native prisoners in the charge of a superintendent and a few soldiers . . . The prisoners were employed in cultivating a sufficient quantity of ground to produce their own food. It was they who had built the superintendent's residence'.[46] Landor did not seem to find this imprisonment disturbing, despite his later observation that the 'native population when in want of a little flour will exert themselves to earn it, by carrying letters, shooting wild ducks with a gun lent to them, driving home cattle or any other easy pursuit'.[47] The willingness of Aboriginal people to work did not prevent them being turned into convicts and unfree labourers. As we saw in Chapter 2 in the section on Australind, Aboriginal convicts worked out their terms doing labour such as arduous postal deliveries on foot over long distances in the southwest, surviving on minimal rations.

There were other ways in which categories of labourer overlapped or were blurred. As the British established isolated coastal settlements around the Australian continent in the nineteenth century, frontier zones proliferated. From Western Australia around the southern coast and Van Diemen's Land, and increasingly further up the east coast, in the scattered contact zones of settlement violence mixed with the more peaceable interactions between settlers and Indigenous people. Interactions exceeded settlers relying on Aboriginal people for labour. Moreover, beside the convicts who were put to work to serve out their sentences up and down the east coast and later in Western Australia, from the 1820s indentured British labourers were brought to the Australian colonies in groups. The first indentured white labourers were contracted by the Australian Agricultural Company for their estate at Port Stephens, but others would follow in Van Diemen's Land, Western Australia, and South Australia.[48] Thus indentured labourers in the Australian colonies were racially diverse. Across Australia settlers employed Indian and Chinese labourers, some brought in small numbers by individual settlers, others arriving under organized schemes. Some Indian workers arrived in Australia individually of their own accord, including those who had been among the thousands of *lascars* crewing the vast numbers of ships plying Indian Ocean and imperial trade routes,

---

[45] Anita King, ' "Conveniently Kept": Aboriginal Imprisonment on Rottnest Island, 1838 to 1904', Honours thesis, School of History, Australian National University, 2011.

[46] Edward Wilson Landor, *The Bushman: Life in a New Country* (1847; republished Twickenham, UK: Senate, 1998), p. 35.

[47] Landor, *The Bushman*, p. 186.

[48] Atkinson and Aveling (eds), *Australians 1838*, p. 121.

and who chose to jump ship in port.[49] In any one settlement, labourers could include a mix of assigned convicts, free or ticket-of-leave workers, servants or indentured labourers from Britain, India, or China, or Aborigines who, especially in these decades, received meagre rations and little else for their labours.

In addition to European indentured workers, various indentured labour schemes brought Indian, Chinese, Pacific Islander, and Maori workers to the Australian colonies in the first half of the nineteenth century. From early in the century some Indians arrived as convicts, while others came as servants brought from India by their British masters and mistresses. We know, for example, about early arrivals in Western Australia, such as Abdulla Zadcock who came as a servant from Bombay before 1832, and Chan Homed and Modsam Nochackaneer who arrived in October 1829 as servants indentured to John L. Morley.[50] In 1816 William Browne brought nine Indian labourers with him from Calcutta to Sydney,[51] and from the 1820s other groups of labourers were brought from India under indenture. Instances included the fourteen servants taken to Port Phillip in 1843, the twenty-five domestic workers including women and children taken to Sydney in 1844, and the fifty people including men, women, and children who arrived in Sydney in 1846.[52] In 1854 Henry Parkes, one of the leaders of the fight for responsible government, himself organized for a group of twenty-four Eurasian men from Madras to be brought to work in Sydney as newspaper compositors. In June 1852 Parkes's newspaper, the *Empire*, had condemned the suggestion of bringing in Eurasians from India, but two years later he defended his own importation, calling these skilled workers 'intelligent and responsible young men', the 'sons of Englishmen by Indian mothers'.[53]

In 1847 Maori and Pacific Islanders were working in the whaling and pastoral industries in New South Wales.[54] The employment of Pacific Islanders escalated in the second half of the century. For example, in the 1860s Mary McConnell and her husband employed 'eight South Sea Islanders' for three years on their station at Cressbrook in Queensland: 'They had by agreement £6 a year and were clothed and fed and their passage paid to and from the islands'.[55] If that rather anodyne rendering of this indentured labour system masks the hardship many islanders suffered, we also know that the Queensland system escalated hugely especially from

[49] On this, see Heather Goodall, Devleena Ghosh, and Lindi Renier Todd, 'Jumping Ship: Indians, Aborigines and Australians Across the Indian Ocean', *Transforming Cultures eJournal* Vol. 1, No. 3 (University of Technology, Sydney, 2008).

[50] Anne Atkinson, *Asian Immigrants to Western Australia 1829–1901* (Nedlands: University of Western Australia Press, 1988), pp. 397, 423.

[51] Alan Dwight, 'The Use of Indian Labourers in New South Wales', *Journal of the Royal Australian Historical Society* Vol. 62, Pt. 2 (September 1976): 114.

[52] James Jupp (ed.), *The Australian People: An Encyclopedia of the Nation, Its People and Their Origins* (Cambridge: Cambridge University Press, 2001), p. 427.

[53] A. W. Martin, *Henry Parkes: A Biography* (Melbourne: Melbourne University Press, 1980), pp. 83, 84, 86.

[54] Janet Doust, 'Setting up Boundaries in Colonial Eastern Australia: Race and Empire', *Australian Historical Studies* Vol. 35 (2004): 159.

[55] Mary McConnell, *Memories of Days Long Gone By* (Brisbane, 1905; self-published), p. 49.

the 1870s, until it was curtailed by immigration restriction acts at the colonial level from 1885 and federally in 1901.

Prior to the large-scale arrival of Chinese prospectors in the gold rush that began in 1851, Chinese workers were brought to the Australian colonies from the 1820s onwards. In 1847, for example, twenty Chinese labourers recruited in Singapore arrived in Western Australia.[56] Particularly between 1848 and 1854, shiploads of indentured Chinese workers were brought by British merchants to work as servants and in the pastoral industry.[57] Ships with Chinese workers arrived in Sydney, Port Phillip, Hobart Town, Moreton Bay, and the Swan River Colony. The *Phillip Laing*, which arrived in Port Phillip in December 1848, for example, brought 219 Asian labourers, 123 of whom were Chinese.[58] One estimate suggests that between 1848 and 1852 more than three thousand Chinese labourers were brought to New South Wales under indenture.[59] While Chinese labourers were usually considered to be valuable and were used for a variety of work, those who sought to take advantage of the schemes that brought Chinese men under indenture were some-times disappointed. Robert Barton chronicled his father's disappointment when he attempted to employ cheap Chinese workers on his sheep station at Boree in the 1850s, when labour was scarce because of the gold rush:

> People who wanted servants could engage Chinese from the ship for a term of three years at a very small monetary wage, with rice and food and some clothes as well. My father got about twenty of these Chinamen and the first thing he set them to work at when they got to the station was to grind the wheat into flour ... However, this arrangement did not last very long. A Chinaman came on a visit one afternoon and told his countrymen who were grinding the wheat to break their engagement as they could only be punished by a few months in gaol and could then go to the goldfields and make big wages ... To have taken them to court would have been a long and tedious trip to the nearest magistrate, and the only punishment they would have got for breaking the agreement was about a month in gaol.[60]

Barton's account illustrates the attractions of indentured labour for employers, as well as how hard it was to keep them during the gold rush.

It is evident from published memoirs and other primary sources from these decades that many of the numerous settlers who had previously lived in India (with the army or otherwise with the East India Company) brought Indian servants with them to Australia. Annie Baxter recorded in her memoirs that when she and her army officer husband arrived in Van Diemen's Land in January 1835, they visited the home of the colonial solicitor-general, whose grounds were 'studded with tents, and at the entrance of these were several Indians, servants to some gentlemen from Madras'.[61] Similarly R. B. Cumberland, for example, who identified himself as 'an

---

[56] Atkinson, *Asian Immigrants to Western Australia*, p. 3.
[57] Jupp, *The Australian People*, pp. 197–8.
[58] Ian Wynd, 'Labour—Supply and Demand in the 1840s', *Investigator: Magazine of the Geelong Historical Society* Vol. 14, No. 1 (March 1979): 32.
[59] Martin, *Henry Parkes*, p. 83.   [60] Barton, *Reminiscences of an Australian Pioneer*, pp. 8–9.
[61] Baxter, *Memories of Tasmania*, p. 5.

Indian Officer' and who first came to Australia on medical leave from service in India, recalled in his memoirs twice bringing Indian servants to Australia. His first residence in Australia consisted of a year spent in Sydney in 1846, on which visit he 'had brought two Indian servants with me, a father and son'.[62] During that first visit he married, then returned to India with his new wife for a further six years of army service, before opting to return to Australia. On this second sojourn Cumberland and his wife brought 'four native servants' with them to Sydney. Eventually they sent these servants back to India, and 'commenced housekeeping with four European female servants and a man'. Cumberland does not explain why they decided to send their servants back to Calcutta; perhaps it was a kindness to the servants. He does, however, note that there had been at least one advantage to employing these Indian servants, during a period when they chose to live outside Sydney in the bush. Seemingly, bushrangers steered clear of their house, choosing to rob their neighbours instead, because 'the thieves were afraid of the four black faces in our kitchen'.[63] While the Cumberlands returned their servants to India, at least some Indian servants brought by their masters and mistresses remained in the Australian colonies.

The employment of non-white domestic servants was so widespread in this period that Emmaline Macarthur, a grandniece of John Macarthur, recalling her home life in Parramatta between 1835 and 1848, recollected that in her father's house convict servants were never 'allowed to enter the home establishment'. Rather the 'maids came from Scotland, [and] our men servants were either free English emigrants or Indians'. Of her own household, she recounted finding 'a clever Indian cook in the kitchen', as well as having 'a negro butler', and 'a Madras manservant'.[64] The 'negro butler' could have been a current or former convict; there were Africans and African Americans among the convicts transported to Australia. More African Americans would come later, in the 1850s, among the diggers who flocked to the gold rush, but those who stayed on were more likely to be self-employed than to become servants.

MIXING WORKERS: THE AUSTRALIAN AGRICULTURAL COMPANY

In various locations, Indian and Chinese labourers intermingled with Aboriginal workers. Edward Landor, who visited southwestern Western Australia in the early 1840s, observed: 'I have noticed that the Coolies of India and the natives of this colony manage to understand one another much sooner than is the case between the latter and the whites',[65] suggesting that Indian indentured labourers were more

---

[62] R. B. Cumberland, *Stray Leaves from the Diary of an Indian Officer* (London: Whitfield, Green and Co., 1865), p. 225.

[63] Cumberland, *Stray Leaves*, pp. 278–89.

[64] Jane de Falbe, *My Dear Miss Macarthur: The Recollections of Emmaline Maria Macarthur (1828–1911)* (Kenthurst, NSW: Kangaroo Press, 1988), pp. 20, 25.

[65] Landor, *The Bushman*, p. 55.

open and willing to communicate with Aboriginal people than at least some settlers. In her memoir of her decades in Australia, Kathleen Lambert recalled of her time on her brother's pastoral station at Montefiores near Wellington in New South Wales in the 1850s that the local labour force included Chinese and Aboriginal workers. At a larger station nearby, the multiple indoor servants including the 'butler' were Chinese while the station hands were Aboriginal. On her brother's smaller station, they had 'Boney', the Chinese cook and gardener, and an Aboriginal man 'Franky' as an outdoor worker. Lambert's colourful anecdotes of station life at Montefiores suggest that there was antagonism between the Chinese and Aboriginal workers, yet represent pastoral station life as mostly very pleasant for the settlers who ruled over this mixed workforce.[66]

We know about the intermixing and mingling of different categories of labourers on the vast estates of the Australian Agricultural Company, at Port Stephens particularly, from the 1820s onwards. The Australian Agricultural Company was formed as a joint stock venture in Britain in 1824 and became a huge pastoralist enterprise in New South Wales. With its provenance of a royal charter and an act of parliament, and a mandate to use its British capital to develop a pastoral enterprise in an unexploited area of New South Wales, the company received a massive land grant of a million acres at Port Stephens, then considered a long way from Sydney.[67] The company was run by a board of directors in London through a colonial committee in Sydney, but supervised by an executive manager at Port Stephens. Its rationale included taking economic advantage of the convict labour system, and its workforce predominantly consisted of convicts. Yet the company's labourers over the decades were remarkably heterogeneous: beside convicts, they included British indentured 'servants', emancipists and other free workers, Aboriginal men and women, and labourers from China and Germany.[68] While the basis of the company's operations was grazing fine-wool sheep to sell fleeces to the European market, the company's labourers built its extensive operations from the ground up and supplied many of the estate's needs. The Aboriginal employees, mainly local Worimi people, 'worked as shepherds (sheep), stockkeepers (cattle), surveyors, hutkeepers, messengers, envoys, constables, boat rowers and builders'.[69]

The Australian Agricultural Company was determined to be an efficient enterprise run on the best contemporary commercial standards, and to that end it kept extensive records. As well as these records, we have an extraordinary account of the company's operations in the 1820s in the form of a detailed narrative written by its first superintendent, Robert Dawson, who was ultimately dismissed in 1828 for failing to produce sufficient profits.

---

[66] Kathleen Lambert ['Lyth'], *The Golden South: Memories of Australian Home Life from 1843 to 1888* (London: Ward and Downey, 1890), pp. 52–64.

[67] John Perkins, 'Convict Labour and the Australian Agricultural Company', in Stephen Nicholas (ed.), *Convict Workers: Reinterpreting Australia's Past* (Cambridge: Cambridge University Press, 1988), pp. 167–8.

[68] Mark Hannah, 'Aboriginal Workers in the Australian Agricultural Company, 1824–1857', *Labour History* No. 82 (May 2002): 17.

[69] Hannah, 'Aboriginal Workers in the Australian Agricultural Company': 17.

Robert Dawson professed great interest in and tolerance towards the Aboriginal people; he certainly took much advantage of their labour, their curiosity, and their goodwill. There is some evidence to support his own claims of his remarkably good relations with the Worimi, though it is also clear that he oversaw a system in which they were not paid in the same way as European labourers. It is very clear from Dawson's account of his time and work at Port Stephens that the Aboriginal workers lived in intimate proximity to the convicts and other European labourers. The Aborigines learned a kind of pidgin English, while Dawson suggests he learned a little of their language. Amongst the many and varied roles assumed by the Aborigines in this remarkable creole community was, for some at least, that of apprehending absconding convicts, whom, according to Dawson, they called 'croppy'. To illustrate the utility and dedication of his Aboriginal employees, Dawson recounts an incident in which an Aboriginal man called Billy Bungaree single-handedly caught a skilled convict worker called Goodwin who had recently run away:

> [Goodwin] was on the opposite bank of the river, skulking behind the trees to avoid being seen. Bungaree called out for a musket directly, put himself across the river in a boat, and in a few minutes tracked, came up with, and secured the man, who was finally delivered up to a constable stationed at a place called Boarul, where he was handcuffed, and locked up a short time before I accidentally called there.
>
> Although there were many fine able-bodied men amongst the natives, still this Bungaree was by far the largest and most resolute man I had seen, and I have no doubt that he would, armed only with his waddy, have secured the runaway. Goodwin and he were perfectly well known to each other, and the account Bungaree gave of the capture was, that as soon as he came within shot of the prisoner, he called to him to stop, threatening to shoot him if he did not.[70]

Dawson continues the anecdote with the further detail that Goodwin tried to fool Billy Bungaree by telling him that he was on an errand in the service of supervisor Dawson himself. Bungaree was sufficiently knowledgeable about the estate's system that he asked to see the pass Goodwin would have had were he on such an errand. Goodwin presented him with a forged pass, which Bungaree refused to believe was valid and hence arrested the escapee. Dawson completes the story with the comment: 'A pair of trousers was always the reward for such a service, and Bungaree was soon at the store with an order for them. The idea of being so taken by a single native appeared to chagrin Goodwin, and added, I have no doubt, to the annoyance of his subsequent sentence to three-months' labour in the chain-gang'.[71] Perhaps the most striking part of this incident is the fact that Billy Bungaree could call for and receive a musket with which to pursue the escaped convict.

Another episode, related by Dawson, that reflects the complex interweaving of the lives of white labourers, Aborigines, and convicts, occurred when an Aborigine named Tom stole a significant quantity of sugar from one of the company stores.

[70] Robert Dawson, *The Present State of Australia* (first published London, 1830; Alburgh: Archival Facsimiles Ltd, 1987), pp. 299–300.
[71] Dawson, *The Present State of Australia*, p. 301.

As Dawson notes, his own considerable authority on the remote and extensive estate included 'the double capacity of master and magistrate'.[72] He thus took decisions about the administration of justice as he saw fit. In this instance, he decided that it was important for Tom to be punished in order to prevent any future such thefts. He therefore asked the Aboriginal workers in this part of the company settlement to bring Tom, who had disappeared, to him. For over two months, the Aborigines said they did not know where Tom was; Dawson was informed that, in fact, Tom occasionally visited their camp at night. Believing he needed to implement his call for Tom to be brought to justice, Dawson gave the Aborigines in the camp an ultimatum: produce Tom or leave the company settlement. When Tom was still not forthcoming, Dawson insisted that the Aborigines should leave; reluctantly, they took their canoes and moved to the opposite side of the harbour. Soon, Dawson received complaints from the 'white families' in the settlement who were unhappy to have lost their Aboriginal workers:

> [They] were without any servants to assist them in their domestic affairs—nobody to carry water, no fish to be had, nor fire-wood, no messengers, &c. &c. In short, the place appeared a gloomy and almost deserted village, whose cheerfulness and conveniences, it was now clearly seen, had in a great measure depended upon these hitherto calumniated outcasts of the world. I was repeatedly asked when the blacks would return, both by men and women, as they did not know what to do without these useful folks.[73]

It was not only the white labouring families who were unhappy about the Aborigines being in exile from the settlement; the latter began to send deputations to Dawson. It was agreed that the Aboriginal group could return, on the understanding that Tom should either stay completely away or be punished.

Within a few days of the group's return, Tom gave himself up, but being taken to Dawson, ran away again. Some days later, he gave himself up again and finally submitted to being punished. Dawson says that he was truly puzzled about what would be a fair punishment given the drawn-out events, and was relieved to find that the Aboriginal group had already thought this through, with a surprising suggestion: that Tom should receive a flogging, but, importantly, by one of themselves. Dawson hesitated to approve this Aboriginal adoption of a convict punishment for one of their own, but was persuaded that the group had decided it was best. Tom was given a dozen lashes by another Aboriginal man, watched by a gathering of other Aborigines, and took them stoically. When it was over, he sought Dawson out to reconcile with him and shake hands. The whole group then assented to Dawson's insistence that there must be no more stealing. Dawson records his deep satisfaction that Tom seemed to harbour no resentment afterwards.[74] This incident suggests that the settlement's Aboriginal workers had not

---

[72] Dawson, *The Present State of Australia*, p. 301.
[73] Dawson, *The Present State of Australia*, pp. 304–5.
[74] Dawson, *The Present State of Australia*, pp. 305–8.

only observed and learnt a good deal about its rules and system, but adapted them to suit their own needs and circumstances; it was a hybrid society indeed.

While Dawson's narrative evinces his own curiosity about and respect for some aspects of Aboriginal culture, much of it is highly self-serving. This is hardly surprising, given that Dawson wrote the book on his return to England after being sacked by the company, and that one of its purposes is his own vindication. But Dawson's account is fascinating as well as self-serving. Its detail enables various angles of analysis, such as Penny Russell's finely wrought study of Dawson's notions of civilized behaviour, with his categorizing of 'individuals in his social universe according to their potential for, progress towards, or departure from, civilisation' regardless of race.[75] We can learn much from his account, too, about how Dawson saw himself in relation to his Aboriginal and other employees. For all of his demonstrated interest in Aboriginal culture, and his repeated defence of their peaceability, inherent good nature, and willingness to be useful, Dawson seems to have enjoyed believing that they regarded him as their master and protector. In his recurrent recording of their supposed conversations with him, he always says they called him 'massa'—meaning master. His repeated ascription of their use of this name for him suggests that he rather liked it.

There are many other pieces of evidence about how he viewed and asserted his own authority. The full title of Dawson's book, in perfect contemporary style, runs to the following: *The Present State of Australia; A Description of the Country, Its Advantages and Prospects, With Reference to Emigration: and a Particular Account of the Manners, Customs, and Condition of Its Aboriginal Inhabitants* by Robert Dawson, Esq., Late Chief Agent of the Australian Agricultural Company.[76] True to the book's title, Dawson presents extensive detail about Aboriginal people's physical condition, including their hunting, food-gathering, dietary and medical practices, their social organization, their practices of scarring and adorning their bodies, their camps and sleeping arrangements, weapons of war, division of labour between the sexes, men's treatment of women, parenting, nursing and caring practices, their languages, religious and spiritual beliefs, annual gatherings, and inter-tribal relations. He assesses and discusses evidence pertaining to current theories about their arrival and dispersal in Australia, including its time span. His great pride in his ethnographic knowledge is very apparent, surpassed only by his pride in what he considers his special rapport with Aboriginal people:

> I was indebted to the natives, who acted as my guides upon every occasion, not only when on horseback, but also in the boat, in which they frequently rowed me up the rivers and various creeks, accompanied often by only one white person. So good an understanding subsisted between us, and so proud were they of the notice I had taken of them, that had it been necessary, I should have had no hesitation in trusting myself alone with them in any situation. The assistance which I derived from them, whether as guides or labourers, exceeded any thing I can describe; and the satisfaction this

[75] Penny Russell, *Savage or Civilised? Manners in Colonial Australia* (Sydney: University of New South Wales Press, 2010), p. 56.
[76] Published in London by Smith, Elder, & Co., Cornhill, 1830.

afforded me, as well as the pleasure I received in the society of these cheerful and obliging people, supported me greatly in the daily performance of the arduous and anxiously responsible duties which I had taken upon myself.[77]

Dawson came to know individual Aborigines very well, such as Wool Bill who acted as his personal servant, enlarging in his narrative on their personalities, and their familial and other relationships with each other.

Nevertheless, he claims in various ways to have enjoyed both special power and authority over the Aboriginal people in the area:

> In all respects I found it necessary to treat them like children, and to watch every opportunity of influencing them by reason and conciliatory treatment, rather than by the exercise of stern authority; but when I found it necessary to be positive I was implicitly obeyed, however unpalatable my order might be to them. My object was never to be unreasonable, by *demanding* any thing which I believed was not necessary to their proper management, and to a right and useful understanding between us. By these means I procured over them an unbounded influence.[78]

Dawson contends that most settlers are ignorant of the nature and capacities of Aboriginal people, not having taken the time and effort to observe them thoroughly; he asserts, rather immodestly, that while no European has yet been in a position to know them fully, 'that in which I stood approached more nearly to it than any other known in that country'.[79]

But it should at the same time be noted that Dawson claimed also to have established comparably good relations and strong authority with the convicts who made up the majority of his labourers at Port Stephens:

> I always proceeded upon the principle, that it was never too late to reform; and considered it my duty to place the convicts in situations where the truth of this should always be apparent to themselves; and I have no recollection, except in one instance, of having returned any convict to the government as hopeless . . . [A]lthough surrounded by large numbers of the very dregs of the dregs of society—of those who had been returned as hopeless by private settlers—still I never upon any occasion slept with my door fastened, nor, to my knowledge, did I ever lose to the value of sixpence from my private property; and although exposed in every possible way by night and by day, being sometimes at a considerable distance from home, I never met with any obstruction or any thing bordering upon an insult from any convict on the grant, during my residence there for a period of two years and two months.[80]

Given Dawson's pride in his rapport with and treatment of his Aboriginal workers, it is all the more significant that, like other settler masters, he chose not to remunerate them in the same way as European workers. During his tenure at Port Stephens, Aborigines were 'paid' with rations, such as flour, tea, sugar, tobacco, maize, biscuits, clay pipes, blankets, trousers, shirts, and frocks.

---

[77] Dawson, *The Present State of Australia*, pp. 28–9.
[78] Dawson, *The Present State of Australia*, pp. 116–17.
[79] Dawson, *The Present State of Australia*, p. 330.
[80] Dawson, *The Present State of Australia*, pp. 301–2.

Mark Hannah, who has studied the labour value and the remuneration of Aboriginal employees of the Australian Agricultural Company from the 1820s to the 1850s, argues that the Aboriginal people themselves and Dawson while he was there saw their sanctuary within the company's settlement as a form of remuneration. By the 1820s, Hannah argues, the Worimi people in the region had suffered sufficient violence from settlers to desire shelter, and it was this which Dawson, with his interest in Aboriginal people and belief in his special relationship with them, offered. Hannah contends, from his analysis of company records, that a system of rations evolved at Port Stephens according to which all workers received particular quantities depending on their job; Aboriginal people received the same rations as others, whether convict, indentured, or free, for the same jobs. The difference lay in wages: by the 1850s, Aboriginal shepherds, for example, were receiving some wages, but at only half the rate paid to European and Chinese shepherds. In earlier years, Aboriginal workers received no cash wages at all. Hannah argues that Aboriginal people accepted their lower rate of remuneration because their primary consideration was to stay as close as they could to their country. In effect, the company, like other employers of Aborigines, exploited their desire to stay on their land as far as possible. Unlike other workers free to move, they were not willing to go elsewhere simply for higher pay.[81]

INDIAN INDENTURED LABOURERS
IN THE AUSTRALIAN COLONIES

Schemes to import indentured Indian labourers were hatched and carried out by various entrepreneurs around the Australian colonies. In Van Diemen's Land and southwest Western Australia, Indian workers were imported by the Prinseps to work their family properties. Charles Prinsep was a wealthy Calcutta lawyer and erstwhile advocate general for the East India Company; the Prinsep family network connected India and the Australian colonies over generations in the nineteenth century. Charles Prinsep believed that there was great potential in trading links between India and the Australian colonies. In the 1820s and 1830s his business undertakings included buying land, importing Indian labourers, and developing trading commodities including horses to be raised in Australia for the Indian market.[82] He first bought a 22,000 acre property near Launceston in 1827 to establish a stud farm, then in 1837 he bought land on the Leschenault Inlet near Bunbury, and moved his horse stud there. Indian labourers who had been imported to work the Van Diemen's Land estate were shipped to Western Australia and in 1838 Thomas Little, a former East India Company soldier and an employee of the Prinseps in Bengal, sailed there from Calcutta to oversee the estate. As well as his

[81] Hannah, 'Aboriginal Workers in the Australian Agricultural Company', pp. 28–30.
[82] Malcolm Allbrook, '"A Triple Empire...United Under One Dominion": Charles Prinsep's Schemes for Exporting Indian Labour to Australia', *South Asia: Journal of South Asian Studies* August 2012, DOI: 10.1080/00856401.2011.649676.

own family, Little took with him a group of thirty-seven Indian workers on five-year contracts with their return passage guaranteed.[83] In 1828 Charles Prinsep urged a scheme under which poor white and mixed-race children would be sent from India to Van Diemen's Land and New South Wales as workers, but the East India Company rejected it.[84] While Indian indentured labourers were never brought to the Australian colonies on the mass scale that Prinsep envisaged— partly because of Australian official and Colonial Office resistance and partly because so many other British colonies competed for such labourers—as late as the 1870s Charles's son Henry Prinsep, who had taken over management of the Western Australian estate in 1866, continued to push such proposals.[85]

Janet Doust, in her study of the colonial New South Wales labour immigration policy, points out how continually this contentious issue recurred. Debate about the importation of non-white labour stretched from 1837 to 1854, preoccupying the Legislative Council, the Sydney press, governors, and the Colonial Office in London. Doust's analysis of petitions for government assistance to import labourers, and of debates in the Legislative Council, shows that a majority of landholders favoured indentured labour, but that less than a third of the elite (particularly magistrates) did so. It was this elite, along with the Colonial Office and several governors, who prevented greater importation of non-white labour than in fact occurred.[86] While ruling officials maintained restrictions on such importation, the continuing demand and debate, and actual schemes that brought non-white workers in, suggest that many landholding settlers either were or wished to become employers of such workers. Doust estimates that between 'December 1837 and March 1846, one hundred and fifty Indian coolies were brought into New South Wales by agents', on top of the Indians brought as servants with masters and mistresses arriving from India.[87]

In her recent essay on the New South Wales debate over importing Indian indentured labour, particularly the early debate from 1836 to 1838, Rose Cullen shows how many of those advocating importing workers had prior experience of India, Mauritius, or both. The debate was sparked by John Mackay who arrived in Sydney from Calcutta in August 1836, after twenty-eight years in India where he had been an indigo planter and merchant. Mackay quickly assessed the Australian colonial demand for labour and began to court support for his scheme to bring in Bengali workers under indenture. In May 1837 Mackay's calls for systematic importation were augmented by similar arguments put forward by J. R. Mayo, who arrived in New South Wales from Mauritius with plans to grow cotton, claiming to have had experience as a planter in the Caribbean and the United States, and to have been in India. In June 1837 Governor Bourke established a committee to consider issues of immigration (both 'Indian and British'), which

---

[83] Allbrook, '"A Triple Empire . . . United Under One Dominion"', p. 13.
[84] Allbrook, '"A Triple Empire . . . United Under One Dominion"', pp. 10–11.
[85] Allbrook, '"A Triple Empire . . . United Under One Dominion"', p. 22.
[86] Doust, 'Setting Up Boundaries in Colonial Eastern Australia', pp. 162–4.
[87] Doust, 'Setting up Boundaries in Colonial Eastern Australia', p. 158.

heard testimony from a range of settlers, including John Broadley Howard who had lived in Bengal for six years, Thomas Porter Biscoe who had worked in the East India Company Civil Service, and John G. Collins who had been in India for eight years.[88] As Cullen shows, the debate over importing Indian labourers occurred in a context where settler knowledge of changing labour patterns elsewhere in the empire came from first-hand observation as well as newspaper accounts and intra-imperial correspondence.[89]

On 8 September 1838, the *South Australian Gazette and Colonial Register* reported on the 'Importation of Indian Laborers'. Refusing to engage in a pro-longed discussion of the issue, the paper limited itself to commenting on evidence from 'the coroner's inquest on the body of a Hill Coolie'. The paper thought its readers would agree it was 'quite clear that these poor men ought to have some protection from the misconduct, neglect, or cupidity of their masters', and would share its 'pleasure in stating that his Excellency the Acting Governor has promptly determined to make formal communications on the subject to the Colonial office and to the Indian Government'.[90] The unfortunate Indian worker, a young Dhangar man called Mungra from the region west of Calcutta, whose death prompted this discussion was one of the group brought by settler Joseph Bruce from Calcutta when he took up a land grant in South Australia in 1838.[91] Bruce brought the first indentured labourers from India to South Australia, about seventeen or eighteen young Dhangar men on five-year bonds, employed them himself, and hired them out to others, but soon left them stranded and destitute when he committed suicide in September the same year.[92]

But the issue of labourers from Asia did not go away. In May 1847 the *South Australian Register* ran a longer piece, commenting on proposals in South Australia for the importation of labourers from China, comparing them to plans in New South Wales for importing labourers from Polynesia. The paper argued that, rather than bringing in 'cooley labour', the colony's government should spend money on assisting destitute labourers in the United Kingdom to emigrate, because British labourers 'would form a permanent addition to our numbers, and would mix, without tainting our population'. Yet Asian labour was not out of the question: 'our fields must be tilled', the *Register* continued, 'our flocks must be watched, our mines must be wrought, and if the labour needed for these purposes, and for which we have paid, is not furnished to us, we are fully justified in adopting whatever means are at our disposal in order to procure an adequate supply'.[93] This defiant attitude on the part of the *Register* matched the continuing practice by some settlers of

[88] Rose Cullen, 'Empire, Indian Indentured Labour and the Colony: The debate over "coolie" labour in New South Wales, 1836–1838', *History Australia* Vol. 9, No. 1 (April 2012): 101.

[89] Cullen, 'Empire, Indian Indentured Labour and the Colony': 84–109.

[90] 'Importation of Indian Laborers', *South Australian Gazette and Colonial Register*, p. 3.

[91] Westrip and Holroyde, *Colonial Cousins*, p. 154; Atkinson and Aveling (eds), *Australians 1838*, pp. 119–20.

[92] Heather Foster, 'The First Indians: The Bruce and Gleeson Indentured Labourers in 19th Century South Australia', *Journal of the Historical Society of South Australia* No. 39 (2011): 21–30.

[93] 'Cooley Labour', *South Australian Register* 26 May 1847, p. 2.

importing non-white labour. Indentured labour schemes that brought Indian workers to Australia may have been more common in New South Wales, Queensland, Victoria, and Western Australia, but we know that there were several in South Australia, from the newspaper reports just cited and other sources too. For example, Westrip and Holroyde contend that in 1848 Indian shepherds were employed 'in the northern reaches of South Australia'.[94]

WHITE SETTLER MANLY AUTHORITY AND EMPLOYING ASIAN AND ABORIGINAL WORKERS

On 17 January 1848, according to a report in the *Sydney Morning Herald*, a 'very respectable meeting of the influential squatters of this district assembled at the Caledonian Hotel, North Brisbane . . . to take into consideration the best mode of introducing coolie labour'.[95] The more extensive report in the *Moreton Bay Courier* described the attendees as 'Stockholders and other employers of labour in the Moreton Bay and Darling Downs districts' and noted that the purpose of the meeting was to form an association 'for the purpose of introducing labourers from India'. Views expressed were that settlers could not rely on labour from Britain, that Indian labourers were ideally suited as shepherds, that white workers would benefit from the expansion of the wool industry, and that the introduction of Indian labourers 'would lead to the growth of sugar, cotton, indigo, rice, and other tropical productions'.[96]

Despite the continuing arrival of groups of indentured labourers from India and China, these squatters' request for the removal of restrictions on the importation of Indian labourers did not succeed until their attention had shifted to Pacific Islanders.[97] The Queensland Polynesian Labourers Act of 1868 drew attention away from the continuing debate over importing Indian labour, yet the Queensland debate recurred in the 1870s and was only quashed with the 1886 repeal of the 1862 Indian Immigration Act.[98] While settler demands for a cheap labour force were so persistent that this Queensland debate was a sequel to the New South Wales debate that had flared sporadically from the late 1830s to the early 1850s, colonial and imperial policy was to limit the numbers of Indian and Chinese labourers allowed into the Australian colonies, and to maintain the colonies in southern Australia predominantly for British settlers, while keeping alive the possibility of a different labour force in the tropical north.[99]

---

[94] Westrip and Holroyde, *Colonial Cousins*, p. 139.
[95] 'Coolie Immigration', *Sydney Morning Herald* Monday 24 January 1848.
[96] 'Domestic Intelligence. Public Meeting—Indian Labour', *Moreton Bay Courier* 22 January 1848, p. 2.
[97] Quinlan, 'Australia 1788–1902', p. 232.
[98] I. N. Moles, 'The Indian Coolie Labour Issue in Queensland', *Historical Society of Queensland Journal* Vol. V, No. 5 (1957): 1350, 1367.
[99] Doust, 'Setting up Boundaries', p. 166. Also on indentured labourers in Australia see Ann Curthoys, 'Liberalism and Exclusionism: A Prehistory of the White Australia Policy', in Laksiri Jayasuriya, David Walker, and Jan Gothard (eds), *Legacies of White Australia: Race, Culture and Nation* (Crawley, WA: University of Western Australia Press, 2003), pp. 8–33.

The January 1848 meeting in North Brisbane was not the first association of pastoralists to pursue the importation of indentured Indian labourers. A similar and indeed connected association had formed in Sydney in 1842, following protracted discussions of the issue in the press and elsewhere. A preliminary meeting had been held in Sydney at the Exchange Rooms on 20 August 1842, and a public meeting in the same venue on 24 September 1842 resulted in the formation of an association of those who supported the removal of restrictions on importing Indian labourers.[100] A related association was formed in Bathurst, which held its first meeting, chaired by Major General Stewart, JP, at Mrs Black's Hotel on 9 November 1842. The Bathurst Association resolved at this meeting to support the Sydney Association's memorial to Lord Stanley to obtain permission 'to import Coolies, or other labourers, from India', and that the governor's support for this petition be solicited.[101] And to the south, also in 1842, an Association for Obtaining Permission to Import Coolies or other Labourers from the East Indies had formed in Geelong, becoming in 1848 the Malay Immigration Society.[102]

In March 1848, the Sydney Indian Labour Association wrote to the Moreton Bay Indian Labour Association to facilitate cooperation in their petitions to colonial and imperial officials. Facing resistance from the New South Wales colonial secretary, they determined to send petitions to the Queen, parliament, and the East India Company board of directors requesting the removal of restrictions on the importation of Indian labourers. The Sydney Association's letter noted that they had also warned the colonial secretary that, if frustrated in their desires for Indian labourers, they would turn their attention to Chinese labourers.[103]

Although their demands ultimately failed, at least for the scale of immigration that they hoped, it is worth paying some attention to the men who attended the meeting and joined the Indian Labour Association of Moreton Bay. The group included several influential and interesting members. One participant is listed as C. W. Wentworth but was quite probably W. C. Wentworth, who was actively involved in importing and employing Indian labourers; in 1845 Wentworth and two partners, Robert Campbell and Robert Towns, imported a group of fifty-one Indian labourers, seventeen to work for each of them on their properties.[104] (See Fig. 3.3.) Wentworth was an outspoken founding member of the Sydney Indian Labour Association.[105] In December 1846 Wentworth took 'Ramdcull', one of his Indian 'hired servants', to court for being absent from work. Ramdcull reportedly had refused to work until he saw a copy of the agreement under which he was indentured to Wentworth; he was denied access to this agreement, fined 33s. 6d., and sentenced to twenty-one days' imprisonment after which he was to return to

[100] 'Indian Labour', *Sydney Morning Herald* 26 August 1842, p. 3 and 26 September 1842, p. 2.
[101] 'Bathurst—Labour', *Sydney Morning Herald* 14 November 1842, pp. 2–3.
[102] Ian Wynd, 'Labour—Supply and Demand in the 1840s', *Investigator: Magazine of the Geelong Historical Society* Vol. 14, No. 1 (March 1979): 28, 32.
[103] 'Indian Labour', *Moreton Bay Courier*, 4 March 1848.
[104] Allbrook, '"A Triple Empire . . . United Under One Dominion"', pp. 16–17.
[105] 'Indian Labour', *Sydney Morning Herald* 26 September 1842, p. 2.

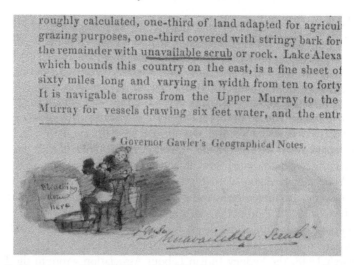

> roughly calculated, one-third of land adapted for agricul
> grazing purposes, one-third covered with stringy bark for
> the remainder with <u>unavailable scrub</u> or rock. Lake Alexa
> which bounds this country on the east, is a fine sheet of
> sixty miles long and varying in width from ten to forty
> It is navigable across from the Upper Murray to the
> Murray for vessels drawing six feet water, and the entr
>
> * Governor Gawler's Geographical Notes.

Fig. 3.3 J. M. Skipper, 'Unavailable scrub'. The figure in the tub may well represent an Indian indentured labourer.

Courtesy of the State Library of South Australia, SLSA: PRG 72/13/1—*South Australian Almanack*, 1841, p. 56 (J. M. Skipper, artist).

Wentworth's employ.[106] Another participant at the Moreton Bay meeting was William Sharp Macleay, eldest son of Colonial Secretary Alexander Macleay, and former commissioner of the British and Spanish Court for the Abolition of the Slave Trade in Havana, Cuba, who had joined his family in Sydney in 1839. His presence in Brisbane at this meeting is curious in that the Macleay family pastoral land was just south of Sydney—perhaps the younger Macleay was considering the possibilities on offer in the northern districts.[107] A founding member of the Sydney Indian Labour Association, listed as G. McLeay, may have been a relative.[108]

The names of some of the men who attended the meeting to form the Indian Labour Association appear in the reports of Crown Lands Commissioners for the Moreton Bay and Darling Downs areas. For example, the report for 1844 on Moreton Bay by Commissioner S. Simpson referred to squatters Mackenzie, Ivory, Balfour, Scott, and Bell—presumably the Colin J. Mackenzie, J. Ivory, John Balfour, G. A. Scott, and I. and A. Bell whose names are listed in newspaper accounts of the Indian Labour Association.[109] Commissioner Simpson also referred to Messrs Archer and Co.; Thomas and David Archer are listed at the meeting. Simpson reported: 'I am sorry to state the Wide Bay Blacks have recently made an irruption among Mr. Archer's cattle. It speaks, however, well for the system of kindness which Mr. Archer has uniformly adopted toward his own tribe at

[106] *Sydney Morning Herald* 3 December 1846, p. 2.

[107] Listed as W. S. McLeay, 'Domestic Intelligence. Public Meeting—Indian Labour', *Moreton Bay Courier* 22 January 1848, p. 2.

[108] 'Indian Labour', *Sydney Morning Herald* 26 September 1842, p. 2.

[109] *Moreton Bay Courier* 22 January 1848, pp. 2–3.

Durandur that they were first to give information of the occurrence and assist in repressing it'. Thus Archer and Simpson together represented Archer as teaching morality, responsibility, and civilization to the Durandur people—with his authority extending to a proprietorial relationship in which they were 'his own tribe'. Simpson goes so far as to claim that the Archers set the local pattern: 'the plan which Messrs Archer and Co first fairly carried out in the north of the district has been generally adopted by the squatters to the south, namely to allow the Aborigines free intercourse with the Head Station and treat their peccadillos with forbearance by which means they appear to take an interest in preventing strange blacks from committing aggressions'.[110]

In Thomas Archer's *Recollections of a Rambling Life*, published in 1897, he narrates his working relationships and dealings with Aboriginal people, repeatedly suggesting his interest in peaceability, albeit on his terms as a settler. Having arrived in Sydney in 1837 as a young man with his family, who already had pastoralist relatives near Bathurst, at first he moved between being a station hand and working as a junior clerk in a Sydney business. Being appointed as an overseer on a family property on the Darling Downs, he found himself: 'sent off with a horse load of provisions and about a dozen blackfellows, to this place [Birallen] to strip bark for erecting the needful huts and woolshed' in order to treat the sheep for scab before they could be driven to the Darling Downs. He recalled:

> During this time I pitched my camp close to my sable companions and became intimately acquainted with this strange and interesting race of people. They belonged to the Wiradury [sic] tribe, the only tribe as far as I know that never committed an outrage on the whites that first settled among them so that in their country peace prevailed between the two races from the outset.[111]

From the Darling Downs to the Moreton Bay area, the 'Wallumbungle [sic] Ranges', the Namoy River, Emu Creek, Cooyar Creek, and the Fitzroy Downs to the Upper Burnett River, as Archer rode the countryside in the process of extending the family pastoralist enterprise, he repeatedly recalls particular 'blackfellows' who accompanied and assisted him, and their usefulness. In establishing Durandur station, Archer's system for employing the Aboriginal people from that specific locale was clearly articulated:

> Many of the blacks helped us by stripping the bark we required for covering the huts, lopping and burning off the heavy trunk, and digging up the soil where the garden was to be with hoes. For these services we paid them with flour, rice, meat and . . . a shirt; also . . . tobacco, for which they soon developed a pronounced taste . . . We tried to distinguish between those who really belonged to the country around us and those from a distance, and encouraged the former to come about us by employing and feeding them when they chose to work, and by not being very hard on them when they preferred stealing to working which was not infrequently the case.[112]

---

[110] S. Simpson CCL, 'Report for Moreton Bay District for the year 1844, January 10th 1845', CO 201/356 AJCP PRO Reel 364.
[111] Thomas Archer, *Recollections of a Rambling Life* (Brisbane: Boolarong Publications, 1988), p. 39.
[112] Archer, *Recollections of a Rambling Life*, p. 70.

Repeatedly, Archer records that Aboriginal workers' 'remuneration' was 'the usual flour and tobacco and an occasional slop shirt'.[113] The possibility of paying Aboriginal workers with monetary wages does not arise.

We can see in the commissioners' reports a discourse that cast squatters as establishing the moral order of the frontier, supposedly teaching Aboriginal people the values of peaceability, respect for squatters' property, and the rewards of employment. These supposed lessons asserted a moral code in which violence was the consequence of disobedience, a violence that was obfuscated in commissioners' reports by language such as 'repressing' the 'occurrence' of an 'irruption among Mr. Archer's cattle'. These same squatters, having created their own moral universe in displacing Aboriginal people from their lands, turned the authority they thus acquired, along with land and wealth, to demands to escalate the importation of Indian labourers. Having become the arbiters of employment codes on the frontier—such as how to exploit Aboriginal labour without deeming it necessary to pay proper wages—they wished to expand their status and authority as masters of non-white workers through increasing the existing importation of Indian and Chinese workers.

The logic of employing Indian indentured labourers and their cheapness compared with European labourers was advocated by settlers across the Australian continent in these decades. Settlers could easily articulate the economic argument for importing them. On 12 January 1842, Edward Gleeson, who would become one of the first settlers of the Clare Valley, provided testimony to the Legislative Council Inquiry into the present state of agricultural and pastoral interests of South Australia. Gleeson brought twenty-four Indian workers with him when he arrived from Calcutta around 1839; he added to these numbers when he took over the labourers brought out by Joseph Bruce after Bruce committed suicide. Gleeson, who had been a civil servant in India, also brought a young mixed-race woman, Mary Thomas, as ayah for his children.[114] Eliza Sarah Mahoney, who arrived as a young settler with her family in 1839, recorded in her memoir: 'While in Adelaide a picturesque sight I remember was the camp under the fine trees in the Parklands of Mr. Gleeson, an Irish gentleman, who had just come from India with his . . . rupees, Arab horses and Indian servants. He afterwards lived at Clare'.[115] Gleeson named his property 'Inchiquin' from his home in Co. Clare, Ireland, and thus bestowed the South Australian region's name; he became the first mayor when Clare was incorporated in 1868.[116] Responding to questions from the Legislative Council Inquiry, Gleeson reported that he habitually employed a mix of European and Indian labourers. Asked whether Indian labourers were useful, he replied: 'Very, quite as much so as Europeans'. Asked whether there were savings to be made in employing Indian labourers, he responded: 'Very great'. Asked about the wages he paid each group, he replied that he paid European labourers '£26 a year and

---

[113] Archer, *Recollections of a Rambling Life*, p. 127.   [114] Foster, 'The First Indians'.

[115] Mahoney, 'The First Settlers at Gawler', p. 77.

[116] 'In the Northern Areas. Clare', in H. T. Burgess (ed.), *The Cyclopedia of South Australia* Volume II (Adelaide: Cyclopedia Co., 1909), p. 468.

rations', while Indian labourers he paid only 'Ten shillings a month [£6 a year] and rations'.[117]

Settlers' arguments in relation to Indian labourers encompassed moral issues as well, just as they did in relation to Aboriginal workers. Two years prior to the meeting at the Caledonian Hotel in North Brisbane, a settler who would attend, Philip Friell of Tent Hill station in the Moreton Bay district, published his case for *The Advantages of Indian Labour in the Australasian Colonies: As Shewn by Certain Details in Regard to the Indian Labourers.* Friell, a former East India Company civil servant,[118] contended that Indian labourers had a 'high appreciation of British character and of British rule'. Indians 'will confide to a European what they will not entrust to any of their own blood, and they look up to him for his assistance in all cases where they are satisfied that the low tone of their own moral standard would be utterly ineffectual to carry them through'.[119] Success in employing Indian indentured labourers lay in the master's wisdom, discretion, and authority. While Indian labourers were 'naturally indolent' and 'naturally suspicious', their employment would be successful and profitable if on pastoral work, under European supervision (not Indian or 'half Caste'), as long as the master is careful not to lose his patience or his temper, and is always 'scrupulously just to them'.[120] For the successful supervision of Indian labourers too, then, the moral qualities and self-discipline (such as patience and ability to keep his temper) of the master were crucial. In Friell's view, with this kind of treatment by a judicious master, 'these men are as good *Christians* as the generality of white laborers [sic] in this country', implying that their worth as labourers could even be measured by religious standards.[121] Friell's own discretion, wisdom, patience, and justice, however, had been called into question the previous year, when a group of eighteen Indian workers walked off his Tent Hill station and pursued legal redress in Brisbane for their mistreatment, non-payment of wages, and inadequate rations. The Indian workers testified that they had been flogged with a whip, a stick, and a stake, one worker having a dog set on him by the superintendent.[122] Friell and his partner Gordon Sanderman (a member of the Sydney Indian Labour Association) subsequently turned their attention towards indentured labourers from China.[123]

---

[117] Despatches re South Australian Indian Labour, Grey to Lord Stanley, February 22nd 1842, enclosing minutes of the *Legislative Council Inquiry into the present state of agricultural and pastoral interests of South Australia*; Evidence of E. B. Gleeson Esq., 12th January 1842, CO13/24, AJCP PRO Reel 588.

[118] Allbrook, '"A Triple Empire... United Under One Dominion"', p. 17.

[119] P. Friell, *The Advantages of Indian Labour in the Australian Colonies, As Shewn by Certain Details in Regard to the Indian Labourers* (Sydney: Richard Thompson, 1846), pp. 4–5.

[120] Friell, *The Advantages of Indian Labour*, pp. 17, 10, 12–13.

[121] Friell, *The Advantages of Indian Labour*, p. 19.

[122] 'Moreton Bay', *Sydney Morning Herald* 10 October 1845, p. 3.

[123] Kay Saunders, *Workers in Bondage: The Origins and Bases of Unfree Labour in Queensland 1824–1916* (St Lucia, Queensland: University of Queensland Press, 1982), p. 14.

CONCLUSION

Integral to settler definitions of white manhood in these decades of rapid Australian colonial expansion was the possibility, the hope, and the actuality of employing Aboriginal people or Indian, Chinese, or Pacific Islander indentured labourers. Being a white free settler thus at least potentially connoted being the master of non-white workers, in arrangements that exploited the economic dependence of Aboriginal people once their lands had been taken, and the poverty of Indian and Chinese workers willing to enter into contracts of indenture.

In order to understand the full meaning of the manly independence and virtue articulated by settlers in the Australian colonies during the struggle for representative and responsible government, we need to include their authority as masters in the changing, hybrid system of labour. If only a fraction of settler men exercised the authority of the legislators and the magistrates who established and adjudicated colonial labour regimes, most were employers of convicts or other labourers. Settlers' authority as masters incorporated the moral order they established with their asserted abilities to distinguish between and juggle different forms of labour and compensation, not least different categories of non-white labour.

Studies of the dense, tangled, and shifting field of European racial thought in the nineteenth century often point towards its hardening around mid-century. British historians, in particular, have shown changes from the humanitarianism of the 1830s that produced the abolition of slavery and the birth of the Aborigines Protection Society, to the harsher racial views evident in the 1850s and 1860s that were buttressed by 'scientific' racial theorizing. Yet as Douglas Lorimer contends, while 'race' increasingly was seen as a physical category, it was thought to manifest in intellectual, moral, and cultural ways. Even as by the 1850s the earlier 'moral idealism' gave way to increasing metropolitan awareness of colonial military force, the decline of indigenous peoples in the path of settler colonialism in Australia and elsewhere was cited as proof of their racial 'inferiority'.[124]

The Australian settler colonies complicate this picture of change by presenting evidence of violent pragmatism throughout the period. Violence towards Aboriginal people marked Australia from its very inception, with a series of highwater marks from the war in late 1820s Van Diemen's Land onwards. As the Australian colonies expanded their militarily enforced grip on increasing swathes of territory from the 1820s, settlers exploited all the varieties of labourer available to them, including convicts, Aborigines, and indentured labourers of different ethnicities. The voracious hunger for land on which to establish pastoral properties and farms created the demand for labour to clear it, cultivate the crops, and tend the stock. That same demand for land put settlers in conflict with its Aboriginal owners, a conflict that settlers often resolved through force. Despite the limited deployment of Aboriginal Protectors in the 1830s and 1840s, as Chapter 6 will demonstrate,

---

[124] Douglas A. Lorimer, *Colour, Class and the Victorians: English Attitudes to the Negro in the mid-nineteenth century* (Leicester: Leicester University Press, 1978), esp. pp. 136, 145; and *Science, Race Relations and Resistance: Britain, 1870–1914* (Manchester: Manchester University Press, 2013), p. 39.

settlers were prepared to hunt and kill Aboriginal people, especially when Aborigines had taken their stock, or attacked themselves or their 'property'. Personal familiarity between Aborigines and settlers did not prevent settler violence. Settlers were glad to make use of Aboriginal people in their vicinity as labourers in a wide range of capacities, compensating them with meagre amounts of food and goods, getting to know them by name, and learning their familial relationships.

But ultimately the land mattered more. As historian John Ferry has vividly expressed it, colonialism was an uncompromising practice of 'take all and give nothing': it was based on the notion of the right to be there, with 'land rights and sovereignty . . . conflated'; the land was simply appropriated, and only a minority of the invaders felt the need for religious or legal justifications for their actions.[125] This was the moral foundation from which colonial self-government emerged.

[125] John Ferry, *Colonial Armidale* (St Lucia, Queensland: University of Queensland Press, 1999), pp. 16–17.

4

Responsible Government
in an Imperial Context

In the 1840s and 1850s the access to land by the settlers and their relationship to it were firmly yoked to political rights. Squatters who, in the early 1840s, wanted seven- or fourteen-year leases to make it worthwhile to build on their pastoral land claims saw the lack of colonial political power as a major obstacle to such permanency. Nothing was more fundamental to settlers than access to land. Land for grazing, farming, and household subsistence often lay at the heart of rationales for moving to the colonies, or for any decision to stay on. The gradual evolution of representative government in the 1840s and then responsible government in the 1850s occurred in tandem with the opening up of new areas to settlers and of lands for sale. Occasionally, settlers expressed their feelings about the land in terms of their moral claims to it, and by extension, their political aspirations and rights. Thomas Browne (also known as Rolf Boldrewood) drew such connections in his memoirs of managing Squattlesea Mere Run on the Eumeralla River in the western district of Victoria in the 1840s and 1850s: 'There were wild beasts (kangaroos and dingoes), Indians (blacks, whose fires in "The Rocks" we could see), a pathless waste, and absolute freedom and independence'.[1] In the lofty upper reaches of settler society, in the richly fertile Longford district south of Launceston, the Archer family paid tribute to their patriarch Joseph Archer following his death in June 1853. Still standing on the magnificent Panshanger estate, the obelisk memorial draws explicit connections among settler land ownership, moral claims, and political rights:

> In memory of Joseph Archer, Esq., the first proprietor of Panshanger and Woodside: one of those early colonists whose perseverance, energy and industry have rendered a large portion of the trackless wilds of this island productive by cultivation and introduced the habits and improvements of civilized life.
>
> These estates present abundant memorials of his usefulness and taste.
>
> Patriotic, disinterested and consistent, he commanded the respect and confidence of the community, and was amongst the foremost in procuring for his adopted country the rights and privileges of a free legislature and responsible government.[2]

---

[1] Rolf Boldrewood [Thomas Alexander Browne], *Old Melbourne Memories* (1884; reprinted Melbourne: William Heinemann, 1969), p. 37.

[2] The obelisk also notes that Archer had arrived in Tasmania in 1821, served as a magistrate, and in 1851 become the first representative member of the Legislative Council for the district of Longford. Memorial text recorded on 6 July 2011 during guided tour of the Panshanger estate.

'Pathless waste' and 'trackless wilds' were hardly casual phrases: their use here signals the nexus between indigenous dispossession and settler claims to both land ownership and political rights. As John C. Weaver has noted, during the vast, rapid frontier conquests of British settler societies in the nineteenth century, the 'word "improvement" was as widely used as "democracy" . . . serving colonizers' justifications for securing [land] title from First Peoples'.[3]

SELF-GOVERNMENT AND DEMOCRATIC INNOVATION

Responsible government in the settler colonies occurred in the context of global moves towards male suffrage that were shaped by liberal ideas of men as political citizens and women as apolitical private beings. In industrializing nations the rise of commerce expanded the middle classes, and middle-class men demanded the political franchise in alignment with their increased cultural authority. In the settler colonies of the British Empire, frontier expansion added new tests of manliness, the attributes associated with highly successful men such as self-discipline and forti-tude. For settlers, racial hierarchies and violent struggles over land were tied to demands for political representation. At the same time, claiming political citizen-ship involved not just the franchise, but the prising of control away from the imperial metropole. In the Australian colonies—as in Canada, South Africa, and New Zealand—political manhood (male suffrage) was linked to the quest for colonial self-government. Hence, in the transition to self-government, Australian settlers and residents reconceived themselves as new actors on the imperial and global stage, forging democratic modernity through constitutional innovation.

Self-government (albeit within the constitutional limits imposed by the British imperial government) occurred in increments in the Australian colonies. In the 1840s the several Australian colonies, starting with New South Wales in 1842, won the principle of partially elected legislative councils. The 1850 Australian Colonies Government Act gave South Australia, Tasmania, and Victoria legislative councils that were two-thirds elected, and lowered the property qualifications for voting in all the colonies.[4] Then in the 1850s, continuing colonial demands for self-government on the Canadian model resulted in new fully articulated constitutions for each colony: constitutions for New South Wales, Tasmania, and Victoria were enacted in 1855, for South Australia in 1856, and in 1859 for Queensland when it separated from New South Wales. Western Australia was on a different schedule, due to its smaller settler population and late introduction of convicts, and would wait until 1890. Each colony now had its own appointed governor representing the monarch, its bicameral legislature, and ministerial governments based on majority

[3] John C. Weaver, 'Concepts of Economic Improvement and the Social Construction of Property Rights: Highlights from the English-Speaking World', in John McLaren, A. R. Buck, and Nancy E. Wright (eds), *Despotic Dominion: Property Rights in British Settler Societies* (Vancouver: UBC Press, 2005), p. 83.

[4] K. S. Inglis, *The Australian Colonists: An exploration of social history 1788–1870* (Carlton, Victoria: Melbourne University Press, 1974), p. 48.

Fig. 4.1 William Strutt, sketch of the opening of the first Victorian parliament under responsible government, 25 November 1856.

Reproduced with the Permission of the Victorian Parliamentary Library and Information Service.

support in the lower house of parliament.[5] (See Fig. 4.1.) Chains of law, administration, and communication extended separately between Westminster and each colonial capital; and the imperial government maintained control of matters including foreign relations.

Other electoral reforms quickly followed, especially in the franchise and methods of voting. Adult male suffrage was established first in South Australia in 1856, then in Victoria in 1857, and in stages in New South Wales in the 1850s, with full adult male suffrage passed in 1858. (Tasmania did not introduce male suffrage at this point, with its largely convict-derived population thought not yet to be capable.[6]) In introducing the vote for all adult men these Australian colonies were in the vanguard of democracy globally; in Britain, full male suffrage would not occur until 1918 along with partial suffrage for women over the age of thirty. Those enfranchised in the first rendition of representative government in New South Wales in 1842 had been substantial property holders: possessors of a freehold estate valued at a minimum of £200 and householders occupying premises valued at a minimum of £20 annually (as well as being subjects of the Crown over the age of twenty-one who were not felons). Gradually the property qualifications for voting were reduced. In 1850, for example, 'An Act for the better Governance of Her Majesty's Australian Colonies (Imperial)' brought the suffrage threshold of freehold

[5] Stuart Macintyre, *A Concise History of Australia*, 3rd ed. (Cambridge: Cambridge University Press, 2009), p. 92.

[6] Marilyn Lake, 'The Gendered and Racialised Self who Claimed the Right to Self-Government', *Journal of Colonialism and Colonial History* Vol. 13, No. 1 (Spring 2012), p. 2.

ownership down to property worth £100 and for a leasehold estate down to £10 annually.[7] Then in 1855 in Victoria, for example, the requirement was lowered again for the House of Assembly: men with a freehold estate valued at £1,000 or a leasehold estate valued at £100 annually could vote for the Legislative Council (seen as the upper house of review with a more restrictive franchise), while those with a freehold estate valued at £50 or a leasehold estate or renting a property valued at a minimum of £10 annually could vote for the Assembly.[8]

Another electoral measure for which the Australian colonies made history was the secret ballot in its Australian-derived form of a printed ballot paper provided by the government. The secret ballot had been one of the demands of the large Chartist reform movement in Britain in the 1830s and 1840s, and was taken up as a demand by radicals. Voting in Britain had been conducted publicly, often by vocal declaration or by a show of hands, and voters were thus susceptible to pressure from employers, landlords, sectarian groups, or others. The secret ballot was therefore seen as an important step for democratic process. It became part of the suite of electoral reforms enacted along with responsible government in the Australian colonies, fully passed first in Victoria in 1856, where the bill to enact it was drafted by Henry S. Chapman, a lawyer member of the Legislative Council. Because Victoria was first to receive the royal assent on this reform, the secret ballot was sometimes called the 'Victorian' ballot; it has also been known as the 'Australian ballot' because of Australia's pioneering role in what has become the dominant international form of voting.[9] As Peter Brent has established, voting in secrecy was already practised in the United States and several continental European countries. It was not secrecy per se that the Australian colonies introduced to the world. What was novel was that voters would, in secret, mark ballot papers provided by the government on which were printed the names of all candidates; in earlier versions of secret voting, voters had taken their own paper ballots with them.[10] Tasmania (where Chapman had briefly served as solicitor general) closely followed Victoria in introducing it.[11] South Australia quickly followed, with the secret ballot included in the colony's new constitution for responsible government passed in 1856. It was introduced in New South Wales in 1858, in Queensland in 1859, and in Western Australia in 1877.

Beside the parliamentary franchise was the municipal franchise which, as in Britain, was based on quite different qualifications and was the source of some anomalies in the voting system. In New South Wales in 1842, when the right to

---

[7] *13 & 14 Victoriae c.59 An Act for the better Governance of Her Majesty's Australian Colonies (Imperial)* 1850.

[8] *18 & 19 Victoriae c.55 An Act to enable Her Majesty to assent to a Bill as amended of the legislature of Victoria to establish a constitution in and for the Colony of Victoria (Imperial)* 1855.

[9] R. S. Neale, 'H. S. Chapman and the "Victorian" Ballot', *Australian Historical Studies* No. 48 (1967): 506–21.

[10] Peter Brent, 'The Rise of the Returning Officer: How Colonial Australia Developed Advanced Electoral Institutions', PhD thesis, Political Science, Australian National University, 2008, pp. 138–41.

[11] Terry Newman, 'Tasmania and the Secret Ballot', *Australian Journal of Politics and History* Vol. 49, No. 1 (2003): 93–101.

vote for the legislative council was restricted to substantial property holders, the municipal franchise was available to men over the age of twenty-one who occupied any premises with an annual value of £25 as long as they had not been in receipt of public charity in the preceding twelve months. But here, too, the voting threshold was lowered and by 1852 in Tasmania any man over twenty-one who occupied premises with an annual value of £10 could vote in municipal elections, while that same year in South Australia any person who either owned or rented any property and had paid their rates could vote. Even though the qualifications for voting for local councils were explicitly different from those for voting for parliament, there was overlap in the use of electoral rolls and this overlap led to some interesting anomalies. For example, the 1858 New South Wales Act, which specified the municipal franchise, referred to 'ratepayers' without explicitly saying male rate-payers only, so some women did vote in subsequent elections.[12]

Such ambiguities abounded: for example, in South Australia the Municipal Corporations Act of 1861 gave the local council vote to 'every person of full age' who either owned or rented any property as long as they had not received public relief and had paid their rates.[13] In Tasmania in 1857 the municipal franchise for rural districts was explicitly limited to men, whereas for Hobart and Launceston it was not. In Victoria in 1863 the ambiguous wording of the Municipalities Amendment Bill was overtly discussed and amended, with the result that women could not become councillors or mayors but clearly were allowed to vote at municipal elections. Because the municipal rolls were used as the basis for parliamentary electoral rolls, some women then voted in the 1864 Victorian parliamentary elections. In 1865 the Victorian parliament acted to prevent women doing so again, by amending the electoral law to stipulate that only 'male persons' enrolled as ratepayers could have the parliamentary franchise.[14]

Electoral anomaly also extended to Aboriginal people. While Queensland and Western Australia explicitly excluded Aboriginal people from the parliamentary franchise, other colonies did not. At the point of Federation in 1901, some Aboriginal people were on the electoral rolls in Victoria and South Australia. Aboriginal enfranchisement was most explicit in South Australia, where at Federation it was estimated that there were around two hundred Aboriginal voters on the rolls, and their right to vote was defended by South Australian representative John Cockburn during the 1897 National Australian Convention debates.[15]

---

[12] F. A. Larcombe, *The Origin of Local Government in New South Wales* Volume 2 (Sydney: Sydney University Press, 1976), p. 152.

[13] *An act to consolidate and amend laws relating to the Corporation of the City of Adelaide and to enable towns and places within the province of South Australia to be incorporated under provisions thereof* 1861, Clauses 11, 14.

[14] See 'Debate on Municipalities Amendment Bill 1863', *Victorian Parliamentary Debates* Vol. 9; 'Debate on the Electoral Law Consolidation Bill 1865', *Victorian Parliamentary Debates* Vol. 11; and Audrey Oldfield, *Woman Suffrage in Australia: A Gift or a Struggle?* (Cambridge: Cambridge University Press, 1992), p. 132.

[15] John Chesterman and Brian Galligan, *Citizens Without Right: Aborigines and Australian Citizenship* (Cambridge: Cambridge University Press, 1997), p. 81; Rita Farrell, 'Women and Citizenship in Colonial Australia', in Patricia Crawford and Philippa Maddern (eds), *Women as*

RESPONSIBLE GOVERNMENT AND
HISTORIOGRAPHICAL INTERPRETATION

The movements and reformers who demanded representative and then responsible government in the Australian colonies have not lacked their historians. As a topic that has long received attention and interest, they have also been the focus of historiographical debate. This debate has focused partly on how to interpret those who stood against colonial authorities on the 1854 Victorian goldfields, some of whom were killed in the bloody military assault on the Eureka Stockade: were they radical and visionary heroes, or were their protests less noble than that? How extensive was the influence of Chartism amongst colonial radicals? How widespread were the urban reform movements, and how should their members be interpreted in class terms? How should we understand the relationship between working-class activists and more middle-class reformers? Class dynamics were unquestionably important, as Peter Cochrane has underscored in his book on the struggle for responsible government in New South Wales, which he sums up as: 'how the eminent landowners of New South Wales plotted to transfer power from Downing Street to themselves, only to see it usurped by their political enemies—the artisans, shopkeepers, merchants and renegade gentry whose power base was Sydney'.[16]

In a recent contribution to this debate, Sean Scalmer argues that we need to recognize how widespread mob action and street riots were in New South Wales, Victoria, and South Australia from the 1840s. This 'collective action' or 'contention', he suggests, drew on older British traditions of election rioting, but should be seen as colonial political agitation, even if at times coloured by sectarian animosities. This widespread collective action was a major reason why male suffrage was achieved in the Australian colonies in the 1850s, partly as a way to contain the threatening mobs, and to achieve social peace. Moreover, the secret ballot was designed to curb political violence and to bring order to election day. Thus colonial democracy should be seen as an outcome of political struggle by working-class agitators, and some of its measures such as the secret ballot should be seen as a means used by 'elites' to limit rioting.[17]

My own concern here is less with the class relations between labouring men and artisan working-class or middle-class reformers. While some of the scholarship to date has considered political connections between Britain and the Australian colonies, such as among Chartists, I suggest that recent historiography has overlooked the extent to which those who pushed self-government had imperial experience and connections elsewhere, and were very aware of developments in Canada especially. Far from being a phenomenon particular to the Australian

Australian Citizens: Underlying Histories (Carlton, Victoria: Melbourne University Press, 2001), p. 120; Philippa Maddern, 'Founding Fathers: Federation the "grand experiment"', in Crawford and Maddern (eds), *Women as Australian Citizens*, p. 11.

[16] Peter Cochrane, *Colonial Ambition: Foundations of Australian Democracy* (Carlton, Victoria: Melbourne University Press, 2006), p. xiii.
[17] Sean Scalmer, 'Containing Contention: Reinterpretation of Democratic Change and Electoral Reform in the Australian Colonies', *Australian Historical Studies* Vol. 42, No. 3 (2011): 337–56.

colonies or shaped exclusively by exigencies there, the movement for responsible government was inherently empire-wide and to be understood fully needs to be seen in an imperial context. Reformers who were at the heart of the movement were mobile, developing their political agendas in more than one metropolitan or colonial context, and bringing previous experience to new locations. Some reform activists participated in imperial philosophical and political networks. Many read newspaper accounts of protests, movements, and electoral reform in other colonies, or treatises by their protagonists. Demands for self-government in the settler colonies were integrally linked to settler colonialism itself as an imperial phenomenon, partly through the agendas and networks of the Wakefieldian systematic colonizers and others who more broadly subscribed to the philosophical radicalism of the 1830s and 1840s. Thus we need to see colonial democratic movements as connected to the expansion of colonial territory, and fully cognizant of frontier struggles over land and the dispossession of indigenous people, as well as having internal class struggles and being limited by their gendered visions.

THE COLONIAL PRESS, IMPERIAL KNOWLEDGE, AND SELF-GOVERNMENT

The nineteenth-century British Empire was oceanic. It was defended by the massive British Army and Navy and enlarged by convicts, settlers, slaves (at least until 1807), and indentured labourers journeying aboard sailing ships, then steamships from the 1850s. And it was sustained by fleets of merchant ships with cargoes of commodities and resources. News and information, too, circulated across the oceans, in dispatches, letters, and newspapers sent by ship.[18] Newspapers circulated around the empire (and the world) from port to port, with colonial editors eagerly awaiting the latest arrivals, so that they could cannibalize the papers for copy. Newspaper editors saw their role as publishing news of interest, and were not constrained by worries over copyright. In the mid-nineteenth century it was standard practice to reprint all or parts of articles and stories from other mastheads, often with attribution, but commonly in a selected, abridged, or edited form liberally interpolated with the editor's own political views.

The Australian colonial press proliferated in the early to middle decades of the century, with multiple newspapers springing up in each of the capital cities, some short-lived and others destined to become venerable (see Fig. 4.2). Among the topics of greatest concern and interest for this burgeoning press were empire-wide issues of political rights and reform, ranging from the abolition of slavery in the early 1830s, to movements for representative and responsible government, as well as more philosophical matters of liberty and citizenship. Colonial newspapers played a direct role in the extended struggle of the 1840s and 1850s for self-government. They informed colonial readers of constitutional change and political

---

[18] On this see Simon J. Potter, *News and the British World: The Emergence of an Imperial Press System, 1876–1922* (Oxford: Clarendon Press, 2003).

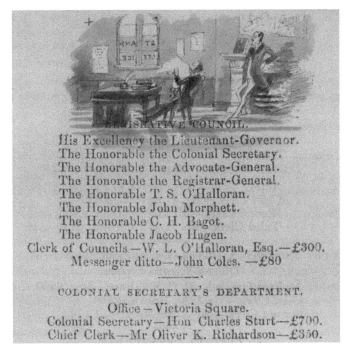

LEGISLATIVE COUNCIL.

His Excellency the Lieutenant-Governor.
The Honorable the Colonial Secretary.
The Honorable the Advocate-General.
The Honorable the Registrar-General.
The Honorable T. S. O'Halloran.
The Honorable John Morphett.
The Honorable C. H. Bagot.
The Honorable Jacob Hagen.
Clerk of Councils—W. L. O'Halloran, Esq.—£300.
Messenger ditto—John Coles. —£80

COLONIAL SECRETARY'S DEPARTMENT.
Office — Victoria Square.
Colonial Secretary—Hon Charles Sturt—£700.
Chief Clerk—Mr Oliver K. Richardson—£350.

Fig. 4.2 J. M. Skipper, 'Office hours from ten to four'.

Courtesy of the State Library of South Australia. SLSA: PRG 72/13/2—*South Australian Almanack*, 1850 (J. M. Skipper, artist).

protests in the other settler colonies, as well as in Europe, the United States, and elsewhere around the world. Frequently, they participated in political debate, with overt demands and enunciated positions on all sorts of questions. Across the range of their own bold political stripes, colonial papers united in their support for greater self-government. In November 1849, for example, the *South Australian Register* 'demanded' legislative reform with a clarion call to fellow settlers: 'The time has arrived when the colonists must throw aside the apathy and inertness which have too long shackled them to the tyranny of the Colonial Office. We must be up and doing'.[19]

One means of focusing on the issue of political and legal rights was to inform readers of matters to do with their absence. In the early 1830s the movement for the abolition of slavery in the British Empire, its eventual legislative success, and the complex consequences for the British slave colonies in the West Indies and South Africa were fertile topics. The *Sydney Herald* in June 1831, for example, reported on dramatic incidents in the British Navy's efforts to patrol the 1807 ban on the slave trade and to intercept slave ships of other nations, then in June 1834 it reported on the smooth transition to emancipation that occurred in the former slave colonies.[20]

---

[19] 'Legislative Reform Demanded', *South Australian Register* 28 November 1849, p. 2.
[20] 'Slave Trade', *Sydney Herald* 27 June 1831, p. 2; *Sydney Herald* 18 June 1834, p. 2.

In 1832, the year before the imperial parliament abolished slavery in all British colonies, the *Herald* trumpeted the moral superiority of the Australian colonies in not having slavery (overlooking the convict system in its stand on principle): 'It is a happy privilege enjoyed by this Country, that no slave population exists in our colony to pollute our soil, and demoralise our social institutions. There is not another Country to the South of the Equator, peopled by Europeans, in which the foul blot of slavery has been washed out by the waters of mercy'.[21]

Colonial papers expressed a sense of the shared interests of all the Australian colonies in the struggle for political representation and self-government, despite their occasional inter-colonial rivalries. In 1849 and 1850 when the Australian Colonies Government Bill was before the British parliament and finally passed by it, extending the representation of settlers in their colonial governments, the politics surrounding the bill and its passage through parliament were followed simultaneously and avidly in New South Wales, Victoria, Van Diemen's Land, and South Australia, the colonies concerned. Similarly, in 1855 when constitutions for full responsible government were being considered in Britain for several of the colonies, again the colonies were united in political anxiety. 'Australian colonists staying in London, or others interested in Australian affairs, look in now and then at Downing-street, and ask whether anything is ever going to be done with the Bills the local Legislatures have so painfully elaborated', the *South Australian Register* reported in June 1855. 'They are invariably sent away with the information that nothing can be done 'till the return of Lord John [Russell] from Vienna; and if the further enquiry is instituted, "When will His Lordship be back?" nobody knows'.[22]

Significantly, the empire-wide movement for settler self-government was followed in detail in relation to other colonial sites as well. The Australian press followed developments in Canada, South Africa, and New Zealand, as well as wars, insurrections, and political upheavals in India, Jamaica, and elsewhere. In June 1834 the *Sydney Herald* gave the heading 'Important!' to its report on the opening of the new Legislative Council in the Cape Colony, South Africa. Its enthusiastic story informed readers that the new government was based on rules 'framed in a liberal spirit, and calculated to work simply and well. They give every Member of Council the right to present public bills'.[23] Looking across the seas to the east as well as the west, Australian papers followed settlements and constitutional developments in New Zealand, too. Perhaps it is unsurprising that the South Australian press was especially enthusiastic about the contributions made by Edward Gibbon Wakefield to the establishment of responsible government there. In August 1854, the Adelaide press included a lengthy report on New Zealand politics that began:

> Our recent files from New Zealand are unusually interesting from the reports they contain of the discussions on constitutional matters that have taken place in the local Legislature. One of the first subjects brought under notice after the meeting of the local Parliament (or General Assembly as they call it) was the question of responsible

---

[21] *Sydney Herald* 24 September 1832, p. 2.
[22] 'The Australian Constitutions', *South Australian Register* 13 June 1855, p. 2.
[23] 'Cape of Good Hope. Important!', *Sydney Herald* 16 June 1834, p. 2.

government. The matter was introduced by Mr. E. G. Wakefield, whose speech, as being the ablest and most important in the debate, we give at considerable length.[24]

Wakefield's speech was then reproduced in three full columns of fine print.

But the major focus of press reports on constitutional developments over the mid-century decades was on Canada, where responsible government was pioneered, and to where the Australian colonies looked for their role model. In the 1830s, Australian newspapers covered the political unrest in Canada, including the struggles of French Canadian settlers in Quebec. Then in 1838 and 1839 there was avid Australian interest in the mission of Lord Durham, sent as viceroy to Canada by the British government to look into settling Canadian affairs and to report on constitutional arrangements. The *Sydney Herald*, for example, in August 1838 printed the correspondence between Lords Glenelg and Durham establishing the latter's mission, then in March 1839 also printed Durham's speech on his early return to England, after his mission had been curtailed, defending its importance and his own judgements. Like other colonial papers, in mid-1839 the *Herald* ran coverage of the Durham Report recommending self-government for the Canadian colonies, later widely regarded as the blueprint for what would become responsible government in the British settler colonies.[25]

In July 1839, the *Herald* seized on the issue of taxation without representation, notoriously the very grievance that had sparked the American Revolution in the 1770s. The paper urged 'the Colonists of New South Wales' to compare their own situation with Canada:

> The question of taxation, in Lower Canada, was the alleged primary grievance which led to the late outbreak in that Province. Now, the people of Lower Canada possess a House of Representatives—they enjoy the privilege of taxing themselves; yet they break out in open insurrection upon the subject of the appropriation of this sum of £100,000. But if the Canadians were justified in acting as they have done in this matter—if they, having a House of Assembly and the right of taxing themselves, were justified in taking up arms in order to insist upon a further control over their revenue of £100,000, what is the character of the treatment of which the Colonists of New South Wales have to complain? Their annual revenue amounts to nearly £400,000; and yet *they* have no House of Assembly—no control at all over the taxes. If a people possessing the privilege of taxing themselve[s], and whose revenue amounts to only about one-fourth of the revenue of this Colony, were justified in their rebellious proceeding, what course ought the Colonists of New South Wales to pursue . . . ?[26]

This was a theme the *Herald* had pursued as early as 1835, and for which the Durham Report provided welcome grist for its mill.

The *Hobart Town Courier* also followed Lord Durham's mission keenly; for example, in May 1839 it reported on the circumstances surrounding and reasons given for his early departure from Canada. Years later, in January 1852, as

---

[24] 'New Zealand Politics', *South Australian Register* 8 August 1854, p. 2.
[25] *Sydney Herald* 17 August 1838, p. 3; 11 March 1839, p. 2; 28 June 1839.
[26] *Sydney Herald* 22 July 1839, p. 2.

Tasmania incrementally won self-government, the *Courier* returned to the subject of the Durham Report, crediting it for shaking up the 'indolent', 'most comfortable', and sleepy authorities at the Colonial Office, who had previously exercised power that was 'wholly irresponsible and abounding in patronage'. Then 'in the midst of their drowsy nonchalance':

> [T]he Durham Report came upon them like an earthquake. From the hour when the *Times* newspaper prevented the official suppression of that remarkable work, the nature of Colonial misgovernment has been understood in the Colonies; the more important dependencies of England have continually sought to obtain a full measure of authority for the management of their own affairs in their own way.[27]

In Tasmania, debate over 'colonial misgovernment' had been especially heated because of the protracted and bitter struggle to end convict transportation.

Even after the achievement of responsible government, Australian colonial papers continued to dwell on it. In June 1857, the now *Sydney Morning Herald* expressed the view that the 'English reader of Australian newspapers will turn with some curiosity and often with still higher interest, to the developments of "Responsible Government"', because while full democracy had not yet been instituted in England, the Australian colonies provided the English with a model of full parliamentary government. In contrast to the slow evolution of democracy in England, settlers in Australia 'within two years, have passed almost from impotence to unrestricted power'.[28] Then, as if to presage the next major constitutional challenge for the Australian colonies, in April 1867 in Queensland the *Brisbane Courier*, for example, printed a long article on the confederation of the Canadian colonies, continuing the tradition of looking to Canada as a political model of great interest.[29]

HENRY S. CHAPMAN: IMPERIAL MOBILITY, POLITICAL REFORM, AND INDIGENOUS LAND RIGHTS

In the welter of literature and debate on colonial constitutional reform in the 1850s, according to the Melbourne paper, the *Argus*, an 1854 pamphlet on 'Parliamentary Government' was especially to be welcomed because of the credentials of its 'able and accomplished' author. The *Argus* described Henry Chapman in the following terms: 'Few men in this hemisphere possess the acquirements and experience necessary for political disquisition in a higher degree than the author of this production. Trained for the Bar, and imbued with the liberal views of the most advanced school of Colonial Reform, he was successively Chief Justice of New

---

[27] 'A Note for Next Year's Debates on Colonial Government', *Courier* (Hobart) 28 January 1852, p. 4.
[28] *Sydney Morning Herald* 18 June 1857, p. 4.
[29] 'The Confederation of British North America', *Brisbane Courier* 23 April 1867, p. 3.

Zealand, and Colonial Secretary in Van Diemen's Land . . . The opinions of such a man on political questions are entitled to great weight'.[30]

To explore and illustrate the ways in which political reformers in the Australian colonies embodied imperial connections and experience, this chapter considers in some detail Henry Samuel Chapman (1803–81), who was one of the leading advocates of responsible government in the white-settler colonies. Chapman was far from alone among the Australian colonial politicians involved in the constitutional reform movement who had cut their political teeth elsewhere, though the extent of his active involvement in multiple British colonies was perhaps greater than most others. Chapman's life story, political persuasions, and writings (including his influential legal judgments) allow us to see how gendered ideas of settler masculinity and manly independence supported claims for self-government—and how they were integrally linked to settler colonialism (particularly Wakefieldian systematic colonization) and indigenous dispossession. In tracing the biography and political opinions of one of its main proponents, we can track the introduction of responsible government as its principles evolved in specific settler–colonial contexts, and were carried and adapted from colony to colony. We can see, too, how such a high-level official expressed his views on indigenous people, before and after his own extensive encounters with them.

Henry Chapman was born into a middle-class family in London in 1803, the son of a civil servant in the Barrack Department (presumably involved in army administration), and was educated at a small private school in Kent and at Newington. He left school at fifteen to become a bank clerk, was forced to give this job up due to eye trouble, then took up work as assistant to a bill broker (financial trader). As a schoolboy his politics were shaped towards republicanism through his acquaintance, via her nephews, with Caroline Princess of Wales, whose disputes with her husband the Prince Regent (the future George IV) polarized the public.[31] In 1821 Chapman was sent to Amsterdam by the bill broker, and during his year there he continued his study of French and German. At age twenty, still employed by the broker, he left Europe for Canada, where he became a mercantile commission agent. Chapman lived in Quebec from 1823 to 1834, sailed back and forth across the Atlantic in pursuit of his work as a merchant, studied law and economics, made friends in radical and reform circles, and in 1833 founded a radical newspaper, the *Montreal Daily Advertiser*. He became interested in the emigration of British settlers to Canada, and, in part because of the political situation of the French in Quebec, interested in representative government in the colonies. Chapman's radical activism in Quebec included meeting Papineau and other members of the French popular movement.[32]

Chapman returned to London in 1835, became involved in radical politics there, and was appointed an assistant commissioner to the enquiry into hand-loom

---

[30] 'Parliamentary Government', *Argus* 27 September 1854, p. 4.
[31] Peter Spiller, *The Chapman Legal Family* (Wellington: Victoria University Press, 1992), p. 18.
[32] R. S. Neale, 'H. S. Chapman and the "Victorian" Ballot', *Australian Historical Studies* Issue 48 (1967): 509.

weaving.[33] His published writings, such as his coverage of Canadian political events in Hansard's *Monthly Repository* and in the *London and Westminster Review*,[34] private correspondence with other activists, and his role as a paid intermediary between the Canadian colonies and the imperial government have been credited with helping foment the Canadian rebellion of 1837, one of the events leading to responsible government there.[35] He studied law in London, and was admitted to the Bar in 1841.

Editing the *Advertiser* in Montreal in 1834–35, Chapman's radical politics led him to espouse Wakefield's systematic colonization as benefitting the lower orders against aristocratic privilege. In his writing on Canadian politics, in fact, he likened the Canadian struggle for political representation to the revolutionary movements sporadically erupting across Europe, as 'a struggle of the many against the few'.[36] In 1837 Chapman began discussing New Zealand with Edward Gibbon Wakefield, and from 1838 he was involved in the hopes and plans for systematic colonization there. Edward Gibbon Wakefield's biographer, Philip Temple, quotes an 1838 letter in which Chapman condemns Wakefield as a dangerous man and a 'clever scoundrel'. Yet later in New Zealand, in a private letter of 1847, Chapman would give a much more sanguine verdict on Wakefield, calling him 'a man of extraordinary energy, activity, boldness of intellect and frankness of manner with much kindness of disposition united with a rather passionate temper'.[37] Perhaps in 1838 Chapman knew Wakefield more by his scandalous reputation than personal association. There is evidence that by 1839 Chapman was a member of a small group of supporters of systematic colonization who met regularly with Wakefield to discuss matters of related political theory.[38] Certainly by 1841 Chapman had become a major collaborator, writing his substantial propaganda treatise in support of the plans for a Wakefieldian settlement at Australind in Western Australia. And the collaboration began several years before that, with Chapman's involvement in the plans for New Zealand. K. R. Miller suggests that around 1840 Chapman was one of Wakefield's most fervent 'disciples', though later as a settler in New Zealand himself by 1850 he had developed specific criticisms of several of the basic tenets of Wakefieldian systematic colonization. Even so, with his hindsight and first-hand experience, in the 1850s Chapman believed that while Wakefield had made a few theoretical errors, he had transformed general English attitudes towards colonization.[39]

[33] Neale, 'H. S. Chapman and the "Victorian" Ballot': 510.

[34] For example, H. S. Chapman, 'Recent Occurrences in Canada', Hansard's *Monthly Repository* February 1836; H. S. Chapman, 'Progress of Events in Canada', *London and Westminster Review* January 1837.

[35] Spiller, *The Chapman Legal Family*, pp. 22–3.

[36] H. S. Chapman, 'Canada', *Monthly Repository* September 1835, pp. 1–2.

[37] Philip Temple, *A Sort of Conscience: The Wakefields* (Auckland: Auckland University Press, 2002), pp. 211, 366–7.

[38] K. R. Miller, 'Henry Samuel Chapman: Colonizer and Colonist', MA (Hons) thesis in history, Canterbury University College, University of New Zealand, 1956, p. 31.

[39] Miller, 'Henry Samuel Chapman: Colonizer and Colonist', pp. 131–52.

Chapman energetically supported the New Zealand Company in its first years, politically and as a newly minted lawyer. From 1840 to 1843 he edited the company's *New Zealand Journal*, writing many of its articles, as well as a variety of treatises in favour of colonization and representative government. His former partner in the *Montreal Daily Advertiser* and good friend from boyhood, Samuel Revans, now in Wellington, also encouraged his interest in New Zealand, and he began actively to consider settling there. Then in 1843, partly because of his New Zealand Company connections, he applied for and was appointed to a newly created judgeship in Wellington, becoming New Zealand's second Supreme Court judge.

During his eight years in Wellington, among many other subjects, he wrote judgments on land grants, judgments that would affect land policy—a crucial issue in a settler colony. Chapman's judgment in the 1847 case *R. v. J.J. Symonds* has been regarded as very influential for New Zealand law, and was also published in New South Wales at the time in recognition of its wider significance for British settler colonies. The case was, in fact, heard in the Auckland Supreme Court, presided over by Chief Justice Martin, but Martin sent it to Chapman in Wellington for his opinion, which was read to the court on 9 June 1847, and with which Martin concurred. Chapman was known to be thorough in the research and reasoning on which he based his opinions. He himself declared at the opening of this judgment that he had sought 'to enunciate the principles upon which our conclusion is based, with more care and particularity than would, under other circumstances, be necessary' because 'this question involves principles of universal application to the respective territorial rights of the Crown, the aboriginal natives, and the European subjects of the Queen; as moreover its decision may affect larger interests than even this Court' was aware of. In explaining his reasoning, Chapman drew on legal precedents in places ranging from Georgia, Connecticut, and Pennsylvania, to the Port Phillip district of New South Wales, in effect showing that the history of British settler colonialism was bound up in this case. The crux of Chapman's judgment was that the Crown had the exclusive right to extinguish native title in land, a decision he supported partly by saying:

> Whatever may be the opinion of jurists as to the strength or weakness of the native title, whatsoever may have been the past vague notions of the natives of this country, whatever may be their present clearer and still growing conception of their own dominion over land, it cannot be too solemnly asserted that it is entitled to be respected; and that it cannot be extinguished (at least in time of peace) otherwise than by the free consent of the native occupiers. But for their protection, and for the sake of humanity, the government is bound to maintain, and the courts to assert, the Queen's exclusive right to extinguish it.[40]

---

[40] *The Queen at the suit of Charles Hunter McIntosh v. John Jermyn Symonds*, Supreme Court of New Zealand, Auckland, April–June 1847. I am grateful to Dr Shaunnagh Dorsett, then of Victoria University of Wellington Law School, for sharing with me her research materials from the Henry Samuel Chapman Collection, Cases in the Supreme Court of New Zealand, from the Hocken Library, University of Otago.

According to legal historian Peter Spiller, Chapman's judgment in *R. v. Symonds* 'came to be regarded as a classic statement on New Zealand land tenure and Maori property rights', which not only clarified the law of land title but also included a 'sympathetic and benevolent treatment' of Maori rights. Chapman's judgment was so important to New Zealand law that in 1938 it was anthologized with a collection of New Zealand privy council cases, and has been variously cited in cases from the 1870s to nearly the end of the twentieth century.[41]

In 1852 the ambitious and peripatetic Chapman moved on to Van Diemen's Land, where he served as colonial secretary for less than a year. It was a job he was pleased to take, partly because it attracted a higher salary and was sufficiently important that his appointment was published in the official government gazette. Moreover, as he explained to his father in a letter:

> The position of the Colonial Secretary is very different from what it was before the introduction of a Representative Council. He was formerly not much more than the Governors [sic] chief clerk. He is now the chief adviser of the Governor in the executive council (which is analogous to the privy council) and it is indeed by the Governor and the Colonial Secretary that the government is carried on . . . In the Legislative Council, the Colonial Secretary is leader of the Government members and party, and if he manages well may be the recognized leader of the house. I have assumed and asserted this position, and circumstances have decidedly favoured me.

He went on to describe to his father the 'very handsome building' of the Council Chamber, and his own position at 'the head of the bench'.[42]

But his tenure in Hobart ended rather abruptly when he and the Legislative Council clashed with the lieutenant-governor over the issue of convict transportation; Chapman, true to his radical principles, favoured the ending of convict transportation as did the majority of the Council. Chapman was dismissed and returned to London for a year. In 1854 he published a treatise (apparently written during his voyage) on responsible government for the Australian colonies, intended both to explain and to advocate the system.

In pushing the adoption of full responsible government in the Australian colonies, Chapman held up its salutary effects in Canada: 'Most persons whose recollection goes fourteen or fifteen years back (for complaint has since been effectually silenced by Responsible Government) have heard something of Canadian grievances, discontent, and finally rebellion; but few are aware of the happy contrast furnished by that great, prosperous and loyal colony since the introduction of a Parliamentary ministry'.[43] Chapman gave full credit to 'Lord Durham's just celebrated Report' for 'this great constitutional reform' in Canada.[44] He argued in

---

[41] Spiller, *The Chapman Legal Family*, pp. 46–7.

[42] Letter from Chapman to his father, Hobart, 11 July 1852, Chapman, Eichelbaum, and Rosenberg Families: Papers, Series 2/3 Henry Samuel Chapman—Tasmanian and Victorian Papers, MS—Papers 8670–066, Archives, Alexander Turnbull Library, National Library of New Zealand.

[43] H. S. Chapman, *Parliamentary Government; or Responsible Ministries for the Australian Colonies* (Hobart: Pratt and Son, 1854), p. 6.

[44] Chapman, *Parliamentary Government*, p. 10.

Fig. 4.3 Stuart A. Donaldson, first premier of New South Wales (portrait, *c.*1860).
State Library of New South Wales P1/484 Digital. a4214084.

contrast that the 1850 act that had revised the constitutions of the Australian colonies had created a hybrid system that was ineffectual, neither full ministerial government nor efficacious executive government, overly dependent on the threat of the stopping of supply. Chapman dismissed the objection that there were not enough men in the Australian colonies capable of holding office (an allusion to Australia's convict past and indeed present), pointing to several capable men currently in office who were settlers, not sent out from Britain, and who 'have proved themselves at least as efficient as those who have been chosen out of the officially trained class'.[45]

Pointing also to New Zealand, where the assembly had recently requested that the principal government officers should be chosen from its own majority group, Chapman argued that the adoption of the system of responsible government in the

[45] Chapman, *Parliamentary Government*, p. 31.

Australian colonies was merely a matter of time (see fig. 4.3). He contended that public men in England who paid attention to colonial affairs were all in favour of such a shift, and that it was becoming generally accepted that it was better for the imperial government to stay out of the internal affairs of the settler colonies. The imperial government should confine itself 'to subjects and questions which concern the empire at large', such as war, peace, and diplomacy, which the colonies ought not to interfere in because they could have no policy on such issues distinct from that of the imperial government. With such an arrangement, he confidently predicted, the imperial bond with the settler colonies would become long-lasting, a lightly felt set of 'chains' that were in effect 'a common citizenship and common allegiance'.[46] It was obvious to the reviewer in Melbourne's *Argus* that several points in Chapman's treatise were directed at the Lieutenant-Governor of Tasmania, Sir William Denison, who had dismissed him for his 'manly and patriotic stand' against convict transportation, but that writer still considered this a pamphlet that 'cannot fail to exert a beneficial influence upon the public mind'.[47]

Having turned down a governorship in the West Indies, in 1854 Chapman chose to return to Australia—but this time to Victoria. In Melbourne he practised law successfully and in 1855 entered politics, being elected at different times to both the Legislative Council and the Legislative Assembly. In the Victorian government he served twice as attorney-general and once very briefly in 1858 as premier.

The platforms Chapman pushed in Victoria included responsible government, equal electoral districts, adult male franchise, election by ballot, and triennial parliaments—positions consistent with his earlier 1830s radicalism, as R. S. Neale has argued.[48] Highlights of Chapman's career in Victoria included his being one of several barristers who gave their services free to defend thirteen of the participants in the Eureka uprising who were charged with high treason. Chapman successfully defended the African American John Joseph, and his success helped the acquittal of the other defendants.[49] Another notable contribution of these years is that he drafted the secret ballot clauses that became Victorian law, devising a system that would largely be adopted elsewhere.[50] He lectured in law at the university and served briefly on the Victorian Supreme Court. In 1864 he returned to New Zealand, this time to the bench in Dunedin. When he retired from the law in 1875, he became chancellor of the University of Otago.[51]

Chapman's commitment to the secret ballot may have been influenced by his first-hand observation of the Canadian elections in December 1834, when there was an open suggestion from Conservatives for employers to wield their power over employees to compel them, during the open voting process, to vote against radicals;

---

[46] Chapman, *Parliamentary Government*, pp. 34–6.
[47] 'Parliamentary Government', *Argus* 27 September 1854, p. 4.
[48] Neale, 'H. S. Chapman and the "Victorian" Ballot': 509–21.
[49] Russel Ward, *The Australian Legend* (Melbourne: Oxford University Press, 1978), p. 133.
[50] Spiller, *The Chapman Legal Family*, pp. 60, 65.
[51] This information is from the *Australian Dictionary of Biography Online* entry on Henry S. Chapman.

a suggestion against which Chapman as a newspaper editor took a clear stand. His activist work for the secret ballot continued in England, where from the mid-1830s he published political tracts in support of the radical agenda, including the ballot. For Chapman the secret ballot was a key component of comprehensive political reform, which he thought should include 'universal' (adult male) suffrage, the abolition of the property qualification for voting, electoral seat redistribution, reforming the House of Lords, and shorter parliamentary terms.[52] In the 1830s Chapman had been a key player in radical and reform circles in London, a frequent correspondent of John Stuart Mill, a follower of Jeremy Bentham as were so many of his contemporary activists, and a writer of many of the influential pamphlets published by the radical leader J. A. Roebuck. He was well connected and involved in many campaigns, writing tracts on the major issues of the mid- to late 1830s, such as the campaign against the Corn Laws which were perceived to benefit the landed gentry and penalize the working classes, and the 1846 repeal of which was seen as a marker of the ascendancy of urban industrial Britain.[53] Peter Brent suggests that in devising his voting system, Henry Chapman was influenced by Bentham who in 1819 had himself designed a more elaborate plan for secret voting. Chapman's contribution in 1856 was to combine voting in secret with the government provision of the printed ballot paper. It became the basis of the 'Australian' secret ballot even though the way that the voter marked the ballot paper would evolve.[54]

Henry Chapman exemplifies the movement of colonial officials among the settler colonies (though he moved to Quebec and to Victoria as a private citizen), and the question of what significance this may have had for political and cultural conceptions at the heart of demands for responsible government. Chapman wrote extensively, over many years, and has left an assortment of papers. In 1843, for example, he published a treatise he called his *New Zealand Portfolio*, an extended case for representative government in the settler colonies. He asserted that settlers in other colonies were watching the impact of the 1839 Durham Report in Canada closely, and that representative government on the Canadian model would be applied across the settler empire; indeed he went so far as to predict that full responsible government, with ministerial officers supported by the majority of the assembly, would ultimately prevail in all self-governing colonies.[55] Yet he nevertheless felt the need to make as convincing a case as possible for the rights of settlers to such representation, and he found a strong basis for his case in their exemplary masculinity. He argued that settlers in the Australasian colonies had become 'really independent men' who had proven their maturity and readiness for self-government. They had shown themselves to be industrious, moral, and—so important an argument in a free trade era—economically productive.[56] Elsewhere

---

[52] Neale, 'H. S. Chapman and the "Victorian" Ballot': 509, 511–13.

[53] Chapman's writings for the 1830s London radical movement are documented in Miller, 'Henry Samuel Chapman: Colonizer and Colonist', esp. pp. 16–21.

[54] Brent, 'The Rise of the Returning Officer', pp. 140–3.

[55] H. S. Chapman, *The New Zealand Portfolio; Embracing a series of papers on subjects of importance to the colonists* (London: Smith, Elder, & Co., 1843), pp. 135–6.

[56] Chapman, *The New Zealand Portfolio*, pp. vii, 122–7.

he claimed that self-government would encourage 'a class of yeomen proprietors', again linking manhood and independence.[57] Indeed, he contended that the very demand for representative self-government by colonial men was seen in England as 'a sort of presumptive proof, that the people are really fit for free institutions'.[58]

At several points in his writing, Chapman shows an awareness of the dispossession at the heart of colonization:

> Wherever we have colonized, there have we both insulted and oppressed. The negro we have forcibly used: the American Indian we could not so use; him, therefore, we have destroyed. The New Zealand native has, by the energy of his character, taught us, that he is neither to be used nor destroyed, so we must make a virtue of necessity, and civilize him.[59]

Significantly, those lines were written before he ever went to New Zealand, though as will become evident Chapman became well acquainted with one Maori man in London. Given this seemingly humanitarian sentiment, Chapman's later lyrical endorsement of the imperial project there, and implicit approbation of the violence at its heart, is noteworthy. On his first voyage to New Zealand, Chapman spent two hours a day studying the Maori language, and his swearing-in ceremony was attended by Maori chiefs.[60] Yet not long afterwards, he wrote privately that the local Maori people were 'a rope of sand, too lazy and filthy to compete with energetic Englishmen' and that they needed to be 'rescued from their barbarity'.[61] In an 1843 publication, written shortly before he would begin to make important judgments on colonial land policy, Chapman asserted: 'No body of colonists ever had larger claims upon the sympathies of their fellow countrymen at home than the first settlers under the [New Zealand] Company'. 'It was a bold adventure theirs,' he goes on, 'to trust themselves, with no better protection than the proud consciousness of their own good intentions, among a set of untamed savages, inhabiting a part of New Zealand scarcely known to Europeans, and where their favourable reception by the denizens of the soil, was … extremely problematical.' The New Zealand Company's land grab, he goes so far as to claim, had 'an air of romance … which modern times have seldom furnished'.[62] In casting the British grabbing of Maori lands as a romantic quest worthy of ancient times, and through his use of terms such as 'no better protection', 'untamed savages', and 'reception by the denizens of the soil', Chapman indicates both an awareness and approval of frontier violence—carried out by the settlers who were such exemplary masculine figures.

Chapman's work as a judge forced him to deal with issues of land possession and dispossession, the very basis of a settler colony. It also exposed him to interactions with Maori, individually and collectively, in ways that perhaps he would not earlier have been able to predict. Probably the most extended such episode occurred in

---

[57] Spiller, *The Chapman Legal Family*, p. 64.
[58] Chapman, *The New Zealand Portfolio*, p. 124.
[59] Quoted in Spiller, *The Chapman Legal Family*, p. 30.
[60] Spiller, *The Chapman Legal Family*, p. 35.
[61] Quoted in Spiller, *The Chapman Legal Family*, p. 40.
[62] Chapman, *The New Zealand Portfolio*, p. iv.

1844 in Taranaki, a region on the west coast of the North Island that would be significant during the New Zealand Wars of the 1860s. Chapman had an unexpected adventure, which we know about partly because it was related at length by one of Chapman's sons, Frederick Revans Chapman, in 1922. Frederick Chapman had followed his father into the law, and also become a judge on the New Zealand Supreme Court, a position he held in 1922 when he delivered a public lecture for the Victoria League in New Plymouth. He used the lecture to recount the story of his father trekking three hundred miles across Taranaki in 1844, a story he pieced together from various records, including his father's anecdotes and a published report of a lecture the elder Chapman gave in Melbourne in 1860.

In 1844 Henry Chapman was the second judge of the New Zealand Supreme Court, living in Wellington; the Chief Justice was William Martin, who resided in Auckland. The two judges arranged to meet to discuss matters relating to the business of the Supreme Court in New Plymouth in Taranaki in December 1844. Henry Chapman could not find a local ship to convey him to New Plymouth, so he arranged with the captain of a small brig sailing to Sydney to drop him off en route. However, the winds played havoc with the ship and its journey to New Plymouth, to a point that the captain and Chapman agreed that the only solution was to land him ashore even though they were some way north of his actual destination. The coastline was not then surveyed, and the captain could only tell Chapman that he was landing somewhere near Albatross Point. Chapman was taken to the beach on a smaller craft, where he jumped to the sand with his belongings, which included a linen tent made by his wife. He was immediately assisted by local Maori, who told him the name of the place, and walked him inland to their '*pā*' or fortified homestead. They pitched his tent for him, fed him with smoked fish and potatoes, and offered to guide him the next morning to a missionary homestead at Kawhia twenty miles away. Early the next morning a group of the Maori set off with Chapman, carrying his belongings. They walked cross country, traversing swamps and streams, arriving at the homestead of the Whiteleys in the afternoon. Mr Whiteley, the missionary, then arranged for four other Maori to guide Chapman on the next stage of his journey, provided him with food and other supplies, and drew him up a detailed plan of the route he should take to New Plymouth, which was eighty miles away. There were no horses, which were apparently considered unsuited to the country anyway. It took Chapman five days of solid walking to reach New Plymouth, where he found the concerned chief justice waiting for him.

Henry Chapman's accounts of this adventure include details of his interactions with the Maori. When he first landed ashore, for instance, he communicated with those who met him in a mixture of English, Maori, and sign language. He describes observing, at one *pā* he encountered, the chief being spoonfed by his attendants because he was in a fasting ritual. He admitted that, during at least one difficult stage of the journey, he had his Maori bearers carry him across swamps because he did not want to get his feet wet. In another instance, where they needed to cross a rapid river, he joined the Maori in swimming across it, and sought to redeem his masculinity (which he felt had suffered a little from being carried across the swamps) by playfully ducking one of his companions, a 'young chief' who had chosen to join the party. He describes indulgently one night when his Maori guides consumed an entire roast pig, leaving him nothing for breakfast, comparing their behaviour to North American indigenous peoples' practice of gorging—a comparison which suggests that he had learnt something of First Nations culture while in Canada.

The strangest part of Henry Chapman's account of his long walk across Taranaki in December and January 1844 occurred after his week-long business meeting with Chief Justice Martin in New Plymouth was over, when he was on the second leg of his cross-country trek, that back to Wellington. Arriving one night at a *pā* south of New Plymouth, Chapman was greeted by a Maori 'chief' he had first met in London a few years earlier. As Chapman told the story, when he had become interested in New Zealand affairs, his curiosity about Maori led him to the London docks where he knew they could be found amongst the sailors on ships from New Zealand. At the docks, he arranged with a ship captain to 'borrow' one of his Maori sailors for a few days, to take home to introduce to friends and relatives. It is not explicit in this account whether the Maori sailor stayed in Chapman's house, though this seems to have been the case. It is explicit, though, that he visited the houses of Chapman's father and father-in-law, and that his reactions to aspects of English houses and servants caused great amusement to the extended Chapman family. The Chapmans apparently showed Emau Niutireni, who described himself as son of Epono, chief of the Taranaki tribe, various London sights including the zoological gardens. And when he left to return to his ship, they gave him numerous gifts. In 1844, when Chapman on his cross-country walk quite coincidentally strayed into Emau Niutireni's *pā* late one evening, Emau served him a meal on crockery that had been given him by the Chapmans in London, on a white tablecloth that had been the gift of others during the same visit. This extraordinary re-encounter, related matter-of-factly in the surviving account of Chapman's walk, speaks to the global mobility of indigenous people even in the early stages of colonialism, as well as to Europeans' unabashed curiosity about them.

Chapman's walk across Taranaki, he reported, also involved passing through a region of tribal warfare, between New Plymouth and Wellington. His Maori guides, fearing for their own safety, abruptly turned back with his approval, while he not only continued his journey but at Wanganui briefly assisted the resident missionary, Mr Taylor, in his self-appointed role of negotiator between the hostile Maori groups.[63]

From the records of Chapman's several weeks of walking, from Albatross Point to Wellington, it is clear that he learnt much about Maori culture—in addition to the fraction of Maori language he already knew—and about their life under British colonialism in that particular region. On the long days of hiking with only his

---

[63] 'A Walk through Taranaki in 1844. Described by the Hon. Mr. Justice Henry Samuel Chapman, of the Supreme Court of New Zealand. A Lecture Delivered at New Plymouth. By the Hon. Mr. Justice Frederick Revans Chapman, of the Supreme Court of New Zealand, Under the auspices of the Victoria League, December 11th, 1922' (*Taranaki Herald and Budget Print*), British Library.

changing guard of Maori guides for company, and his nights of camping out or staying at the various *pā* whose hospitality enabled his journey, he must surely have learnt something of their individual and communal stories as well as their historical circumstances.

Chapman's writings and his encounters in London and New Zealand are significant on this point, because nearly all the extensive histories to date on responsible government, in the Australian colonies at least, not only minimize the imperial dimensions, but they have not drawn any connections with frontier violence. Rather the figures that populate their pages are urban men, variously radical or conservative, who seem blithely unaware of the moving frontier, and the continuing dispossession of indigenous people and violent clashes. Only very recent work has begun to draw these important connections.[64] In the great swathe of accounts of mid-nineteenth century political maturation in Australia, questions of bloodshed and racial conflict do not arise.[65] And Chapman is of particular interest in this context precisely *because* he was a radical, a well-intentioned reformer, and apparently well-liked by nearly all who knew him.

In Chapman's 1843 *New Zealand Portfolio*, he contended that while responsible government was inevitable across the settler colonies, it was justified in different ways in the various colonies, according to the particular interactions settlers had with the local indigenous populations. Such interactions required different forms of masculine strength. In relation to systematic colonization in Australia, Chapman advocated the civilization of Aboriginal people through their transformation into a peasant or labouring class. In New Zealand, his emphasis was more on the brute force necessary to establish British control—a kind of settler heroism. Despite his erstwhile humanitarian sentiments and own encounters with Maori people who had rendered him great personal assistance, in December 1845 Chapman commented in a letter to his father that Governor Fitzroy had a 'sort of monomania:—a notion that the Europeans were bent on destroying the natives and that the natives could do no wrong'.[66]

The exemplary masculinity required in the colonization of Australia was slightly different from the heroic force required in New Zealand. Chapman argued that settlers in the Australasian colonies had become 'really independent men' who had proven their maturity and readiness for self-government. But what made them even more evidently fit for self-government was their capacity to become masters of non-white and indigenous labour. We see this in his propagandist vision for the

[64] Jessie Mitchell, ' "Are we in Danger of a Hostile Visit from the Aborigines?" Dispossession and the Rise of Self-Government in New South Wales', *Australian Historical Studies* Vol. 40, No. 3 (2009): 294–307.

[65] This historiography includes Peter Cochrane, *Colonial Ambition: Foundations of Australian Democracy* (Carlton, Victoria: Melbourne University Press, 2006); John Hirst, *The Strange Birth of Colonial Democracy: New South Wales 1848–1884* (Crows Nest: Allen & Unwin, 1988); Terry Irving, *The Southern Tree of Liberty: The Democratic Movement in New South Wales before 1856* (Sydney: Federation Press, 2006); A. G. L. Shaw (ed.), *Great Britain and the Colonies 1815–1865* (London: Methuen, 1970); and John M. Ward, *Colonial Self-Government: The British Experience 1759–1856* (London: Macmillan, 1976).

[66] Quoted in Temple, *A Sort of Conscience*, p. 362.

establishment of Australind. The evidence of the subsequent exploitation of Aboriginal labour in Australind and its surrounding area confirms Chapman's notion of white settlers as the employers and masters of Aboriginal people, whom they were supposedly civilizing.

When Chapman arrived in New Zealand at the end of 1843 to assume the position of judge, he himself acquired a black man servant—seemingly of African descent, though it is unclear of what origin. The servant had been trained as a carpenter, worked as a ship's steward, and had multiple skills: Chapman described him as 'a treasure'.[67] Perhaps Chapman's familiarity with the London docks had facilitated finding such a valued servant, though he apparently found him in Auckland, where arriving sailors could have come from around the world. A nursery maid hired around the same time was 'half-caste', presumably meaning of part-Maori descent. Chapman and his wife Kate were sufficiently satisfied with both servants that they took them to Hobart: 'We are comfortably off for servants', he reported to his father in September 1852. 'We have a capital man servant whom I brought from New Zealand. I give him £25 and livery. Ellen our half caste girl is nursery made [sic]. We have a woman cook and a housemaid who also assists in the nursery. This is the same as our indoor establishment in New Zealand.'[68] Chapman himself, then, knew the experience of being master to a non-white servant, including one whom he dressed in livery.

Chapman extolled emigration for women as much as for men. Systematic colonization emphasized the migration of couples and families, not just single men, and Chapman argued that South Australia, New Zealand, and Australind all depended on the 'cheerful emigration of young women of refinement, who have been accustomed from infancy to a species of society which the older colonies were destitute of, but which in our newer colonies they themselves help to form'.[69] But his focus was on the settler men, those who constituted 'the nations of Englishmen to which the spirit of colonization has given birth'.[70] And central to the status of Englishmen in the settler colonies, in his view, would be their position as masters of labourers—labourers who would include Europeans, some from elsewhere such as Indian and Chinese indentured workers, and not least, from among the indigenous people.

CONCLUSION

While the story of Australind and Henry Chapman's writings provide us with insight into conceptions of white settler masculinity in these decades, Chapman's career, writings, and advocacy of responsible government for the settler colonies

[67] Miller, 'Henry Samuel Chapman: Colonizer and Colonist,' pp. 92–4.
[68] Letter to his father from Hobart, 11 July 1852, Chapman, Eichelbaum, and Rosenberg Families: Papers, Series 2/3 Henry Samuel Chapman—Tasmanian and Victorian Papers, MS—Papers 8670–066, Archives, Alexander Turnbull Library, National Library of New Zealand.
[69] Chapman, *The New Settlement of Australind*, p. 11.
[70] Chapman, *The New Settlement of Australind*, p. 11.

shed light on the political dimensions of contemporary understandings of manly qualities. Settler men, like Chapman himself, Marshall Clifton, and Mr George Eliot the resident magistrate whom Louisa Clifton married, saw their status as masters of workers of different races, and at once as patriarchs in their families and communities. While arguments for responsible government in the Australian colonies and other parts of the settler empire were founded on the rights of men to representation, the presumed status of white settler men as political subjects included their dominion over both women and non-white workers. Given the convict status of some of these workers—such as the Aboriginal mailmen in southwestern Western Australia, who worked only for rations, not wages, to serve out terms for offences they may not have known they were committing—the white settler men were masters in a system partially more akin to slavery or indentured labour than to the wage labour of Britain.

Because Henry Chapman was one of the leading advocates of responsible government in the settler colonies, his writings provide an example of how we can use masculinity as an analytic category in relation to liberalism, democracy, responsible government, and settler colonialism in the mid-nineteenth century. They also show that we need to see these as globally connected ideas and movements. Moreover, ideas of white-settler men's rights and authority formed in this period would shape the Australian colonial polity for the rest of the nineteenth century, contribute to ideas of white privilege and exclusion transnationally, and leave a tenacious legacy for the new Australian nation in the twentieth century.

In nineteenth-century Canada, New Zealand, the West Indies, Cape Colony, and the Australian colonies, settlers struggled to assert their social respectability. Claims that they were replicating the nobler aspects of British civilization formed a central plank in their campaigns for political representation, alongside their inheritance of rights to English liberty. For a metropolitan reading public that thrived on sensational stories of colonial violence, mishap, and degeneracy, colonials had to erect an alternative vision of the settler colonies as stable, prosperous, and upright societies in the face of frontier conflict and warfare. Settlers sought to show that colonial society participated in new Victorian prescriptions for middle-class respectability. For the Australian colonies, ideas of gender—especially the social and economic independence integral to full manhood—were at the heart of struggles over the status of emancipated convicts, class relations, access to land, and, ultimately, claims for self-government. In August 1859 the *South Australian Register*, defending the system of responsible government from criticism that it, too, was fallible to political error and arguing for the inherent moral superiority of democracy, saw gender as the crux of the matter: 'the community that is master of its own actions, while it may sometimes go wrong, is certain in the end to manifest more manliness of character . . . It is the power of self-government that makes a nation of men'.[71]

---

[71] 'Responsible Government', *South Australian Register* 25 August 1859, p. 2.

The achievement of representative and responsible government in the 1840s and 1850s took the Australian colonies from being Britain's distant, ocean-bound gaols to the stature of internationally visible pioneers of democracy and political reform. For settlers, their claims to the land that they took from its previous occupiers were bound up in their manly morality and their desire to be political actors with voting rights. Settlers in Australia could and did look to the precedents set in Canada for models of political rights and colonial self-government, and some among them, such as Chapman, even drew comparisons between the indigenous cultures of all three countries, including New Zealand, in their arguments. However, for women in the Australian colonies who vociferously protested their exclusion from the political rights of responsible government, Canada would prove less of a model than the women's movements emerging in the United States and elsewhere.

5

Settler Women, Work, and Debating the Gender of Citizenship

From July 1858 to January 1859, the reading public in Sydney and to a lesser extent Melbourne was able to subscribe to the *Spectator,* which described itself as a *Journal of Literature and Art For the Cultivation of the Memorable and the Beautiful.* Edited by the enterprising but transient Cora Anna Weekes who had arrived in Sydney after producing other short-lived journals in Texas and California, the *Spectator* presented its readers with a range of articles on gender relations and the status and condition of women. Weekes said she was English-born, and like so many other women and men in this period, took advantage of shipping routes and settler colonies. It is evident that she was a feminist. In the *Spectator*'s third number, for example, a disquisition on 'Woman's Influence in Developing Individual and Social Character' contended: 'Mankind are rising through commerce, civilization, and missions, only as woman is restored to her proper position in the family and the economy of society. In proportion as she is degraded from her appointed sphere, society is dislocated, confidence is destroyed, selfishness reins [sic], and the victims of vice bear the marks of divine vengeance on their persons and characters'.[1] Short-lived though the *Spectator* was, its continued twice-monthly publication for six months was one element in the debate on gender roles that percolated across the Australian colonies in the 1850s. Related to the questions of citizenship that were fundamental to the achievement of responsible government, Australian colonial interest in women's conditions and relations between the sexes was shaped, too, by the contemporary international women's movement. Notwithstanding the transnational nature of this debate, in the Australian colonies it had specific inflections due to the legacies of the convict system, the experiences of settlers in colonial towns and the vast Australian bush, and the gold rush that erupted in 1851.

Gender relations in the mid-nineteenth-century Australian colonies were, in part, shaped by convict society and its legacies, including conceptions of the patriarchal family. Historian Kirsty Reid argues that in Van Diemen's Land at least the whole colony was founded on a patriarchal model of authority. Reid traces shifting ways in which idealized notions of fatherhood, family, and masculinity were invoked in colonial governance and social order, or were used to critique them and to call for reform. She looks at the new visions from the 1820s of the settler

---

[1] *Spectator* 31 July 1858 (Vol. I, No. 3), p. 34.

household as 'a miniature "panopticon"' in which assignment would instil 'a moral and ordered femininity' in convict women, and make convict men into 'useful and industrious' agricultural labourers.[2] Not only was the gendered reform of convicts at stake. Settler families were imagined as vehicles of proper fatherhood and moral masculinity, by which the state itself could be judged, and through which 'independent and self-governing men formed the lynchpin of a liberal and self-governing empire'.[3] As Reid shows, the masculinities of both convicts and settlers were directly linked to the simultaneous production of correlated femininities.

As outlined in Chapter 4, the British Parliament enacted constitutions for responsible government in the Australian colonies as follows: New South Wales, Victoria, and Tasmania all in 1855, South Australia in 1856, and Queensland in 1859. While Western Australia was not given responsible government until 1890, this clustering of the achievement of self-government in the other colonies, with male suffrage also achieved during these years in South Australia, Victoria, and New South Wales, enables us to see a broad pattern of newly articulated gender roles in the 1850s. The authors of the major history of Australian women, *Creating A Nation*, have eloquently delineated the profound social significance of these changes: there was a 'new space for men to act in, on stages such as courts, newspaper columns, mechanics' institutes, trades societies, public meetings, political associations, and finally the ballot box and parliament. Men discovered a new way to think of themselves, as political citizens with a voice in their own government. Those women who tried to speak on their own behalf were told that their role was to be governed'.[4] But the women who did speak on their own behalf contributed to contemporary debate over this new definition of political citizenship as explicitly masculine.

This new division had roots in the eighteenth century, in the Enlightenment thinking that produced the American and French Revolutions, according to which the individual with rights to life, liberty, happiness, fraternity, and property was the privileged white male. Feminists of the late eighteenth century, such as Mary Wollstonecraft and Olympe de Gouges, had been dismissed. When the Chartist movement of the 1830s and 1840s was first founded in England, it called for universal suffrage including women, but later even the Chartists turned away from this ideal. Much of the political agitation in Britain of the 1830s to 1850s was led by men of the respectable working classes, such as those with skilled trades, who were adamant that the male head of household was the breadwinner, and that women should not take men's jobs in the workplace, or be political citizens in the public sphere. In fact, around the empire women of the poorer classes continued to work, not only as servants but in a range of small businesses. In mid-nineteenth-century Sydney, for example, as Catherine Bishop has recently shown, a substantial

---

[2] Kirsty Reid, *Gender, Crime and Empire: Convicts, Settlers and the State in Early Colonial Australia* (Manchester: Manchester University Press, 2007), pp. 125–6.

[3] Reid, *Gender, Crime and Empire*, p. 256.

[4] Patricia Grimshaw, Marilyn Lake, Ann McGrath, and Marian Quartly, *Creating a Nation* (Ringwood, Victoria: McPhee Gribble, 1994), p. 94.

proportion of women ran shops, inns, and boarding houses, while some were teachers, actresses, and held other jobs.[5]

But in the colonies, too, there were masculinist ideas. In the 1840s and 1850s, those who advocated self-government in the settler colonies, including the Australian colonies, developed a discourse about settler men and their worthiness for political rights. As we saw in Chapter 4, the leading advocate of responsible government, Henry Chapman, claimed that settlers exhibited exemplary masculinity. He argued that settlers in the Australasian colonies had become 'really independent men' who had proven their maturity and readiness for self-government. They had shown themselves to be industrious, moral, and economically productive.[6] Further, he claimed that self-government would encourage 'a class of yeomen proprietors', again linking manhood and independence.[7] It was a formulation with great contemporary currency, echoed, for example, by the *South Australian Register* in June 1850 with its declaration that: 'All men are by nature free and independent, and have certain inalienable rights'.[8] For some mid-century political theorists, the manly independence required for self-government was characteristic of both adult men and mature nations, and clearly excluded women.[9]

In the Australian press in the 1840s and 1850s, as the struggle for representative and then responsible government played out, the term 'universal suffrage' was endlessly discussed and defined. It was the topic of a debating society meeting in Melbourne in June 1842, where the Hon. Mr Murray expressed his misgivings and questioned a speaker who advocated universal suffrage. 'Did [the speaker] intend to include all, without even excepting women?', Mr Murray asked.[10] In Adelaide in April 1851, at an election meeting, a Mr Hagen dismissed the term 'universal suffrage' as too broad:

> The term 'universal suffrage' in its most limited sense must include the wandering black natives; he thought no man could possibly think of giving them the franchise, though in saying this he did not mean to say that he would make colour of a man's skin per se a test of political qualification.... [I]n the most extensive sense, universal suffrage ... must include women and young children.[11]

Despite such opposition, universal suffrage, meaning settler men only, was the consensus. No doubt there was no conscious irony when the *South Australian Register* reported in September 1850 that 'the local press to a man pronounced for universal suffrage'.[12]

---

[5] Catherine Bishop, 'Commerce Was a Woman: Women in Business in Colonial Sydney and Wellington', PhD thesis, School of History, Australian National University, 2012.

[6] H. S. Chapman, *The New Zealand Portfolio; Embracing a series of papers on subjects of importance to the colonists* (London: Smith and Elder, 1843), pp. vii, 122–7.

[7] Peter Spiller, *The Chapman Legal Family* (Wellington: Victoria University Press, 1992), p. 64.

[8] *South Australian Register* 25 June 1850, p. 3.

[9] Marilyn Lake, 'The Gendered and Racialised Self who Claimed the Right to Self-Government', *Journal of Colonialism and Colonial History* Vol. 13, No. 1 (Spring 2012), p. 1.

[10] 'Port Phillip. Debating Society – Universal Suffrage', *Australasian Chronicle* 14 June 1842, p. 2.

[11] *South Australian Register* 28 April 1851, p. 2.

[12] *South Australian Register* 26 September 1850, p. 2.

DEBATING THE GENDER OF CITIZENSHIP
IN THE 1850s AUSTRALIAN COLONIES

Reading across genres of sources allows us to trace conceptions of gender linked to political citizenship around the time of responsible government in the 1850s, and to glimpse the significance of the changes and the debate among settler women and men. The introduction of representative and then responsible government into the Australian colonies brought democracy, in a form that was both early and somewhat progressive by international standards. But, like elsewhere in the world, it was a masculine preserve; the enfranchisement of men created a new division between the sexes. This was a radical departure: ordinary men would now be political subjects and voters, able to stand for parliament, while women were excluded from politics and thus labelled different in a new way. Settler men became political actors while settler women were excluded from those rights. It was generally assumed that men and women were different. Yet some women in these years were active in public, intellectual, and cultural life, and there is ample evidence to allow us to consider the negotiation and articulation of gender difference at the time of the granting of colonial self-government. As Joan Wallach Scott has pointed out in relation to the Western world, the 'Victorian ideology of domesticity' was not 'created whole' without dissension, but was rather 'the constant subject of great differences of opinion'.[13]

Around the Australian colonies, gender differences and their import were widely debated. For example, '[i]n 1853 the tradesmen and artisans of Perth, meeting at the Swan River Mechanics Institute, spent three nights debating the topic "whether Women do or would possess the same amount of Intellect as man if they had the same advantages"', concluding in the negative. The debaters contended that 'women are incapable of equalling the man and taking the rules of Government into their own hands'. These men at the Mechanics' Institute went so far as to say: 'Women have never had and never can have the same amount of Intellect and no one among us considers his wife is superior in Intellect to himself or superior in Governing powers'. As earlier historians have suggested, this all points to close connections between the idea of democracy as it evolved, and the idea of patriarchy.[14] By the 1850s settler society, with its gendered structure rooted in the exploitation, reform, and governance of convicts as Reid argues, was firmly founded on this reconsolidated and new form of patriarchy in which men became enfranchised citizens.

The Australian press ran various articles concerning women's political rights, their interest in politics, and the issue of whether they belonged in the private or the public sphere. In Tasmania in 1857, a proposal was debated to provide a public gallery for women from which to observe the legislative chambers and listen to political debate. Either some were already doing so, or wished to. One concerned

---

[13] Joan Wallach Scott, *Gender and the Politics of History* (New York: Columbia University Press, 1999), p. 43.
[14] Grimshaw et al., *Creating a Nation*, pp. 102 and 104–5.

commentator wrote to the editor of the *Hobart Town Daily Courier* on 23 May 1857, trying to convince women that they should not sit in the parliamentary gallery: 'the wiser numbers of the fair sex must by this time be satisfied that little enjoyment can be derived from listening to the debates of a colonial Parliament'. Parliamentary debate was too rough for women's ears, this writer thought: 'it only remains for [women] to consider whether any supposed beneficial influence which their presence might exercise is not too dearly purchased by the sacrifice of their own feelings of delicacy and refinement—whether that influence cannot be exerted more beneficially and more surely in the privacy of HOME, than in the oppressive and tainted atmosphere of a public debating hall'. In this letter-writer's view, women did not belong in the political realm even as listeners, as he hoped to convince the newspaper's 'fair readers who are thoughtlessly inclined to indulge an unprofitable curiosity'.[15]

In August 1859 a debate was held in the Ipswich School of Arts in Queensland, on the question: 'Would it be right to admit women to equal political privileges with the men?' A Mr Cramp argued in favour of women's rights, saying: 'that woman is morally and intellectually capable of exercising the franchise, and taking a part in politics; that having been in all ages a conservator of peace, her influence would be beneficial. Good Queens, and women who had defended their country, proved their capability to govern'. Perhaps in reply to Mr Violet, who 'made a sensation by an unique [sic] speech against the ladies interfering in politics, based on Scripture', Dr Challinor argued that 'Scripture had been misquoted', and that it did not contain anything 'to discountenance the privilege of voting'. Moreover, he contended:

> It is expedient for the country whose women are thoroughly versed in sound politics. Washington's mother made him the defender of liberty. Women capable of conducting large businesses had a right to vote: nor has nature made such a difference as should bar their right to political privileges.[16]

The debate, which seemed to include only male participants, was to be continued the following week.

As Mary Ryan has shown of the evolving public sphere in the United States in the mid-nineteenth century, despite their overt political exclusion, women inserted themselves into public life and political debate in various ways.[17] While the public sphere in the Australian colonies was quite different from that of the contemporaneous United States for a range of historically specific reasons, in both parts of the settler–colonial world it was changing, and some women's active engagement with it was one of the forces driving change. Despite their exclusion from the franchise as it was forged in the 1850s, women expressed their political views in a variety of ways. In Melbourne in February 1851, a meeting of the Australasian League against convict

---

[15] *Hobart Town Daily Courier* 23 May 1857.

[16] Others argued the other side; *Moreton Bay Courier* 10 August 1859, p. 2.

[17] Mary P. Ryan, *Women in Public: Between Banners and Ballots, 1825–1880* (Baltimore: Johns Hopkins University Press, 1990).

Fig. 5.1 S. T. Gill, 'First subscription ball, Ballarat, 1854'.
State Library of New South Wales DG V*/ SpColl/ Gill/19 Digital. a1528401.

transportation drew a crowd of nearly two hundred, of whom 'a very large proportion belonged to the fairer portion of the creation'. A Mrs Dalgarno was one of the speakers, and used the occasion, not only to expound her anti-transportation views, but also to advocate the inclusion of women in local government: 'She had heard of things going wrong in the City Council, and she did not at all wonder at it. Let them only try as a remedy, appointing half their Councillors from the women, and she was sure this would cure it'.[18] Historian Clare Wright argues that women were integral, outspoken, and bold participants in the political disturbances on the Ballarat goldfields in 1854, actively stirring popular democratic opinion in the turbulent protests leading up to the Eureka Stockade.[19] (See Fig. 5.1.)

This activism, according to Wright, was not limited to the Victorian goldfields in the early 1850s, but was sufficiently widespread and had such impact that it needs to be recognized as an early, short-lived moment when women demanded emancipation. Women's calls for political rights had become such a prominent part of public discourse in Victoria in 1853 to 1854 that they became the subject of satire. In 1854 a journalist and comic playwright William Akhurst wrote a farce called

[18] 'Tea Meeting', *Argus* (Melbourne) 15 February 1851, p. 4.
[19] Clare Wright, '"New Brooms They Say Sweep Clean": Women's Political Activism on the Ballarat Goldfields, 1854', *Australian Historical Studies* Vol. 39, No. 3 (2008): 305–21. See also Clare Wright, *The Forgotten Rebels of Eureka* (Melbourne: Text Publishing, 2013).

'Rights of Woman', which was staged in Melbourne. A major protagonist in the play was 'a strong-minded lady who is a Pupil of the New Age and a firm supporter of the Rights of Woman', and the play further boasted a song entitled 'Woman's Rights'.[20]

A few women openly challenged the assumption that men were their intellectual superiors, and urged women's political involvement. Several letters published in the *Sydney Morning Herald* in 1857 and 1858 expressed views of privileged women. 'Sarah Sands' argued against democracy for men, on the basis that women of the upper classes would lose the little influence they had:

> What! Is it not enough, that they should debar us from the franchise, but that they should also seek to deprive us of what little influence we have in the social scale?[21]

Openly arguing for the privilege of 'rank', 'Sarah Sands' called on all women to oppose the Electoral Reform League because one of its leaders had criticized women who spent too much on finery: 'I repudiate this League, and demand all of my sex to exert their influence to oppose it. It is antagonistic to us, its principals . . . are inimical to our interests and subversive of our influence'.[22]

Others accepted the rights of men to political and social equality, but asked that women be included:

> Are there any valid reasons for refusing this privilege to women, who, but for their sex—the accident of birth—would, by the present laws, be entitled to it? I opine that numerous positive evils result to women, and through women to society at large, in consequence of that policy which restricts the franchise to male persons only; and that there are no objections to a more equitable distribution of civil rights, which will bear the test of calm, impartial, scrutiny.
>
> In the first place, Sir, it seems to me that this restrictive policy introduces a principle into our polity as, to my thinking, erroneous. It applies a physical condition as a test of moral fitness.[23]

'H.' contended further that 'the claims of women to participation in the elective franchise' were 'a question deeply interesting to a large proportion of your readers, and one which will well bear ventilation just now'.[24] These examples all show the extent to which issues of women's exclusion from politics, their rights, and their roles were discussed and debated around 1850s Australia, including by women. In the 1860s and 1870s the issue continued to percolate, if at a slightly lower temperature, with articles and letters on women's political rights appearing in newspapers ranging from the *Queanbeyan Age and General Advertiser* in June 1861, to the *Launceston Examiner* in June 1867, and the *Queenslander* in April

---

[20] Clare Wright, 'Golden Opportunities: The Early Origins of Women's Suffrage in Victoria', *Victorian Historical Journal* Vol. 79, No. 2 (Nov. 2008), p. 215.

[21] Sarah Sands, *Sydney Morning Herald* 13 August 1857, from *The Push from the Bush: A Bulletin of Social History* No. 25 (Oct. 1987), p. 54.

[22] Sarah Sands, *Sydney Morning Herald* 13 August 1857.

[23] 'H.', Letter to the editor, *Sydney Morning Herald* 2 July 1858, p. 5.

[24] 'H.', Letter to the editor, *Sydney Morning Herald*.

1871, among others.[25] Not surprisingly, there was a spike of interest in the issue in the colonial press in 1866 and 1867, with the passage of the British Reform Act that enfranchised artisanal men, and John Stuart Mill's championing of the issue of women's suffrage in the House of Commons.[26]

CAROLINE CHISHOLM: ADVOCATING MIGRATION AND SPEAKING UP

Caroline Chisholm (1808–77) has been commemorated more than any other woman who figured in nineteenth-century Australian history, except for the imperial monarch Queen Victoria herself. From 1967 to 1992 Chisholm's portrait featured on the Australian five-dollar note in the first series of the nation's decimal currency. The federal electoral division of Chisholm, which covers an area of approximately sixty-five square kilometres of Melbourne's eastern suburbs, is named after her. A suburb of Canberra is named for her, as is Chisholm Street in another Canberra suburb, that of Ainslie. Roman Catholic colleges in Melbourne and Sydney are named for her, as are state schools in Canberra and southwestern Sydney, and a school in Northampton, England, near where she was born and where she is buried. A charitable society in Victoria and a theological library in Melbourne are named in her memory, as are a retirement village and nursing home in Sydney, and a Catholic centre for the study of ethical issues in health care. Reflected in this broad range of commemorative naming, Caroline Chisholm figures in Australian public memory as 'the emigrants' friend', a social worker who devoted herself to the cause of emigration from Britain in the mid-nineteenth century, particularly to helping poor single young women and families.

Yet this simple near-saintly image of Chisholm's untiring work in the 1840s and 1850s for the Australian colonies' social and moral uplift hides more than it reveals, both about Chisholm's life and about the part of Australian history for which she is something of a metonym. The emphasis on Chisholm as a woman involved in philanthropy belies her remarkable achievements and the extent of her political influence. In tying her to the charitable work associated with women of her period, this image diminishes her significance as a highly visible migration proponent, in some ways a counterpart to Edward Gibbon Wakefield even though his strength was in theory and propaganda while hers was in action. Chisholm was concerned with the demographic and economic potential of migration; as Jan Kociumbas has put it, she was 'essentially a female political economist'.[27] Moreover, the thumbnail biography that is publicly known of her omits the significance of her early years in India, the connections between the Indian and Australian colonies in those decades,

[25] 'Who Should Elect Members of Parliament', *Queanbeyan Age and General Advertiser* 27 June 1861, p. 4 (reprinted from the *Illawarra Mercury*); 'Female Suffrage', *Launceston Examiner* 8 June 1867, p. 6; 'Female Suffrage', *Queenslander* 22 April 1871, p. 2.

[26] For example, 'The Debate on Female Suffrage', *Sydney Morning Herald* 29 July 1867, p. 3.

[27] Jan Kociumbas, *The Oxford History of Australia: Possessions, 1770–1860* Volume 2 (South Melbourne, Victoria: Oxford University Press, 1992), p. 184.

Fig. 5.2 Caroline Chisholm, lithograph portrait by Thomas Fairland (published by M. I. Laidler, 1851).
National Library of Australia, an9267591.

and the ways in which we need to see the mid-nineteenth-century colonies in their wider imperial context. (See Fig. 5.2.)

Chisholm's story speaks to the significance of settlers from India in early colonial Australia, not least those with military backgrounds. It also illustrates nicely some of the themes in this volume: that serendipity was often involved in settlers' movements, that they were surprisingly mobile, took chances as they arose—and had often been exposed to colonial racial hierarchies elsewhere. Born Caroline Jones in 1808, to a yeoman farming family in Northampton, in 1830 she married Captain Archibald Chisholm who served in the East India Company army. Archibald Chisholm was Roman Catholic; Caroline converted to Catholicism on their marriage but at the same time obtained his agreement that he would support her in whatever social reform work she took up. The first two years of their marriage were spent in Brighton, after which Archibald returned to his army service in Madras. Caroline soon followed, and the six years she spent in India produced more than her first two sons. Caroline Chisholm chose as her first cause that of the suitable education of the daughters of the company's ordinary white soldiers, establishing the Female School of Industry for the Daughters of European Soldiers. As she explained in an 1852 pamphlet that recorded something of her life story:

> Mrs. Chisholm was at Madras, in India, with her husband, who was an officer in the Indian army. She was sorry to see the young girls, the daughters of soldiers, brought up in the barracks: not taught to read or write, or sew, or cook, or anything that would enable them to become good useful wives when they grew up, beside all the bad language and bad examples that were to be seen and heard among the soldiers. So she set to work, collected subscriptions from a great many gentlemen, including the governor, Sir Charles Adam, and raised enough to establish an Institution, where the young girls were taken care of, and instructed by herself and other ladies in everything useful.... This Institution is carried on to this day, and receives the orphans of soldiers.[28]

It is unclear if any of the girls in the school were mixed-race, though certainly some of the daughters of European soldiers in Madras at the time would have been.

While Caroline Chisholm's career would be largely devoted to purposeful migration from Britain to Australia, her own arrival in the Australian colonies was shaped more by circumstance. In 1838 Archibald was given leave, which they decided to spend in Australia rather than returning to England because of its climate and its proximity. With their two young sons and three Indian servants, they embarked on the *Emerald Isle*, a ship chartered by the Australian Association of Bengal which sought to develop relations between the Indian and Australian colonies—the sort of relations that Australind's name and aspirations represented. It was a particularly long voyage. The ship had to spend a month en route at Mauritius for repairs, then another month in Adelaide. They stopped at Hobart for a further three weeks, before finally arriving in Sydney in late 1838. The Chisholms settled in a cottage at Windsor on the western edge of Sydney where their third son was born in 1839. In 1840 imperial imperatives prevailed again, when Archibald was recalled to service due to the outbreak of war between Britain and China. Rather than returning to India or England, Caroline chose to stay in Sydney with their children.[29]

Despite the fact that the demographic balance and social health of settler Australia would become Caroline Chisholm's life's work, like many other settlers she did not stay permanently. In 1846, the Chisholms returned to England after Archibald retired from the army; there Caroline actively pursued her work in support of Australian colonization, especially establishing the Family Colonization Loan Society that became her major project. In 1851 Archibald, who subordinated his post-army career to hers, returned to Australia to anchor the work in the colonies. Meanwhile Caroline stayed to tour, lecture, raise money, exert her influence, and write letters and pamphlets. Chisholm's success included the launching of the *Caroline Chisholm*, which in September 1853 embarked on its

---

[28] *The Story of the Life of Mrs. Caroline Chisholm, The Emigrant's Friend, and Her Adventure in Australia* (London: Trelawney Saunders, Charing Cross, 1852), p. 4.
[29] Margaret Kiddle, *Caroline Chisholm* (Carlton, Victoria: Melbourne University Press, 1950), pp. 4–5.

first voyage with emigrants to Australia. In 1854, Caroline herself returned to the colonies and continued her high-profile advocacy of the migration of women and families. After she developed a kidney problem in 1857, the family moved to Kyneton in Victoria where Archibald served as a magistrate and their elder sons ran a shop. Returning to Sydney for medical treatment, Caroline was impelled by financial necessity to run a girls' school in Newtown. In 1866 the elder Chisholms returned to England, where they lived out their lives obscurely and modestly.[30] Chisholm's 1852 biography summed up her early work for Australian colonization thus: 'By [her] system of homes, register offices, and journeys through the bush, between 1839 and 1846, she was the means of settling comfortably, as servants or farmers, more than eleven thousand souls'.[31]

Chisholm's pride in her work was in good part due to its success, measurable in the numbers of poor emigrants who settled in Australia with her help and the women for whom she arranged jobs as servants in the interior. From 1849 the Family Colonization Loan Society, her particular achievement, operated as a kind of cooperative or friendly society for those with modest means. The society accepted contributions from intending poor settlers or their relatives, lent them the balance of their passages, helped them to find positions on arrival, and then collected the balance owing on lenient terms. But she was also conscious of her own fortitude in establishing her servants' registry system in the colonies' backblocks. Her 1852 biography notes that many of the young women whom she helped to find jobs would not otherwise have dared to venture into the bush despite the availability of good wages there: 'They were frightened by foolish stories about blacks and robbers'.[32] Chisholm, in contrast, saw herself as brave and practical. Anticipating the celebrated women travellers in Africa and the Middle East of the later nineteenth and early twentieth centuries, she claimed to have 'met with many curious adventures in travelling where no lady, and very few white women, had ever been before'.[33]

Charles Dickens, a famous contemporary of Chisholm's, who knew her quite well, fictionalized her work in racialized and imperial terms. In fact Dickens supported Chisholm's work for poor British emigrants and in 1851–52 even advertised the Family Colonization Loan Society in his *Household Words*. Nevertheless it is widely considered that in his 1852–53 novel *Bleak House*, Dickens drew a satirical portrait of Chisholm with his character Mrs Jellyby. Mrs Jellyby is a well-known philanthropist living in London with her meek, subservient husband and brood of children. She devotes almost all her waking hours and energy to her 'African project' which aimed: 'by this time next year to have from a hundred and fifty to two hundred families cultivating coffee and educating the natives of Borrioboola-Gha, on the left bank of the Niger'.[34] According to Chisholm's

---

[30] Judith Iltis, 'Chisholm, Caroline (1808–1877)', *Australian Dictionary of Biography*, National Centre of Biography, Australian National University, http://adb.anu.edu.au/biography/chisholm-caroline-1894/text2231, accessed 22 November 2013.

[31] *The Story of the Life of Mrs. Caroline Chisholm*, p. 13.

[32] *The Story of the Life of Mrs. Caroline Chisholm*, p. 7.

[33] *The Story of the Life of Mrs. Caroline Chisholm*, p. 10.

[34] Charles Dickens, *Bleak House* (1853; London: Oxford University Press, 1948), p. 37.

biographer Margaret Kiddle, this fictional scheme alluded to an actual scheme of ten years earlier, the African Civilization Society and Niger Association, which had sought to establish a model farm and Christian mission on the Upper Niger River and thus to open the area to British trade. An expedition had been sent and a colony founded, which failed within a year. Kiddle notes that part of the evidence for Mrs Jellyby being modelled on Chisholm is that, unlike the real African Civilization Society and Niger Association, Mrs Jellyby's Borrioboola-Gha scheme involved the settlement of British families.[35]

Mrs Jellyby is wholly preoccupied with her endless correspondence for her African project, and oblivious to her dirty and neglected brood. When visitors arrive at the house, one small boy has just got his head stuck in the iron fence railings, soon after which another falls down an entire flight of stairs, both incidents escaping Mrs Jellyby's attention. The house is dusty, untidy, littered with paper, and lacking in normal comforts; fires are unlit, candles inadequate, and the cook is an inebriate. At dinner, Mrs Jellyby had so much correspondence that there were 'four envelopes in the gravy at once'.[36] Worse, Mrs Jellyby herself is dishevelled, her hair unbrushed, and her dress gaping at the back, held together only with stay-lace.[37] Kiddle contends that, although Chisholm had six children by this point, and that her house may have been somewhat disorderly due to her running something of a training school for servants destined for Australia in her kitchen, she did not neglect her household, her children, or her appearance.[38]

Given that Chisholm's first social reform project, in Madras, had been a school for girls, perhaps the cruellest aspect of the Mrs Jellyby caricature is that of her daughter Caddy (Caroline) Jellyby. Mrs Jellyby relies on her eldest daughter as her 'amanuensis', dictating letters to her so ceaselessly that the girl was not only 'in such a state of ink' but that she was 'jaded and unhealthy-looking' and although 'by no means plain' was poorly shod and had 'no article of dress upon her, from a pin upwards, that was in its proper condition or its right place'.[39] Worse, Miss Jellyby is desperately unhappy. She admits to a kind visitor that she detests the Africa project and her mother's endless talk of it, feels that her mother has neglected her parental duty, and that she herself is uneducated in everything but writing. Unlike other girls whom she envies, she cannot speak French, knows neither geography nor sewing, nor can she play music, dance, or sing.[40]

It may have been partly this fictional portrayal of Chisholm's daughter that especially provoked feminist editor and lecturer Cora Anna Weekes to lambast Dickens's Mrs Jellyby, in December 1859 in Sydney. In her public lecture at the School of Arts on the subject of 'Female Heroism in the Nineteenth Century', Weekes elaborated on the themes of womanly virtue, the contemporary movement 'to enlarge the sphere of [women's] activity and usefulness', and 'Woman's Rights'. Weekes took Mrs Jellyby to be an attack on supporters of women's rights, that made the cause 'as ridiculous as a vivid fancy and a fine eye for contrasts can make it'.

[35] Kiddle, *Caroline Chisholm*, pp. 165–6.   [36] Dickens, *Bleak House*, p. 40.
[37] Dickens, *Bleak House*, pp. 35–7.   [38] Kiddle, *Caroline Chisholm*, pp. 167–8.
[39] Dickens, *Bleak House*, pp. 37–8.   [40] Dickens, *Bleak House*, pp. 43–8.

By suggesting that women who 'go earnestly and directly to a good work' forget their domestic obligations and responsibilities are absurd and unfeminine, Dickens had flung his sketch 'in the face of every earnest woman who makes an effort to elevate the condition of her sex'.[41] While Weekes did not mention Chisholm by name, her extended criticism of Dickens's caricature to a Sydney audience at the height of Chisholm's fame suggests that they likely made the connection.

One reason that Weekes's audience may well have understood the connection to Chisholm was that Chisholm herself gave several well-attended public lectures in Sydney in the period from 1859 to 1861. Although she always included references to her own work in facilitating migration to Australia—even mentioning particular people whom she had helped—Chisholm did not confine herself to that subject, lecturing on matters from the early closing of public houses and shops, to the opening up of access to the land to farmers of modest means, to the reasons for subscribing to newspapers, and to the secret ballot and universal suffrage. Able to command audiences, she chose to use her celebrity to exert her influence on political matters of the day. Women comprised part of her audience. Indeed, on 10 December 1860, when Chisholm gave a lecture at the Temperance Hall in Pitt Street on the subject of land buyers' access to selection, according to the *Sydney Morning Herald* it was to such 'a very large audience' that: 'Shortly after the doors were thrown open, the hall rapidly filled with persons of both sexes, until it became so densely crowded that, before even the lecture commenced, it was necessary to provide for numbers of ladies upon the platform'.[42] The *Empire* reported that there was a 'large proportion of ladies' as well as 'men of all classes'. Despite the fact that New South Wales was in the middle of an election campaign, 'Not one of our most popular candidates has been listened to by a more numerous and enthusiastic audience'.[43]

In a lecture the previous year, Chisholm had assertively addressed women's right to express their political views:

> [S]ome people seemed to speak as if they thought that no woman ought to have any opinions whatever as regarded politics; but she had seen a good deal of life, and had herself seen good cause to adopt certain well-defined political opinions; and she would fearlessly remark that the political evils to which she was about to advert did exist, and could not continue to exist except through the blunders of political leaders.[44]

The 'political evils' included those who sought to limit landholding and political office to the wealthy, and those who stood in the way of colonial democracy, parliamentary representation, and universal suffrage. She spoke in favour of the secret ballot, which was already operating elsewhere in the Australian colonies and

---

[41] Cora Anna Weekes, 'Female Heroism in the Nineteenth Century', the *Spectator: Journal of Literature and Art For the Cultivation of the Memorable and the Beautiful* Vol. II, No. 13, 22 January 1859, pp. 1–2.

[42] 'Mrs Chisholm upon free selection before survey', *Sydney Morning Herald* 11 December 1860, p. 4.

[43] 'Lecture on Free Selection before Survey, by Mrs Chisholm', *Empire* [Sydney] 11 December 1860, p. 5.

[44] 'Mrs Chisholm's Lecture', *Sydney Morning Herald* 9 July 1859, p. 7.

had been recently introduced in New South Wales, and urged the further cause of the payment of members of parliament. The ballot, in her view, was such a signal attribute of the Australian colonial political system that 'it was worth coming sixteen thousand miles to get hold of it'. Returning to the topic of women's right to political speech, she reasserted: 'Serious objections had been urged against a lady appearing before the public, but she would state her reasons for taking that course . . . [S]he did not want her experience to die with her, but if she had one good thought she wished to impart it'.[45] In her December 1860 public lecture at the Temperance Hall, the chair, a Mr Hanson, suggested as a witty compliment that Mrs Chisholm should be elected as a member of parliament: 'Mrs Chisholm would make a most excellent representative in the Assembly, a very useful check on some of the proceedings in Macquarie-street. He would recommend them to put Mrs Chisholm in at the head of the poll'. In her response in kind, Chisholm mentioned that she was currently teaching English to some Chinese men, and had run into one of her pupils at a public meeting. Noting that this pupil understood the role of public meetings in keeping social order, and alluding to recent anti-Chinese protests on gold-mining fields and discussion of restrictions on their immigration, she asserted that: 'If they were to send her into the House as their representative, she would not pledge herself to vote against the Chinese. She told them now because it was better to tell them now than after she had been in the House'.[46] Chisholm was jesting in response to Mr Hanson's wit, yet perhaps she actually could imagine herself as a member of parliament.

Though Chisholm is not usually associated with the nineteenth-century women's movement, Cora Anna Weekes saw Dickens's satirical rendering of her as an attack on its proponents. Given Chisholm's Sydney public speeches, she may well have accepted that linking, at least to the contemporary debate over gender and political authority. Certainly her high public visibility and decades-long career in advocacy, lobbying, lecturing, and fund-raising rendered her a publicly political woman.

CATHERINE HELEN SPENCE: WRITING WOMEN'S RIGHTS IN THE GOLD RUSH AND AFTER

When in 1894 South Australia became the first Australian colony to give women the vote, it was partly because of its progressive Liberals, but it was also because of the organized women's movement there, a movement whose genealogy stretched back to the middle of the century. Catherine Helen Spence (1825–1910), one of the movement's leaders, was a pioneering reformer whose feminist thought and advocacy of proportional representation transcended South Australia and had an international impact (see Fig. 5.3). Spence arrived in Adelaide as a migrant from

---

[45] 'Mrs Chisholm's Lecture', *Sydney Morning Herald*, 9 July 1859, p. 7.
[46] 'Lecture on Free Selection before Survey, by Mrs Chisholm', *Empire* [Sydney] 11 December 1860, p. 5.

Fig. 5.3 Catherine Helen Spence, 1865, unknown London photographer.
State Library of New South Wales P1/1610 Digital. a4363010.

Scotland with her family in 1839 when she was thirteen and the colony just three years old. As Susan Magarey has argued, we can see in Spence's writings of the 1850s and early 1860s the first formulations of what would later become her public activism for electoral reform and women's voting rights. In her novels, not least those from this period, Magarey argues, 'Spence challenged the patriarchal dominance of Australian culture' with her 'rebel' heroines, her focus on the financial bases of women's lives, and her female characters' engagement with public culture and political issues.[47]

---

[47] Susan Magarey, *Unbridling the Tongues of Women: A biography of Catherine Helen Spence* (Sydney: Hale & Iremonger, 1985), pp. 66, 71.

Spence spurred the debate about women's issues through her novels, including *Clara Morison* (1854) and *Mr. Hogarth's Will* (1865). Spence wrote *Clara Morison* to prove that women emigrating from Britain to Australia were not just destined to be or useful as wives. Morison is a genteel young Scottish woman who is orphaned and compelled by her uncle to migrate from Edinburgh to Adelaide. Despite family expectations that Morison will land a job as a governess, soon after arrival she has no choice but to work as a servant. She endures both menial work and servile status, but manages to do so with dignity and self-respect. She not only makes a few friends in the colony but stumbles on a family of her cousins whose hospitality rescues her from domestic service, and in the end is rewarded with a very happy marriage to a successful pastoralist in the mid-north. Morison herself is not an activist, though she is literary, holds firm opinions, and shows a consciousness of women's subordination. Another character is Margaret Elliot, an alter ego for Spence, who refuses to marry despite two offers, is independent, knowledgeable and opinionated, runs her family's household, and criticizes social attitudes towards spinsters. Margaret is regarded by Adelaide society as a bluestocking, due to her intellectual abilities and pursuits: 'She studied mathematics with George and law with Gilbert; she read the driest books, and made extracts from them in an old ledger ... She read all the newspapers she could get hold of, and was as well acquainted with current history as with Magnall's[sic] Questions'.[48] Not only educated and intelligent, Margaret Elliot was passionately interested in politics:

> Margaret's [letter to Clara] was filled with politics; she told Clara what the Council ought to do during the session, but what they would not do, and gave her own ideas on what would actually be done; quoted some speeches in Parliament on colonial questions, and enlarged on the ignorance of the British public with regard to their dependencies; deprecated the policy of the Governor of Van Diemen's Land in writing home for more convicts, and hoped that the Home Government would not consent to such a suicidal request.[49]

While the fictional Margaret conveys Spence's overtly feminist message, Jennifer Rutherford suggests that *Clara Morison* is a colonial version of Jane Austen in its domestic interiors, with its feminist sensibility 'set against the political debates' of the 1850s colonies.[50] *Clara Morison* suggests that women play crucial social roles and questions their exclusion from the public world.

Mr. Hogarth's Will was first published in instalments in 1864, then as a novel in 1865. It is set in the late 1850s and early 1860s, and tackles directly the question of women's ability to make a living, the limited options open to them, and the relative advantages of these options. It is a protest against women's exclusion from the professions and respectable, well-paid jobs. The central character, Jane Melville, has

---

[48] *Mangnall's Questions* was a widely used school text associated with a well-known Yorkshire girls' school. Catherine Helen Spence, *Clara Morison* (first published John W. Parker and Son, 1854; Adelaide: Rigby Ltd, 1971), p. 160.

[49] Spence, *Clara Morison*, p. 343.

[50] Jennifer Rutherford, *The Gauche Intruder: Freud, Lacan and the White Australian Fantasy* (Carlton South, Victoria: Melbourne University Press, 2000), p. 39.

been well educated in Scotland, and wants to have a career in a field such as banking or publishing, but men will not employ her. She finds a job as a governess and housekeeper, migrates to Australia, then marries, but after marriage still wishes to play a role in the wider world. The novel deals with politics and electoral reform, even supporting women's right to the vote.[51]

Spence's early novels were written when few women in the Australian colonies were able to publish. One of the more successful novels from the same era is Caroline Woolmer Leakey's *The Broad Arrow*. First published in London in 1859 and Hobart in 1860, *The Broad Arrow* is a bathetic tale of a middle-class young Englishwoman wrongly convicted of child murder, and sentenced to transportation for life in Tasmania, who seems to take every opportunity to put others ahead of herself. A mawkish, religious, and morally inspired novel, it represents women as either middle-class invalids or rough servants, and did nothing to challenge gender prescriptions of women's limitations—quite a contrast to Spence's work.[52] The first novel published in South Australia itself (Spence's early novels were published in England) was *Marian, or The Light of Some One's Home, A Tale of Australian Life in the Bush* by Maud Jean Franc (the pen name of Matilda Jane Evans) published in 1859. *Marian* was considerably more conventional than *Clara Morison* in its gender politics, the tale of a governess from London who adapts well to her farmstead home at Mt Barker and marries one of the sons. Its heroine was more assertive, independent, and happier than the protagonist of *The Broad Arrow*, yet the novel's serious religious purpose and acceptance of most social conventions meant it also differed from Spence's work.[53]

There were particular reasons why the early 1850s was a moment when some South Australian women were able to exert greater independence. As Catherine Helen Spence documents in *Clara Morison*, referring to the effects of the 'gold-fever' exodus to Victoria from Adelaide by Christmas 1852:

> The clerks out of employment, supernumerary shopmen, failing tradesmen, parasol-menders, and piano-tuners, went first, but now everyone is going, without regard to circumstances or families . . . Our butcher's man has dwindled into a small boy, who tells us he's the only man in the shop. Our baker drives his own cart, and you see women driving about quite independently now.[54]

Even in early 1851, prior to the major discovery of gold in New South Wales and Victoria, the departure of men from the Australian colonies to the California gold rush had led to women's expanded roles in business. When Clara Morison first arrives in Adelaide, and is looking for lodgings, a Mr Campbell advises her to go to Mrs Handy's boarding house: 'Mrs. Handy's house was thought very well

[51] Catherine Helen Spence, *Mr. Hogarth's Will* (first published London: Richard Bentley, 1865; Ringwood, Victoria: Penguin Books, 1988), pp. 274–5.
[52] Oline Keese [Caroline Woolmer Leakey], *The Broad Arrow, Being Passages from the History of Maida Gwynnham, a 'Lifer'* (first published London, 1859; London: Richard Bentley, 1887).
[53] Barbara Wall, *Our Own Matilda: Matilda Jane Evans, 1827–1886, Pioneer Woman and Novelist* (Kent Town, South Australia: Wakefield Press, 1994), Ch. 5.
[54] Spence, *Clara Morison*, pp. 170, 172.

conducted; ... Mr. Handy had gone to California on a gold-hunting expedition, and though he had been gone more than a year, did not speak of coming back soon; but ... in his absence, the boarding-house was very creditably managed by Mrs. Handy'.[55] Much later, Mr Handy finally returns from the Victorian goldfields, where he had been led by his failure in California, and is lavishly throwing around his winnings. Even then 'Mrs. Handy was still doing her best to keep her boarders together, for she saw that her husband's habits of steady industry were completely broken up, and that she must depend hence-forward on her own exertions'.[56] The relative absence of men for a period in the early 1850s, in all likelihood, may have helped to prepare for the gender debates of the mid-1850s.

TRACKING DEVELOPMENTS OVERSEAS

Settlers in the Australian colonies were well aware of the emergence of women's rights groups in Britain around 1850, and at Seneca Falls in the United States in 1848. A colonial man visiting London sent a report on changes there back to the *Sydney Morning Herald* in January 1851, complaining of new attitudes among women, not least their presence in his club. He described his astonishment and disapproval at finding that: 'Numbers of elegantly dressed women, were lounging luxuriously in easy chairs, in their especial drawing room, evidently as much at home at their club, as my wife was in her own house, and amongst her children'.[57]

In April 1851, for example, the *South Australian Register* reported on 'A Woman's Rights Convention ... held at Worcester, Massachusetts'. As the paper reported, resolutions passed at that convention included: 'That women are clearly entitled to the right of suffrage, and to be considered eligible to office ... That as ... women alone can learn by experience, and prove by works, what is their rightful sphere of duties, we recommend as *next steps*, that they should demand a *co-equal share* in the formation and administration of Laws—Municipal, State, and Nation—through Legislative Assemblies, Courts, and Executive offices'.[58] In February 1857, the *Hobart Town Mercury* reported on the 'Women's Rights Convention' recently held in New York State and presided over by Lucy Stone, which resolved, among other items, that: '[T]he main power of the woman's right movement lies in this—that whilst always demanding for woman better education, better employment, and better laws, it has always kept steadily in view the one cardinal demand for the right of suffrage, asking in a democracy the symbol and the guarantee of all other rights'.[59] In July 1858, the *South Australian Advertiser* noted:

---

[55] Spence, *Clara Morison*, p. 22.   [56] Spence, *Clara Morison*, p. 383.
[57] 'Contributions from Home', *Sydney Morning Herald* 4 January 1851, p. 4.
[58] *South Australian Register* 25 April 1851, p. 2.
[59] 'Women's Rights Convention', *Hobart Town Mercury* 25 February 1857, p. 3.

Should the ladies of South Australia take it into their heads to demand such an alteration in the Electoral Act as will confer upon them the right of voting for representatives in Parliament, it may be well for them to know that their claims are not without precedent as we find by a letter in the *National Intelligencer*, that women formerly possessed, and at various times exercised, the elective franchise in the State of New Jersey ... [I]n 1790 a prominent quaker member of the Assembly ... had sufficient influence to have [an election law] so drawn as to read "he or she" when referring to qualified voters ... No change of this phraseology was made until 1807, and women often voted ... In the Presidential contest of 1800 there were many instances of their voting in different parts of the State. At an election in Hunterdon county in 1802 even some women of colour were allowed to vote, and their ballots elected a member of the Legislature.[60]

Such interest in women's voting rights elsewhere occurred in the context of the constant parsing of the term 'universal suffrage', a low-level and often mocking refrain about whether it should include women and others.

Of course, these shifts in gender ideology occurred in many places around the world. In South Africa, gender definitions were a core part of the changes from British rule around 1800 to the 1853 constitution for representative government.[61] In Lower Canada, some women had voted in elections in the first half of the nineteenth century, a right that was taken away from them in 1849 following its union with Upper Canada.[62] Historian Cecilia Morgan argues that in the 1840s Upper Canadian papers 'published satirical articles and broadsides lampooning those in the United States who campaigned for women's rights (including the right to vote)'.[63] As Morgan's point makes clear, from the 1830s women's suffrage had become a visible issue in the United States, linked to the movement to abolish slavery.

FRANCHISE ANOMALIES

Moreover, in the 1850s anomalies emerged in relation to women's ability to vote for municipal elections in various parts of the Australian colonies. As noted in the last chapter, in Tasmania in 1857 the municipal franchise for rural districts was explicitly limited to men, whereas for Hobart and Launceston it was not. Next, the 1858 New South Wales Act, which specified the municipal franchise, referred to 'ratepayers' without explicitly saying male ratepayers only, so some women did vote in subsequent elections, such as Elizabeth Cadman in the 1859 Waverley Council

---

[60] *South Australian Advertiser* 13 July 1858, p. 3.

[61] Kirsten McKenzie, 'Replacing Wollstonecraft's Models: Gender, Respectability and Colonial Political Rights in Middle-Class Cape Town, c.1800–1850', in Joy Damousi and Katherine Ellinghaus (eds), *Citizenship, Women and Social Justice* (Melbourne: History Department, University of Melbourne, 1999), pp. 79–88.

[62] Bettina Bradbury, *Wife to Widow: Lives, Laws, and Politics in Nineteenth-Century Montreal* (Vancouver: UBC Press, 2011), pp. 260–88.

[63] Cecilia Morgan, *Public Men and Virtuous Women: The Gendered Languages of Religion and Politics in Upper Canada, 1791–1850* (Toronto: University of Toronto Press, 1996), p. 198.

elections in Sydney.[64] In 1861, in South Australia the Municipal Corporations Act gave the local council vote to 'every person of full age' who either owned or rented any property, as long as they had not received public relief and had paid their rates.[65] In Victoria in 1863 the ambiguous wording of the Municipalities Amendment Bill was overtly discussed and amended, with the result that women could not become councillors or mayors but clearly were allowed to vote at municipal elections. Because the municipal rolls were used as the basis for parliamentary electoral rolls, some women then voted in the 1864 Victorian parliamentary elections. In 1865 the Victorian parliament acted to prevent women doing so again, by amending the electoral law to stipulate that only 'male persons' enrolled as ratepayers could have the parliamentary franchise.[66] Despite the ambiguities, debates, and back-filling, this meant that in the 1850s and 1860s some women in various colonies had the experience of voting, and some continued to enjoy the municipal franchise. In this area, women in the Australian colonies were a little ahead of their metropolitan counterparts. In Britain, women's right to vote at local government elections was established by parliament in a legislative amendment in 1869. In 1872, though, this right was limited to unmarried women ratepayers.[67]

There were other links, too, between responsible government and electoral reform in the mid-century Australian colonies, and the fact that some of the Australian colonies in the 1890s and then the nation in 1902 were among the first states in the world to enfranchise women. Marian Sawer has argued that the Australian colonies' early adoption of the secret ballot was a key factor. Prior to the secret ballot, election days in Australia, like elsewhere, were often violent events with much public drunkenness, raucous behaviour and brawls, and intimidation near the polling places. It was easy then to claim that voting was not advisable for a 'lady'. With the secret ballot, when voting places became safe and seemly, and election days became quieter affairs, it was much harder to argue that voting was a threat to a woman's safety or respectability.[68]

---

[64] F. A. Larcombe, *The Origin of Local Government in New South Wales* Volume 2 (Sydney: Sydney University Press, 1976), p. 152; J. Selkirk Provis and Keith A. Johnson, *Cadman's Cottage: The Life and Times of John Cadman in Colonial Sydney 1798–1848* (Sydney: J. S. Provis & K. A. Johnson, 1972), p. 120.

[65] *An act to consolidate and amend laws relating to the Corporation of the City of Adelaide and to enable towns and places within the province of South Australia to be incorporated under provisions thereof* 1861, Clauses 11, 14.

[66] See 'Debate on Municipalities Amendment Bill 1863', *Victorian Parliamentary Debates* Vol. 9; 'Debate on the Electoral Law Consolidation Bill 1865', *Victorian Parliamentary Debates* Vol. 11; and Audrey Oldfield, *Woman Suffrage in Australia: A Gift or a Struggle?* (Cambridge: Cambridge University Press, 1992), p. 132.

[67] Patricia Hollis, *Ladies Elect: Women in English Local Government 1865–1914* (Oxford: Clarendon Press, 1987), p. 7.

[68] Marian Sawer (ed.), *Elections: Full, Free & Fair* (Leichhardt, New South Wales: Federation Press, 2001), p. 12.

COLONIALISM AND WOMEN'S WORK

While settlers in the Australian colonies were aware that women's political rights were a matter of debate and controversy overseas as well as at home, at least some of those who read the newspapers and participated in civic life were also well aware that the mid-century women's movement demanded that women should have access to wider choices of employment. One person who drew public attention to this issue was, again, Cora Anna Weekes.

On 30 December 1858, Weekes delivered a public lecture at the Sydney School of Arts on the topic of 'Female Heroism in the Nineteenth Century'. The *Sydney Morning Herald* reported that the lecture had been attended by about sixty people and that it was 'principally an advocacy of Women's Rights'.[69] The warp and woof of Weekes's lecture came from the religiosity and biblical references that saturated dominant public discourse in the mid-nineteenth century. The main 'heroines' with whom she illustrated her talk were the American prison reformer Miss Dix, and the British nurse and health reformer Florence Nightingale whose leadership of military nurses during the Crimean War of 1854–56 had made her an imperial household word. The tenor of Weekes's lecture was overtly feminist, even as she denied claiming the suffrage for women. Her principal demand, she admonished her Australian audience, was that: 'It is the imperative duty of society to find, immediately, additional means of honest and respectable employment for females!' Alluding graphically and poetically to the ubiquitous and tragic lives of prostitutes, forced into such a terrible life by desperation, she argued that women were confined to too few occupations:

> How many situations in life are open to industrious young women? Are they employed in printing houses, in jewellers' shops, in studios, chemists' establishments, and other light occupations? No! They are only dressmakers, or school mistresses, or drapers' assistants, and no more!

She had devoted her own life, Weekes testified, 'to give equal facilities to women as are possessed by men towards earning a[n] honest livelihood'.[70]

Other issues of the *Spectator* continued the theme of employment for women. One demanded:

> Shall not Woman be permitted to work with brain as well as with fingers? Look around you, citizens of Sydney, at the hundreds of poor unfortunates who throng the streets and crowd the 'labour offices' in search of employment. Think of the large numbers of respectable and delicately nurtured females, thrown by some ruthless stroke upon the mercies of the world, and struggling in menial occupations.[71]

---

[69] *Sydney Morning Herald* 31 December 1858, p. 5.
[70] Elizabeth Webby (ed.), *Colonial Voices: Letters, Diaries, Journalism and Other Accounts of Nineteenth-Century Australia* (St Lucia, Queensland: University of Queensland Press, 1989), pp. 322–3, 329, 480.
[71] Quoted in Patricia Clarke, *Pen Portraits: Women writers and journalists in nineteenth century Australia* (Sydney: Pandora, 1988), pp. 71–2.

The paper continued to publish pieces on women's rights, including some from overseas. On 27 November 1858 it reprinted an essay by the Rev. John L. Blake of Boston on 'The Rights of Women'.[72] The previous issue of October 1858 had informed its Australian readers about the prize being offered by the Lyons Imperial Academy of Science for the best essay on the subject of how to raise women's wages to the same level as those of men, and how to open up new careers for women.[73]

In her doctoral research Catherine Bishop has unsettled previous assumptions about women's supposedly minor participation in the economy in Sydney (and Wellington, New Zealand) from the 1830s to the 1860s. While historians have long known that colonial women in this period were not all convicts, domestic servants, or housewives, Bishop has extensively cross-checked shipping lists, births, deaths, and marriages indexes, trade directories, rates registers, newspaper advertisements, banking, insolvency, and other records to show that women's engagement in commerce was considerably more extensive than we had realized. From this painstaking research, Bishop has discovered that:

> There were milliners, dressmakers and straw bonnet-makers, grocers, general dealers and tobacconists, schoolteachers, music professors and dancing mistresses, publicans, boarding house keepers, and restaurateurs, laundresses, actresses and brothel-keepers, along with the occasional plumber, undertaker, printer and taxidermist. Some women arrived with experience running a business in England, others reinvented themselves upon immigration, on marriage or after being widowed. They were variously spinsters, wives, mothers and widows. They included ex-convicts, immigrants and colonial-born women and they were running businesses alone, with female partners or with husbands and/or adult children.[74]

Even the legal system of coverture, under which married women had no legal identity separate from that of their husbands and could not own property, did not stop women engaging in small business, though it did mean they were vulnerable to husbands who were insolvent for any reason, and could only collect debts through their husbands.[75] Bishop contends that, contrary to the upper-middle-class ideology of separate spheres, these women 'were from the "shopkeeper" class and their labour was both expected and valued. They were respected for their enterprise'. In colonial towns across the empire and the United States, in places not yet industrialized, 'businesswomen remained present, visible and valued'.[76]

Other scholars have similarly questioned the power of the 'cult of domesticity', or the notion of 'the angel in the house', in shaping the actuality of women's lives, in places ranging from the Australian bush to provincial United States, and parts of Europe. Scholarly consensus now seems to be that the ideology of separate spheres was a benchmark of respectability, which to some extent did influence women's choices, but that it was only one factor among many shaping women's decisions. Women were aware of the ideology but negotiated their way around and through it,

---

[72] Rev. John L. Blake, 'The Rights of Women', *Spectator* 27 November 1858, pp. 141–3.
[73] 'Work for Women', *Spectator* 30 October 1858, p. 111.
[74] Bishop, 'Commerce Was a Woman', p. 7.   [75] Bishop, 'Commerce Was a Woman', Ch. 4.
[76] Bishop, 'Commerce Was a Woman', p. 315.

prepared to reject or subvert it as they needed. Economic necessity, location, family circumstances and attitudes, marital and class status, were also factors in women's decisions about their participation in small business, farming, or other ways of earning a livelihood.[77]

Back in 1983, pioneer of women's history Patricia Grimshaw argued that women on the Australian frontier needed to work to contribute to family income.[78] And there are plentiful documentary sources that bear out her point. Sarah Musgrave's recollections of her life on pastoral stations in mid-nineteenth-century New South Wales provide clues that women who considered themselves respectable or genteel performed the same labour as men, and that, inversely, at least some men performed domestic labour. News of the 1849 Californian gold-rush reached Burrangong when Musgrave was thirteen years old. With the sudden exodus of would-be gold seekers, labour quickly became short; Musgrave recalled how, at Burrangong, she took the place of a man as shepherd. Sometime later, when a drought threatened the sheep on the station, Musgrave admits in her memoirs that: 'I and Jane Robertson (a girlfriend) worked at the station, drawing water from out of the homestead well and running it into troughs for the sheep. Commencing at daylight, we would work until ten o'clock at night and by this diligent labour we kept the sheep supplied for twelve months. Then the drought broke'.[79] But the transgression of gendered labour expectations could work both ways. Musgrave reports that when she married, it was not possible to find a domestic servant, and she herself had never learnt to cook. Fortunately, her new husband was able to teach her how to cope with domestic duties: 'He was a good cook and housekeeper, and I an apt pupil. So it was not long before I could carry on without his guidance'.[80]

Spence's writing is far from being the only evidence that some women in South Australia questioned contemporary gender prescriptions. In December 1851 recent Adelaide settler Emily Clark mentioned in her diary 'a certain Mrs. Brown who keeps a book-seller's shop', and a few months later commented on the Misses Catchside who

> [H]ave been drying raisins, and some excellent currants. They are fearless and independent women, and have already killed several snakes. They manage the garden entirely also the horses cows and poultry. One day they wanted firewood, so they harnessed the horse and collected fallen branches in the paddock. They mow lucerne for the animals and when their brother was harvesting his crop, they each reaped for five hours every day.[81]

---

[77] For valuable insights into this topic, I am indebted to the excellent work of Margriet Fokken during her research internship with me at the Australian National University in 2010, which counted towards her Research Masters degree in Modern History and International Relations at the University of Gröningen, the Netherlands.

[78] Patricia Grimshaw, 'The Australian Family: An Historical Interpretation', in A. Burns, G. Bottomley, and P. Jools (eds), *The Family in the Modern World* (Sydney: George Allen & Unwin, 1983), p. 38.

[79] Sarah Musgrave, *The Wayback* (1926; republished West Wyalong, NSW: Bland District Historical Society, 4th ed., 1979), pp. 25 and 39.

[80] Musgrave, *The Wayback*, p. 46.

[81] South Australia State Library, PRG389/9 Recollections of Miss Caroline Emily Clark completed by her sister Mrs Joseph Crompton. Extracts from the diary of Miss Caroline Emily Clark, pp. 123, 125–6.

While Clark's focus here is on women's skills and economic contributions, her telling phrase 'fearless and independent women' alerts us to her interest in gender constrictions.

These examples from New South Wales and South Australia reflect, to some extent, the particular exigencies caused by the Californian and Australian gold rushes from 1849 through the 1850s and even into the 1860s. Yet other sources show us that, well prior to the gold rush, settler women were prepared to undertake unfamiliar and demanding forms of labour when it was required. Following the unofficial arrival of settlers from Van Diemen's Land at Port Phillip Bay in 1835, and the spurious 'treaty' struck with the Kulin people, the settlement of what in 1850 became the colony of Victoria occurred in a furious episode of land grabbing. Settlers poured into the region, scouted out fertile tracts, and installed themselves, while dislodging the Indigenous people by force. In 1845 Katherine Kirkland published a memoir of her experiences inland from the Port Phillip region in the years from 1839. As the editors introduced her memoir:

> The wilds of Australia present at this time some strange scenes. Persons of all characters, and every variety of previous habits, are there planting themselves as sheep-farmers, each family being generally placed in some rude hut in the centre of its 'run', or sheep-walk, rarely at less than five miles' distance from another. Thus transferred all at once from parlour life in [Britain], perhaps from some learned or elegant profession, into a primeval solitude, and left to their own resources, a change of life and occupation is induced such as we have no experience of in civilised climes.[82]

While evidently unused to performing domestic labour herself, and critical of the shortcomings she observed in colonial servants, Kirkland nevertheless adapted quickly enough. Even on the trip inland to the family's run, she made 'a good supply of ketchup' from mushrooms she gathered, helped an established settler to make 'some fritters of flour and water' that she declared 'the best things I had ever ate', and as soon as she settled into her own hut devised various dishes and taught her servant to cook them. When the servant began to rebel (and could do so because there were no others), Kirkland had to do the washing, and took over the management of the dairy cows.[83]

Kirkland learnt to enjoy life in the bush, priding herself on the management of the dairy, raising chickens, and overseeing the establishment of a vegetable garden and berry bushes. She admitted that she 'really liked managing the dairy', even copying the local Aboriginal women by making a basket in which to hang her baby close to her while she was working in the dairy.[84] Her cooking skills improved such that she records with pride the dishes she provided at their house for a neighbour-hood New Year's Feast, on 1 January 1841, including kangaroo soup and parrot pie as well as the traditional roast turkey.[85] Her practical skills developed to such a level that she coped with several accidents, including a spring-cart overturning in a creek;

---

[82] Katherine Kirkland, 'Life in the Bush: By a Lady', *Chambers's Miscellany of Useful and Entertaining Tracts* Vol. 1, No. 8 (Edinburgh: William and Robert Chambers, 1845), p. 1.
[83] Kirkland, 'Life in the Bush', pp. 7, 9, 11, 15.
[84] Kirkland, 'Life in the Bush', p. 16.　　　[85] Kirkland, 'Life in the Bush', p. 23.

having to make a splint for an injured leg from a tea-box and part of her own dress; and even helping to save the farm they moved to nearer Melbourne when it was surrounded by a bushfire in February 1841. Before compelled to return to Britain by financial adversity and ill health, she briefly opened a boarding school in Melbourne.[86] Kirkland's narrative frankly admits the challenges of bush life, while revealing her pleasure in its novelties and her own accomplishments.

As well as women's preparedness to be adaptive and resilient in strange colonial circumstances, some women workers arrived through organized schemes, especially schemes to bring out young women as servants. An episode that occurred in 1855–56 in Willunga, a small town in South Australia, allows us to see a little of the lives of Irish servant girls in the bush. Servant girls had been part of the fabric of colonial Australia from its inception, initially, of course, as convicts serving out their sentences. Kirkland noted in her memoir of the Port Phillip settlement that, whereas servants previously had been in very short supply and could command high wages, in early 1841 several ships arrived with immigrants, and young women could be seen walking the streets inquiring if anyone needed a servant. She and her husband allowed several young women who had just arrived to live in their detached kitchen in their Melbourne house, until they could find places elsewhere.[87] We know from Jan Gothard's book *Blue China* that between 1860 and 1900 nearly 90,000 'single British women accepted an assisted passage to one of the six Australian colonies', helped by colonial governments keen to bring out domestic servants.[88] As Gothard points out, these numbers were multiple times larger than the women sent out earlier as convicts.[89] Such schemes to bring labouring women to the colonies actually started in the 1850s in South Australia, Victoria, Tasmania, and Western Australia. From Marie Steiner's research we know detailed stories of some of the poor British (mostly Irish) young women sent to South Australia in 1855; how they were managed by a Female Immigration Board, and accommodated in special servants' depots set up in country towns.

The first such depot was established in Willunga, south of Adelaide, and now the heart of the McLaren Vale food and wine area. Willunga's attractions had been noticed early and it was occupied by Europeans from 1839. By July 1855 when the first servants' depot was set up, there were nearly 2,500 settlers in the district. Conditions were makeshift for these potential servants; the first party of thirty-nine female immigrants had to take their cooking utensils and bedding with them from Adelaide; their accommodation included bunks in the local court house, and most of the girls had no shoes or boots.[90] The governor had laid down rules that 'no girl should be readmitted [to the depot] who had refused employment with

[86] Kirkland, 'Life in the Bush', p. 32.   [87] Kirkland, 'Life in the Bush', pp. 31–2.
[88] Jan Gothard, *Blue China: Single Female Migration to Colonial Australia* (Carlton, Victoria: Melbourne University Press, 2001), p. 2.
[89] Gothard, *Blue China*, p. 9.
[90] Marie Steiner, *Servants Depots in Colonial South Australia* (Kent Town, South Australia: Wakefield Press, 2009), pp. 33–5.

wages of 2/6 per week and meals for three months'.[91] By early August, seventeen of the thirty-nine had taken positions.

But the Willunga servants' depot was short-lived. When it was closed down in January 1856, sixty-one young women had been sent there from Adelaide, though there is no record of how many had found employment, or what happened to those who did not. One reason for the short lifespan of the Willunga servants' depot was a dispute that broke out between the young women and the chair of the Willunga District Council, Mr Smith Kell, in October 1855, a dispute exacerbated by religious tensions between the mostly Catholic girls and Kell's assertive Protestantism. The ruckus on 10 October was serious enough that Kell later described it as 'a great disturbance at the depot, so much that I was obliged to call in the police'.[92] Others reported that the majority of the young women at the depot were 'bent on a row', and that Mr Kell had been 'repulsed by the females from the place'.[93] Kell had attempted to forbid the young women still at the depot from visiting their friends at their new places of employment. It was this denial of their freedom that had incensed them. As the matron responsible for the women pointed out, their desperation for jobs and for contact with each other was such that they were willing to walk barefoot for miles on country tracks.

From this small set of historical records detailing this dispute, which made it as far as the governor's desk in Adelaide, we can glimpse this brief episode in the lives of poor Irish young women, who had sailed halfway around the world, only to be sent out to a bush village in the hopes of being employed by local settlers as servants—in conditions that were likely often rough. These brief records allow us to conjure a little the uncertainties and travails of the poor young labouring women who were the targets of such colonial labour schemes.

Finally, we turn to a memoir that relates the life of a girl and young woman in much more privileged and mostly urban circumstances, yet whose life, too, was shaped by the exigencies of colonialism and whose story also allows us a few insights into genteel women's paid employment and its determinants. Kathleen Lambert migrated to New South Wales with her family as a teenage girl in 1843. From the memoir she published in 1890, we only learn a little about her parents. Her father had a business partner who met them on arrival in Sydney. Her mother had never wanted to come, strongly disliked the colony, and died five years after their arrival. Some indications suggest that the family was upper middle-class. Their first house on Elizabeth Street had six rooms plus the servants' quarters, and Lambert speaks of her father's letters of introduction to cultured gentlemen and their families. Her parents, according to Lambert, were themselves well-educated and highly literate, and the family read together: 'We had Byron, Scott, Wordsworth, Campbell, Rogers, Shelley, Pope, and Moore as our guests of an evening: Bulwer, Thackeray, and Dickens, the latter personally known to my father'.[94] Lambert and her sisters

---

[91] Steiner, *Servants Depots*, p. 36.   [92] Steiner, *Servants Depots*, p. 37.
[93] Steiner, *Servants Depots*, pp. 37 and 43.
[94] Kathleen Lambert ('Lyth'), *The Golden South: Memories of Australian Home Life, 1843–1888* (London: Ward and Downey, 1890), p. 13.

began their education in Sydney under the tutelage of 'a French lady' who taught them French, music, and singing. The following year they were sent to a boarding school in Liverpool, forty miles from Sydney, which she found attractive and comfortable, being run by 'a highly educated woman and a true Christian'.[95]

While this all speaks of affluence and privilege, it was not to last. After a year of boarding school, Kathleen became a governess. She seems intent to render as pleasant this first experience as a governess, perhaps masking what may have been her father's declining income. She calls her employers 'English gentle folks'. Mr Johnson was a solicitor, and she claims that while living in their house in Newtown she 'had access to an excellent library, and also mixed in the best society as well as with the best musical talent of the colony'.[96] After three years in this position, which she describes as 'an ideal one', when her mother died she returned home to manage the house for her father—by now a more modest cottage in Glebe.

In the early 1850s, Kathleen and her sisters decamped from Sydney to their brother's station household in the bush at Montefiores near Wellington in central New South Wales. Soon after arrival, Lambert announces, her 'troubles began' when her brother's cook died. With servants scarce, expensive and unreliable, she took on the household management herself, having to learn skills such as bread-making. They had to fetch water from a well, a task assigned to her fourteen-year-old sister. After a while, the household acquired Chinese and Aboriginal servants and workers, whom Kathleen managed. She describes in detail one night when the Aboriginal men got drunk, and one beat his wife, who fled into their household for shelter; and she describes, too, the Chinese cook's opium smoking and its effects.[97] Whether despite these and other challenges or perhaps because of them, Lambert claimed to enjoy her three years managing a bush homestead and the curiosities, informalities, and sociability of bush life. When her brother married, he no longer needed her services and she returned to governessing in Sydney, again describing her employment as comfortable, pleasant, and genteel. Lambert's memoir shows that even middle-class mid-century colonial women could move between unpaid familial household management, and respectable paid work, as circumstances demanded, and in Lambert's case, at least, see both forms of employment as consonant with self-respect and social contribution.

CONCLUSION

In the Australian colonies, responsible government was brought in hand-in-hand with male suffrage. This was significantly ahead of many places in the world, including Britain—where the 1867 Reform Act expanded the categories of men who could vote, as did the 1884 Reform Act, but it was not until 1918 that full male suffrage was introduced there. Settler men became political subjects, while settler women were excluded from those rights. Years later, one woman remembered

[95] Lambert, *The Golden South*, p. 18.   [96] Lambert, *The Golden South*, p. 35.
[97] Lambert, *The Golden South*, Ch. 7.

how at the early elections under the new system: 'All masculines were agog with a natural sense of importance' on election day.[98] Yet there was debate over politics and gender issues from the 1850s. In July 1858, for example, 'Justitia' wrote to the editor of the *Sydney Morning Herald* on the subject of women and politics, protesting women's political, civil, and educational disabilities, the system in which women 'have their ambition mortified from their youth upward', and calling for 'the removal of those disqualifications which appear so glaringly unjust, and so injurious in their results'.[99]

The debate over women's political rights and roles that was part of colonial public life in the 1850s was a direct product of the campaigns for and winning of responsible government. As settler men were enfranchised and gained political authority, the question of women's simultaneous exclusion from political rights became a contentious issue. It was one component of the transnational debate over women's political and legal rights that had erupted in places from London to Seneca Falls, New York, in the 1840s, but it was at once inflected with meanings specific to Australian colonial circumstances. Gender ideology in the Australian colonies in the mid-century decades was shaped by influences that included the social project to reform convicts, and exigencies of the bush that meant settler women and girls encountered challenges unlike those in Europe. Women's enforced pragmatism and practical skills acquired in the bush and in gold-rush conditions, the varied hardships, and the physical freedoms of colonial girlhood, added particular colonial dimensions to ideas of women's capabilities. Kathleen Lambert, for example, recalled one summer of her early years in Sydney, when she and her sisters bathed in the harbour at the Domain every day, calling it 'delightful' and noting that most Australian women could swim—in the 1840s![100] Such physical activity fed into what later became the idealized notion of 'the Australian girl'.

By the 1880s in South Australia a women's movement had emerged with Catherine Helen Spence as one of its leaders. South Australia enfranchised women in 1894, the first Australian colony to do so, due to the colony's women's movement and its progressive liberal government led by Charles Cameron Kingston (1850–1908). Western Australia followed in 1899 and from 1902 white women could vote in Commonwealth elections. Indeed, in 1902 Australia became the first nation where women could vote and stand for election to the new federal parliament. But this was a racially exclusive franchise. Patricia Grimshaw has shown the ways in which, in settler colonies around the Pacific Ocean, racial politics variously influenced the outcomes of late-nineteenth-century debates over women's suffrage. In New Zealand, Maori women were enfranchised along with white women in 1893 because settler politicians saw this as the best political expedient, given Maori men's earlier enfranchisement. In contrast, even in the southeastern

---

[98] *The Push from the Bush: A Bulletin of Social History* No. 25, Oct. 1987, p. 53, quoting Joy Damousi, 'Socialist Women in Australia: 1890–1920', *Melbourne Historical Journal* Vol. 17 (1985): 66.
[99] 'Justitia', letter to the editor on 'Women and Politics', *Sydney Morning Herald* 7 July 1858, p. 8.
[100] Lambert, *The Golden South*, pp. 31–2.

Australian colonies where Aborigines had some limited voting rights, Aboriginal men and women were excluded from the new national franchise when white women were particularly included.[101] Aboriginal exclusion from the vote was just one aspect of their exclusion from national citizenship. While white women faced significant continuing disparities in employment and wages, they had become political citizens. What is significant here is that the pervasive gender debate of the 1850s, and the fact that at least some women resisted their newly articulated political exclusion, formed an important early stage in this protracted struggle.

[101] Patricia Grimshaw, 'Settler Anxieties, Indigenous Peoples, and Women's Suffrage in the Colonies of Australia, New Zealand, and Hawai'i, 1888–1902', in Karen Offen (ed.), *Globalizing Feminisms 1789–1945* (London: Routledge, 2010), pp. 111–21.

6

Frontier Violence and Political Manhood

In the very decades when Australian men struggled for and won representative government and then responsible government in most colonies, the frontier shifted rapidly as settlers violently forced Aboriginal people from their lands. Increasingly, sheep and cattle grazed on lands grabbed by pastoralists. Definitions of manhood (meaning both male adulthood and manly qualities) on the frontier in settler societies were influenced by those shaped in colonial urban centres and the imperial metropole, including mid-nineteenth-century notions of manly independence, self-control, and reason. But the exigencies of settler colonialism and the widespread use of frontier violence put alternative, discrepant definitions in tension with these notions—definitions that emphasized physical strength and endurance, horse-riding, shooting, and hunting skills,[1] and, in a quieter register, included the use of extreme violence towards Aboriginal people.

Yet settler manhood—its nature, rights, and responsibilities—was a matter of contest and debate. Elizabeth Elbourne has shown that the morality of British settlers in the Australian colonies (and in South Africa, Canada, and New Zealand) was a major concern of the 1835–36 imperial parliamentary select committee that investigated the treatment of indigenous peoples and sought an evangelical revolution. Elbourne shows the ambiguity and circularity of argument over indigenous and settler rights, while pointing to the centrality of virtue and vice as organizing principles that served to 'downplay the issue of the morality of land sales'.[2] The committee's two-volume report represented settler colonies as 'sites of peculiarly unchecked white male sin; indeed, of an almost exaggerated hyper-masculinity, as men indulged in unrestrained appetites to have sex, to exploit resources, and to kill'.[3] Just as up to 1833 slaveholders in other parts of the empire had defended themselves against abolitionist criticism, settlers felt the need to assert their own virtue against characterizations of them as vicious. From the 1830s various settlers and systematic colonizers constructed a discourse of the virtuous free settler. In New South Wales, for example, in the furore over the execution of seven white men for the 1838 Myall Creek massacre of Aborigines, the *Sydney Herald*

---

[1] Elizabeth Vibert, 'Real men hunt buffalo: Masculinity, race and class in British fur traders' narratives', in Catherine Hall (ed.), *Cultures of Empire: Colonizers in Britain and the Empire in the Nineteenth and Twentieth Centuries: A Reader* (New York: Routledge, 2000).

[2] Elizabeth Elbourne, 'The Sins of the Settler: The 1835–36 Select Committee on Aborigines and Debates over Virtue and Conquest in the Early-Nineteenth Century British White Settler Empire', *Journal of Colonialism and Colonial History* 4: 3 (2003): 68.

[3] Elbourne, 'The Sins of the Settler', 28.

particularly framed its defence of the murderers by constructing an image of moral but embattled settlers on the colonial frontier: ' "respectable", "honest", "men of the world" whose engagement in the violence of Aboriginal dispossession was an unfortunate but vital element in their role as protectors of their families, servants and property and as cultivators of the barren landscape'.[4]

Australia's mythology of the stoic, egalitarian bushman and the ethos of mateship—so evocatively articulated and historicized in 1958 by historian Russel Ward as *The Australian Legend*—has served to obscure the violence, especially the interracial violence, of frontier history. Ward does occasionally refer to violence, and even links it to gender. For example, he notes one source saying: 'The Australian boy . . . can fight like an Irishman', and elsewhere he cites a mid-century description of urban toughs making a standard practice of knocking down the hats of their social betters as they entered the theatre. He comments on these by suggesting that such behaviour should be seen as the 'inevitable concomitant' of qualities such as 'readiness' and 'manly independence'.[5] While Ward saw such occasional violence in positive terms as evidence of the manliness of his 'nomad tribe' and urban toughs, his overarching mythologizing of the bushmen is blind to the pervasive violence towards indigenous people that characterized the frontier in the mid-century decades he studied. *The Australian Legend* is densely packed with nuggets of historical detail and, in fact, Ward mentions telling instances of such violence, but he does not integrate that evidence into his larger romantic picture. Rather, as Henry Reynolds has eloquently argued, Ward's mythological vision of the bush erases Aboriginal people as a presence and the pervasive frontier violence perpetrated against them. Reynolds contends sharply: 'Members of the nomad tribe were in the forefront of the border wars. They manned the punitive expeditions, large and small. Many of them shot Aborigines and in turn they lived in fear of a spear in the back and knew of fellow workers who had been bludgeoned to death'.[6] Reynolds admits that early in his career he was influenced by Ward, and only slowly was forced by his own research to see how blind and romanticized a rendering of the bushmen Ward had produced. He asks pointedly: 'How did a fine, creative historian like Russel Ward not see, not notice the pistols nonchalantly thrust through the belt of his noble frontiersman, the carbine slung across the shoulder, the abundant ammunition, the bloodstained hands? . . . One answer is that an unexpurgated account of settlement robs the bushman of his glamour'.[7]

In contrast to Ward, John Ferry's evocation of gender relations and ideology in *Colonial Armidale* is less blind. Ferry dealt directly and forthrightly with frontier violence in the New England region of northern New South Wales, providing clear

---

[4] Rebecca Wood, 'Frontier Violence and the Bush Legend: The *Sydney Herald*'s Response to the Myall Creek Massacre Trials and the Creation of Colonial Identity', *History Australia* Vol. 6, No. 3 (2009): 67.10.

[5] Russel Ward, *The Australian Legend* (South Melbourne: Oxford University Press, 1958), pp. 65–6.

[6] Henry Reynolds, *Why Weren't We Told? A personal search for the truth about our history* (Camberwell, Victoria: Penguin Books, 1999), p. 130.

[7] Reynolds, *Why Weren't We Told?*, pp. 131–2.

evidence of the violence involved in dispossessing the indigenous people there.[8] Ferry discusses the construction and significance of masculinities in nineteenth-century Armidale, importantly showing that they were linked to racial violence: 'The frontier bushwhack was an ejaculation of male violence. It was an expression of extreme masculinism'.[9] The men Ferry discusses were of the squatter and official class—the class above the 'nomad tribe' of bushmen whom Ward evokes so fondly and romantically in *The Australian Legend*. Yet the violence is there in Ward, too, but buried rather than highlighted. Ward inserts evidence in passing which shows that he was aware of what he calls at one point 'racist passions, always felt for Aborigines'.[10] He notes, too, the brutal violence white men sometimes wielded against Aboriginal women. He quotes an 1840 source on interracial violence and venereal disease thus: 'I am told it is no uncommon thing for these rascals to sleep all night with a Lubra . . . and if she poxes him or in any way offends him perhaps Shoot her before 12 next day. I am certain it is a thing which has frequently occurred'.[11] John Ferry's foregrounding of the violence perpetrated by at least some of Armidale's founding fathers, such as the Everett brothers and Commissioner George Macdonald, points to connections between frontier violence and political authority.

This chapter suggests that there is another unacknowledged Australian legend that needs to be called into question—the legend that self-government in the Australian colonies was won by a progressive reform movement that operated in a purely political realm divorced from the messy realities of the frontier. It challenges the latter legend by considering various forms of violence that shaped the reaches of settler society in the early to mid-nineteenth century, and teasing out ways in which these forms of violence were connected to constructions of manhood, not least ideas of settler manhood that would feed into claims for political authority.

BUSHRANGERS

Among the graves in the cemetery at Beechworth, the historic gold-mining town in northern Victoria, is that of John Watt who was 'shot by bushrangers' in 1872. Watt had arrived in Australia in 1858 at the age of twenty-five, worked on the surveying of the boundary line dividing Victoria from New South Wales, moved to the Beechworth area, and become the publican of the Woogaree Hotel. On the night of 15 October 1872 two armed bushrangers held up first the post office and then the hotel. Watt and another man were shot, Watt receiving a severe shotgun wound of which he died ten days later.[12] While Watt's murder occurred in the

---

[8] John Ferry, *Colonial Armidale* (St Lucia, Queensland: University of Queensland Press, 1999), Ch. 2.

[9] Ferry, *Colonial Armidale*, p. 130.   [10] Ward, *The Australian Legend*, p. 129.

[11] Ward, *The Australian Legend*, p. 98.

[12] Ian Hyndman, 'Tour of Historic Graves at Beechworth Cemetery' (Beechworth Cemetery Trust), no. 6.

Fig. 6.1 William Strutt (1825–1915), 'Bushrangers, Victoria, Australia, 1852' (1887). Oil on canvas, 73.0 cm × 154.0 cm.

The University of Melbourne Art Collection. Gift of the Russell and Mab Grimwade Bequest 1973. 1973.0038.000.000.

region that would become associated with the infamous Ned Kelly, bushrangers were a scourge of the Australian bush across the continent from the beginning of the nineteenth century. Their pervasive presence and the fear they engendered helped to shape the culture of violence that lurked beyond the major towns. (See Fig. 6.1.)

As settlers pushed out the boundaries of the colonized areas, often in defiance of official limits, frontier contact zones proliferated in the expanses of country beyond full control of authorities and the law. The Australian bush was so vast, especially on the mainland, that there were always regions and places for convicts to escape to and in which Aborigines could find refuge and shelter. In the decades of rapid settler expansion from the 1820s, rural and frontier areas became characterized by property theft and violence, a mix of bushranging and interracial conflict over land. At some times and in some places, the two occurred in tandem. Bushrangers were a mixed group. 'Black Caesar', known as Australia's first bushranger, was of African descent, a convict who had been sentenced in England for stealing money and who arrived with the First Fleet. In 1795 Caesar fled into the bush near Sydney where he survived for months before being shot in February 1796.[13] In the few cases of Aboriginal 'bushrangers', violent resistance to white settlers merged with behaviour regarded as outlaw or criminal.

Perhaps the most famous Aboriginal bushranger was Mosquito or Musquito (1780–1825), an Aboriginal resistance leader and tracker. Musquito was probably an Eora man, born on the north shore of Port Jackson. In 1805 he was involved in raids on settlers on the Hawkesbury and Georges rivers, raids which were not unlike

---

[13] Cassandra Pybus, *Black Founders: The Unknown Story of Australia's first black settlers* (Sydney: University of New South Wales Press, 2006), pp. 3, 134–5.

bushranging, but were acts of resistance to white invasion. He was arrested and sent to Norfolk Island for eight years. In 1813 he was sent from Norfolk Island to Launceston in Van Diemen's Land, where he became a blacktracker—work that involved, ironically enough, tracking white bushrangers. Musquito again turned to bushranging, saying that the ostracism he received from white convicts had driven him to it. In 1823 and 1824 he and his gang killed several stock-keepers on the island's east coast. Musquito was wounded, captured, and charged with aiding and abetting murder; he was hanged on 25 February 1825. Musquito's story shows how blurred the boundaries could be between bushranging and violent Aboriginal resistance to the settlers.[14]

Statistics of convictions for bushranging in the Australian colonies—including those charged with highway robbery, robbery under arms, horse-stealing, and escaped convicts who committed robbery while on the run—begin in the late eighteenth century, and show it rising after the turn of the nineteenth century. In Van Diemen's Land the decade with the most convictions was the 1820s (also the time of the Black War waged against Aborigines), while in Victoria the 1850s (the gold rush decade) was the high point. Bushranging in New South Wales was at its worst in the 1860s, with the 1830s being the second worst decade, followed by the 1840s.[15]

Convicts who escaped and managed to evade pursuit and capture often turned to bushranging to survive; such escapees constituted a major source of bushrangers in the early to mid-century. In later decades, they were augmented by those with more criminal motives. According to settler Thomas Murray-Prior, who arrived in New South Wales in 1839:

> It was only to be expected that among such a multitude of lawless characters, some desperate & daring men would be found ready to break from authority & constitute themselves the leaders of a reckless gang. Such a convict—goaded by the desire for revenge for tyranny either real or imaginary—would escape & take to the bush— would form a gang of followers, providing himself & them with arms & ammunition by bailing up & robbing stores & travellers.[16]

There is some evidence that bushrangers included convicts who escaped from the harsh conditions of work gangs on inland public projects such as the Great North Road connecting Sydney to northern New South Wales. The use of flogging and the punitive ball-and-chain meant that some convicts ran away from work gangs to escape the harsh conditions, even though it meant surviving hand to mouth in the bush. Some bushrangers were assigned convicts who ran away from their pastoralist masters. In 1830 the New South Wales Legislative Council passed a Bushranging

---

[14] Naomi Parry, 'Musquito (1780–1825)', *Australian Dictionary of Biography*, National Centre of Biography, Australian National University, http://adb.anu.edu.au/biography/musquito-13124/text23749, accessed 7 November 2012.

[15] Stephan Williams (compiler), *The Book of a Thousand Bushrangers* (Woden, ACT: Popinjay Publications, 1993).

[16] Thomas Murray-Prior memoir, Rosa Praed Papers, OM64-1/3/1/1, State Library of Queensland, p. 20.

Act (in force until 1842), that made it legal for *anyone* to arrest someone found on the road with firearms who looked like they might commit a robbery. There was contemporary debate about this act, because it reversed the usual presumption of innocence, but the widespread impact of bushranging lent it support. Fear of bushranging became something of a colonial panic. The Bushranging Act also gave wide powers to police and magistrates.

Bushrangers were such a part of frontier life in the mid-nineteenth century that stories circulated widely among settlers. Kathleen Lambert, who ran her brother's household for a time in the 1850s on his station at Montefiores near Wellington in central New South Wales, recalled bushrangers as part of life in the region, not least because the gold escorts would pass through on their way from the nearby goldfields. Bushrangers were attracted to gold, but would target station homesteads sufficiently commonly that settlers learned strategies to cope with them. Lambert recounts the story of one settler wife on a station near Bathurst who 'rode into town to obtain the money the bushrangers insisted on receiving before they would release her husband and others'. In another instance, the women of the property were forced by bushrangers to cook a meal for them, then play the piano and dance with them. Lambert insists that 'Australian women in many instances displayed great courage and coolness when brought in contact with bushrangers'.[17] While the great majority of bushrangers were men, it was not exclusively so: for example, Bridget Fairless was hanged for highway robbery.[18]

Bushranging was one of the interconnected forms of violence that riddled the settler frontier. As David Roberts has evocatively described the early New England frontier in the 1830s, workers blurred with outlaws, shepherds could become bushrangers, allegiances could shift swiftly, and pastoralists often could not trust their assigned convicts or even other workers enough to be able to rely on them in the event of an attack.[19] Fear and violence were commonly intertwined.

MOUNTED POLICE, BORDER POLICE, AND THE NATIVE POLICE

Early nineteenth-century New South Wales posed significant challenges to its emerging policing and justice system. As Bruce Kercher found in his examination of the motley roll of cases considered by the New South Wales Supreme Court between 1824 and 1836, judges heard stories 'about showers of Aboriginal spears, brutal attacks on Aborigines, escaped convicts, piracy on the high seas, gun battles with bushrangers, [and] convict mutinies'.[20] By the 1820s official and settler

[17] Kathleen Lambert ['Lyth'], *The Golden South: Memories of Australian Home Life from 1843 to 1888* (London: Ward and Downey, 1890), p. 68.

[18] Bruce Kercher, *Outsiders: Tales from the Supreme Court of NSW, 1824–1836* (Melbourne: Australian Scholarly Publishing, 2006), p. 5.

[19] David Andrew Roberts, 'The Frontier', in Alan Atkinson et al. (eds), *High Lean Country: Land, people and memory in New England* (Sydney: Allen and Unwin, 2006), p. 102.

[20] Kercher, *Outsiders*, p. 1.

Fig. 6.2 Godfrey Charles Mundy, 'Encounter. Mounted police and blacks', 1840. Drawing: pen and ink.

National Library of Australia, vn6149301.

anxieties about maintaining control of convicts were exacerbated by the rise of bushranging and Aboriginal violent resistance. In 1825 the Mounted Police was formed as a special force to bring order to frontier areas. Members of the force were recruited from British Army regiments stationed in the colony: they wore military-style uniforms, kept their military status, and were posted in scattered places. The Mounted Police was hailed as successful and was in demand from magistrates in the outer districts, despite ambiguous lines of command between the two. As bushranging escalated, the Mounted Police numbers were increased, from forty-six in New South Wales in 1826, to 104 in 1830, and at its peak in 1839 a strength of 144.[21]

There is evidence that the Mounted Police was unrestrained in its attacks on Aborigines (see Fig. 6.2). Nevertheless, in 1839 concern about the continuing violence between settlers and Aborigines led to the formation of a new and separate force for the more remote areas outside the limits of official settlement: the Border Police would work under the authority of the Crown Lands Commissioners (who will be discussed in the next section). According to legal historian David Neal, the

---

[21] David Neal, *The Rule of Law in a Penal Colony: Law and Power in Early New South Wales* (Cambridge: Cambridge University Press, 1991), pp. 150–1.

calibre of those who joined the Border Police and their conditions of service were the worst of the colonial police forces. Border Police constables included convicts on no pay (though full rations), they had no uniforms, and had to build their own huts; their numbers reached a high of eighty-six in 1845 before they were closed down in 1847.[22] The irony of convicts being employed as police was not singular to the Border Police; even Sydney Police included convicts, especially in its early years.

From the 1840s, colonial police forces were augmented by Aboriginal troopers, recruited because settlers had been forced to recognize that Aborigines' skills in tracking in the bush made them far superior to white forces for work beyond the towns. While 'black trackers' would be used across the continent well into the twentieth century, Aboriginal police forces began to be employed in the Port Phillip district in 1842, and the northern areas of New South Wales in 1848. The northern force, which would be passed on to the Queensland government at separation, rose to a high of ninety-six in 1852, then a second large peak of 206 in 1878. The Native Police Force had white officers (a model well established in other parts of the British Empire, such as the East India Company army) but troopers were mounted, wore full and recognizable uniforms, and were well equipped with guns and ammunition. An organizing principle of the Native Police, especially in the north, was that Aboriginal men were deployed in areas not their own country, so that the people they policed were not from their own ethnic or kinship groups, did not speak their language, and were regarded as foreigners. Each troop was deliberately composed of different language groups to prevent group solidarity that might undermine the white officer's authority.

Another principle, as with Aboriginal workers in all areas of employment, was that they were paid significantly less than white police. Native Police troops were widely regarded as highly effective agents of colonial rule in frontier areas, partly because of their tracking skills, and partly because they were allowed to operate with little public scrutiny. Settlers, for the most part, were glad that they were so effective in dampening Aboriginal resistance and did not choose to question their methods.[23]

Thomas Murray-Prior, an early settler of southern Queensland whose own involvement in frontier warfare will be discussed later in this chapter, recorded in his memoir of the period from the 1840s to the 1860s, details of how the Native Police worked. In his account, it is clear that the settlers relied on the Native Police to carry out the worst of the killings, though many did not hesitate to conduct their own murderous attacks on Aboriginal groups when they deemed it necessary. Murray-Prior recounted an episode that he suggests helped to conclude the frontier 'war' in which he was involved in the late 1850s:

[22] Neal, *The Rule of Law in a Penal Colony*, pp. 151–3.
[23] This paragraph is based on Henry Reynolds, *With the White People: The Crucial Role of Aborigines in the Exploration and Development of Australia* (Ringwood, Victoria: Penguin Books, 1990), Ch. 2 'Black Troopers'.

A party of 8 or 10 [Native] police were with an officer on the Lower Dawson. The country was very scrubby & broken. It was almost impossible for the pursuers to penetrate into the scrub—the natives used to shew themselves occasionally & jeer at the police—tell them to come on & catch them.—Where force would not do, stratagem might, thought the troopers, so they said to their [white] officer . . . Horses are no good here . . . You are no good in scrub . . . We boys will go into the scrub unarmed & induce the wild blacks to go hunting with us in a friendly way . . . Accordingly next morning early they all stripped, piled their arms—& started with paddy melon sticks (a paddy melon is a small kangaroo) for a hunt, & easily persuaded the natives to join them, seeing that they were unarmed, & after the hunt to come with them to their camp. These blacks were on the warpath—they were all men of one family,—the father & 8 sons—They came into camp, & had a grand feed. The police watched their opportunity, jumped up, got their carbines, & before the myalls [wild blacks] knew what they were about, they shot the old man & 7 others. The 8th got away.[24]

The Native Police, Murray-Prior noted rather self-servingly, were 'always the worst against the wilder blacks'.[25]

The attack that Murray-Prior described may have been fairly representative of the operations of the Native Police in Queensland, whose method for reprisal raids commonly involved surrounding Aboriginal camps (particularly vulnerable at dawn) and opening fire. As Jonathan Richards has argued, it is important to recognize that: 'the Native Police should be regarded as a military force, albeit an odd or irregular one'.[26] Led by white officers, many of whom had prior military experience in a range of colonial locations, the Native Police forces were connected to imperial army networks through individual ties and to the wider British Empire (and other European empires) through common structures, methods, and imperatives. Richards points out that the use by Queensland Native Police of horses, firearms, postal and telegraph systems, as well as its terrible tactics, were all 'typical under the rules of frontier colonialism'.[27]

CROWN LANDS COMMISSIONERS
IN NEW SOUTH WALES, 1830–50

From 1836 onwards, commissioners for Crown Lands were appointed in some areas, particularly in the Port Phillip district, overlapping with missionaries and protectors in their roles of reporting on the contact zones of cultural encounter, frontier violence, and indigenous displacement. In areas further north in New South Wales the first commissioners were appointed from 1837. Commissioners'

[24] Thomas Murray-Prior memoir, Rosa Praed Papers, OM64-1/3/1/1, State Library of Queensland, pp. 37–8.
[25] Thomas Murray-Prior memoir, p. 13.
[26] Jonathan Richards, *The Secret War: A True History of Queensland's Native Police* (St Lucia, Queensland: University of Queensland Press, 2008), p. 8.
[27] Richards, *The Secret War*, pp. 11–12.

jobs included collecting statistics, renewing squatters' licences, surveying local resources, and reporting on race relations and violence. The race relations part of their portfolio was in response to the charges of the Select Committee. Commissioners for Crown Lands were typically prosperous land-holding settlers, the gentry of their frontier regions, the class from which magistrates were also drawn. Commissioners' reports went first to Sydney, but were also forwarded to London, valued as first-hand testimony of the colonial frontier.

Hilary Golder has proffered some very interesting observations on the records of the commissioners of Crown Lands in New South Wales in the late 1830s and early 1840s.[28] These records, which Golder claims have been underused by historians, cover what were known as the 'Unsettled Districts' from 1837 onwards. The job of commissioners was created to produce colonial knowledge of the frontier. They were to visit the stations in their districts and to count and report on the numbers of people, buildings, and livestock, the uses of the country, and supplies of water and wood. It was also the commissioners' responsibility to monitor crime—such as bushranging and unlicensed tree felling—and to report on race relations and violence, whether interracial or intraracial. Commissioners were given police—often convicts—to assist them in their work. Not least, they were to investigate any violent deaths.

However, there were contradictions built into the role of Crown Lands commissioners. They doubled as protectors of Aborigines, yet they were active agents of frontier expansion. Some were squatters themselves, even though they were supposed to monitor other squatters—and some had been government surveyors. Golder contends that the commissioners under-reported the numbers of violent deaths, and not surprisingly given their contradictory roles, their reports show that there was a blurring between official police actions and vigilante reprisal raids against Aborigines. Using terms such as 'engagement', 'affray', and 'collision,' the commissioners' reports made it difficult for officials in Sydney to know the true nature of frontier violence, even when they wanted to.[29] Despite these obfuscations, apparently even the governor at times raised questions about the reports. From Golder's careful reading of these records, it is clear that awareness of frontier violence was part of the *raison d'etre* of the commissioners, and that it filtered through from their reports to officials in Sydney. This points to the likelihood that those who were pushing for self-government were hardly innocent about the frontier, and it confirms what John Ferry describes as the 'language of colonialism' in which 'Aboriginal violence was described in detail with all the hyperbole of horror' while 'European violence was dissembled by euphemism'.[30]

Heather Goodall has also drawn on the reports of the commissioners for Crown Lands in her study of Commissioner Richard Bligh of the Macintyre River district in the late 1840s, in which she vividly demonstrates the tensions inherent in

---

[28] Hilary Golder, *Evidence and Accountability: Revisiting and Reading the Public Record* (Royal Exchange: History Council of New South Wales, 2006).

[29] Golder, *Evidence and Accountability*, pp. 6–16.   [30] Ferry, *Colonial Armidale*, p. 20.

commissioners' work.[31] Goodall reveals how rich a source the records of the commissioners for Crown Lands are in her finely constructed account of Commissioner Richard Bligh's vexed attempts to administer British law on the Macintyre River area of New South Wales between 1847 and 1856. Bligh's attempts to bring to justice white men who had killed Aboriginal people were foiled by the strong culture of silence among the settlers, despite their varying views about the responsibility and morality of those involved. Goodall demonstrates through her careful analysis of the records that ideas of gender were centrally tied to the conflicts between white and Indigenous people over land and livelihood, law and justice. Just as Commissioner Bligh's attempts to instil order and administer justice were linked to his understanding of his paternal and masculine responsibilities, one of the Pikampul men whose lives were devastated by the invasion and conflict in the area also reacted at least in part through his conceptions of his manly duties. Authority, livelihood, land, and masculinity, Goodall shows, were bound up together.[32]

The reports written by commissioners reflect a moral universe in which violence was seen as the inevitable if extreme result of non-cooperation. Aboriginal people who bent themselves to settlers' demands and needs, who engaged in labouring for settlers, or otherwise showed themselves compliant (no doubt due to their own desperate struggle for survival), were discussed in terms of virtue and utility. Those who did not were castigated in terms that supposedly cumulatively justified the use of violence. In this moral universe, settlers cast themselves as the vehicles of moral redemption for Aboriginal people, in offering opportunities for the labouring work that would bring them into civilization.

For example, in 1841 J. C. S. Handt, the commissioner for Crown Lands reporting on Moreton Bay, suggested an age and gender difference among indigenous peoples' disposition to labour:

> The Aboriginal natives of these parts are less tractable than those who have been longer among civilized people; many of them, however, . . . are useful in doing any rough work. The middle-aged and old men will in general do some work, and at the German Mission, the women are found useful likewise, but it is seldom that the young men are willing to do anything in the way of work.

He immediately made clear, though, that this was not formal labour for wages. Rather, Aboriginal people were 'paid' with 'plenty to eat while they are at work, and a good quantity of provisions in the evening to take into the bush for their family'. The settlers' attitude towards Aboriginal labour was quite distinct from that towards Indian and Chinese workers. Commissioner Handt's report obfuscated Europeans' role in frontier violence with the glib note that: 'some hostilities have taken place between the Aborigines and the settlers in which some on both sides

[31] Heather Goodall, 'Authority under challenge: Pikampul land and Queen Victoria's law during the British invasion of Australia', Ch. 13 in Martin Daunton and Rick Halpern (eds), *Empire and Others: British Encounters with Indigenous Peoples, 1600–1850* (Philadelphia: University of Pennsylvania Press, 1999).

[32] Goodall, 'Authority under challenge', pp. 260–79.

have lost their lives'.[33] In 1842 Handt continued to claim that Aboriginal people 'who have been with the white people are in some degree civilized having become useful in performing common manual labour', implying that such labour was beneficial for Aboriginal people despite his simultaneous noting of the fact that 'many of them, children not excepted are infected with venereal disease'.[34]

Also in 1842, Graham D. Hunter, commissioner of Crown Lands for the District of Bligh, registered his opinion that: 'it is during this period when stations are newly formed that any outrage takes place on the part of the Aborigines; and when a proper feeling is formed with the white people, and no improper conduct on part of the whites, there is little risk to be run of any outrage being committed'—suggesting that the Aborigines were responsible both for the violence and for learning the 'proper feeling' that would enable peace.[35] Similarly, in December 1842, J. Allman, the commissioner for Crown Lands for the Wellington district northwest of Bathurst, argued that working for settlers equated to virtuous behaviour: 'Those natives with whom I have been in communication on the Lower Lachlan all appear to be quiet and well-behaved, and are of considerable service to the stockholders in many respects'. These 'good Aborigines' stood in contrast to 'the natives on the Lower Bogan, who are inclined to be troublesome and to take advantage of any opportunity afforded them of making aggressions against the whites'.[36]

A recurrent theme of the commissioners' reports is the need for wisdom and discretion on the part of settler men. S. Simpson, commissioner for the Moreton Bay district in 1844, saw this as the critical factor:

> Everything... depends upon the judicious management of the proprietor or superin-tendent of the station in preventing any improper intercourse between the gins and his men and taking care that they are fairly and honestly dealt with for any little services they render.[37]

There are repeated references in the reports to settler men taking indigenous women—a pattern of sexual assault and kidnapping of which commissioners were well aware, and which they condemned in their reports, but with little or no evidence that they sought to repress or intervene in such behaviour. There are references to other crimes by settlers, such as Thomas Coutts on the Clarence River who was prosecuted for poisoning Aboriginal people. Commissioner Fry, referring to this in his January 1848 report, blamed Coutts for provoking the subsequent murder by 'the Blacks' of one of his workers. Fry condemned Coutts's 'treatment of

---

[33] L. [sic] C. S. Handt, CCL, 'Report...relative to the condition of the Aborigines at Moreton Bay, 1841', CCL (and Missionary) Reports for 1841, CO 201/318, AJCP PRO Reel 338, pp. 203 ff.

[34] J. C. S. Handt, CCL, 'Report of the transactions relative to the Aborigines in the District of Moreton Bay for the year 1842', CO 210/332, AJCP PRO Reel 347.

[35] Graham D. Hunter, CCL, 'Report on the conditions of the Aboriginal Natives in the District of Bligh for 1842', CO 210/332, AJCP PRO Reel 347.

[36] The Lower Bogan area is northwest of Parkes in central New South Wales. J. Allman, CCL, 'Report for Wellington, 31 December 1842', CO 210/332, AJCP PRO Reel 347.

[37] S. Simpson, CCL, 'Report of the State of the Aborigines in the District of Moreton Bay, 1 January 1844', CO 210/344, AJCP PRO Reel 356.

the natives' as 'distinguished by the most barbarous inhumanity'.[38] The commissioners' reports, then, sought to support the legal code and to establish a moral code of settler behaviour.

At the same time the reports continued to use euphemisms for violence *against* Aboriginal people, words such as 'collision', 'pursuit', 'harshness', and 'severity', or direct terms such as 'bloodshed', 'kill', and 'justifiably shot', while attacks *by* Aborigines were emotively termed 'atrocity', 'murder', 'aggressions', and 'outrages'. Such carefully chosen terms helped to build the case that settlers, who could evaluate different kinds of violence, were establishing civilized order even as they committed violent acts when supposedly necessary.

Reports also registered change over time in patterns of Aboriginal employment. By 1851 commissioners' reports noted the widespread increase of Aboriginal employment because of the gold rush, and their more commonly being paid partly in wages. Edgar Beckham reported for the Lachlan district that Aborigines 'would work more willingly for money than anything else'. Robert Massie reported for New England that Aboriginal workers 'have been in considerable repute as shepherds, grooms and even house servants . . . and in some cases they have been receiving wages at the rate of £20 per annum'.[39] Thus the distinction between Aboriginal labour and indentured Asian labour began to narrow. Moreover, in some instances, Aboriginal workers were compared favourably to Asian indentured labourers. In the Burnett district of what is now Queensland, in January 1853 Commissioner M. C. O'Connell reported:

> [T]he past twelve months present some features in the conduct of the Aborigines which seem to give promise of a possibility of inuring them to profitable industrial employment owing to the scarcity of European labour and the intractableness of the Chinese who have been imported to supply the deficiency . . . In these emergencies the Aborigines have willingly and cheerfully lent their aid . . . [On] the establishment of Messrs Strathdee [they have] tended with care and fidelity upward of 16,000 sheep. At the Messrs Lawless also I saw them the only person [sic] employed to aid the proprietors in pressing and packing wool at the shearing time.[40]

In 1858 Commissioner Arthur Hallinan reported of the Wide Bay (south of Maryborough) and Burnett district that beside working on stations 'the Blacks . . . are also employed in the towns getting wood and water'.[41]

Still in the late 1850s, commissioners' reports evince a belief that race relations depended in part on the morality and wisdom of the settler men themselves. Commissioner Wiseman reported in January 1857 for the Leichhardt district of

[38] Oliver Fry, CCL, 'Report for the Clarence River District, 17 January 1848', CO 201/397, AJCP PRO Reel 392.

[39] Reports of the Commissioners of Crown Lands on the State of the Aborigines for 1851, in Governors' Despatches to the Secretary of State for the Colonies, Vol. 71, 1852, Mitchell A1260 (CY 1944) commencing at Frame 679.

[40] Commissioner for Crown Lands M. C. O'Connell, Report for the Burnett District, 6 January 1853, CO 201/467, AJCP PRO Reel 645.

[41] Commissioner Arthur E. Hallinan, Report for the District of Wide Bay and Burnett, 31 December 1858, CO 201/508, AJCP PRO Reel 674.

south-central Queensland that Aboriginal people 'are very glad to live near a station' and that employment on stations was common. At Gracemere station, belonging to Charles Archer and his brothers, there had been no trouble because of Archer 'not allowing any of the Native Police or his own servants to interfere with or carry away by force the wives or daughters of the savages'. On the Elliots' station, in contrast, the 'frequent collisions' were because 'both the Messrs Elliot were men of easy, indolent disposition who could exercise no moral control over their servants either white or black'.[42]

THOMAS MURRAY-PRIOR IN NORTHERN NEW SOUTH WALES/QUEENSLAND: VIGILANTE VIOLENCE AND POLITICS

Thomas Murray-Prior (1819–92), a leading Queensland pastoralist, plantation owner, civil servant, and politician, affords us a case study with which to build on the reports of settlers who served as Crown Lands commissioners in New South Wales, to investigate how, in settler society, frontier violence was accepted within evolving definitions of manhood and hence political responsibility.[43] Murray-Prior also happened to produce a daughter who left a body of memoirs and fiction about her childhood on the Queensland frontier and the frontier's connections to colonial politics.

From the mid-1840s, Murray-Prior owned and ran pastoral properties in what was then the tense early-frontier region of northern New South Wales. From 1844 to 1850 he ran Broomelton in the Logan River district (just south of Brisbane) in partnership with Hugh Aikman, as well as Bungroopim Station in the same area at least from 1848 to 1849. Then in September 1853 he sold Broomelton and in 1854 bought Hawkwood in the Burnett region (inland from Maryborough). In 1858 he sold Hawkwood and bought a banana plantation at Ormiston near Cleveland in what is now a coastal area of Brisbane, and from there in 1864 bought another pastoral station, Maroon, in the Fassifern district.[44] His temporary abandonment of pastoral properties for a banana plantation was apparently linked to the 1857 killing by Aborigines of a neighbouring settler family, the Frasers, in the Burnett area. We know about Murray-Prior's involvement in the reprisal party consisting of settlers and their Aboriginal workers, thanks to his own memoir and other records, and the memoirs of his eldest daughter Rosa Praed, particularly her

---

[42] Commissioner W. H. Wiseman, Report for the Leichhardt District, 7 January 1857, CO 210/ 498, AJCP PRO Reel 666.

[43] Elsewhere I have discussed Thomas Murray-Prior as a significant case study for examining connections among race relations, the frontier, and settler government: 'Frontier Violence and Settler Manhood', published keynote address from the 2007 Australian Historical Association regional conference, *History Australia* Vol. 6, No. 1 (April 2009): 09.1–09.15.

[44] H. J. Gibbney, 'Murray-Prior, Thomas Lodge (1819–1892)', *Australian Dictionary of Biography* Volume 5 (Melbourne: Melbourne University Press, 1974), pp. 323–4.

books *Australian Life: Black and White* and *My Australian Girlhood*.[45] Gordon Reid's study of the massacre of the Fraser family at Hornet Bank station, which will feature in Chapter 7 of this volume, draws extensively on Thomas Murray-Prior's records to discuss his involvement in the reprisal parties.[46]

Murray-Prior was born in Somerset, England, in 1819 to a middle-class family, and was educated at a school in Brussels and privately in England. His father was an officer of the Hussars who fought at Waterloo at the end of the Napoleonic War campaigns.[47] Thomas Murray-Prior did a brief stint, not in the army like his father, rather in the navy on HMS *Donegal*, but resigned and in 1839 left for Sydney. In the memoir Murray-Prior dictated to his wife in the 1880s, at Rosa's request, he saw himself as one of a cohort of young settlers: 'about 1838 or 39 a number of young men—most of them cadets of good family, came out to the colony—some of these were undergraduates of Oxford & Cambridge some the sons of soldiers—sailors—& younger sons of county men who could not get commissions or appointments'.[48] He first spent time in the Maitland and Tamworth regions of New South Wales before heading north to the Moreton Bay area in what is now Queensland.

Murray-Prior's eldest daughter Rosa Caroline, born in 1851, became Rosa Praed, a successful writer from 1880 to the 1920s. In several of her works Praed drew on her memories of her childhood in the 1850s and 1860s, as well as material provided to her by her father and others. The violence of territorial conquest and interracial murder on the Queensland frontier in those decades was so pervasive that, writing in London in the 1880s, Praed claimed 'I have not ceased to dream that I am on an out-station besieged by Blacks; and during many a night do I fly through the endless forests, and hide in stony gullies, pursued by my aboriginal as ruthlessly as was ever De Quincy by his Malay'.[49] Praed recalled that the white men she grew up among were always armed, and that the fear and anticipation of attack and reprisals shaped life for both settlers and Aborigines.

The Aboriginal men who found employment on the pastoral and grazing runs of the settlers were crucial actors in daily life on the colonial frontier. The demands made on them by squatters included not only their routine duties but also participating in violent attacks. Often such workers, such as the Native Police, were Aboriginal men from another region, who felt no kinship to the local people under attack. The 'boys', as they were demeaningly called, on Praed's father's station were 'Bean-Tree, Dick, Freddy, and Tombo'; Praed notes that they 'had adopted, as far as possible, the customs of the white men'. They:

---

[45] Mrs Campbell Praed, *Australian Life: Black and White* (London: Chapman and Hall, 1885) and Rosa Campbell-Praed, *My Australian Girlhood* (London: Fisher Unwin, 1902).

[46] Gordon Reid, *A Nest of Hornets: The Massacre of the Fraser Family at Hornet Bank Station, Central Queensland, 1857, and Related Events* (Melbourne: Oxford University Press, 1982).

[47] On the significance of Peninsular War veterans, from earlier in the Napoleonic Wars, to the settlement of the Australian colonies, see Christine Wright, *Wellington's Men in Australia: Peninsular War Veterans and the Making of Empire c.1820–40* (Basingstoke: Palgrave Macmillan, 2011).

[48] Thomas Murray-Prior memoir, Rosa Praed Papers, OM64-1/3/1/1, State Library of Queensland.

[49] Praed, *Australian Life*, pp. 27–8.

would not do menial work, but rode among the cattle, looked for lost sheep, and brought up the horses. Their moleskins were always white. They wore Crimean shirts, with coloured handkerchiefs knotted above one shoulder and under the other, and sang songs in their own language set to operatic airs.[50]

Praed may have been drawing on her own memory here, but she was also drawing on her father's description of his workers at this time. Murray-Prior noted that Billy, one of his 'black boys', had served in the Native Police, part of a group recruited from the distant Murray River and brought to the region by their commandant Mr H. Walker. Murray-Prior recorded, too, that it was Mary-Anne, Billy's wife and the family's domestic servant, who kept the Aboriginal station-hands' clothes so clean. 'I used to be quite proud of my boys', he noted in this passage.[51]

After local indigenous people, the Jiman, attacked one of the station homesteads and killed eleven white people, mostly members of the Fraser family who owned the station, a revenge party comprised only of men set out to conduct reprisals on those supposed to be responsible. Significantly, the party included three of the 'black boys', who were armed like the white men. The trust and manly status that these Aboriginal men held as part of the reprisal party was earned partly through their declared preparedness to kill, articulated during the expedition planning. Praed reports that her father instructed the others to kill only the adult men, but some in the group argued for killing the women and children too—including Tombo. Murray-Prior, however, 'held firm to the traditions of English warfare',[52] insisting that only men were to be considered combatants and targets. According to Praed, like the Europeans, the itinerant Aborigines saw connections between combat and masculinity. In the ensuing unequal fight in which numbers of Aborigines died but no white men, according to her father, one particular Aboriginal man 'stood forth bravely and fought like a man'[53]—a gendered stance that did him little good against the white men's guns. The significance of violence for shaping frontier masculinity is most apparent in Tombo's willingness to argue for killing Aboriginal women and children. It is unclear whether Tombo was sincere in this argument, or whether he mounted it for rhetorical effect with which to stake a gendered claim. While such evidence is mediated and fragmentary, it is sufficient to show negotiations between Aboriginal and settler men over manly behaviour.

Praed's knowledge of the actual acts of violence came largely from her father's memories of these years, which she asked him to record in the 1880s, apparently intending to draw on them in her writing. Praed was only six years old at the time of the Hornet Bank station killings in 1857 and the subsequent reprisal murders of Aborigines. The Jiman people of the Upper Dawson River region were under increasing pressure from white squatters taking their land, and low-level hostilities between them and the settlers had become endemic. There is evidence, too, that shepherds and Native Police troopers in the area were routinely raping Jiman

---

[50] Praed, *Australian Life*, p. 35.
[51] Thomas Murray-Prior memoir, p. 52.
[52] Praed, *Australian Life*, p. 80.
[53] Praed, *Australian Life*, p. 84.

women and, moreover, that sons of the Fraser family were doing so as well, despite their mother trying to prevent them. This ongoing low-level warfare and culture of rape culminated in the planned attack by local Aboriginal people on the Hornet Bank station. On 27 October 1857, a large group of Aborigines attacked the Hornet Bank station homestead of the Fraser family on the Dawson River, killed all the males there except one who survived, raped the mother and two of her daughters, and then killed the women and children. In sum, eleven white people, including several of the Frasers' employees, were killed.

Subsequent reprisals were protracted and resulted in the deaths of significantly more Aboriginal people than the whites killed. Reprisals included vigilante expeditions by local settlers and attacks by Native Police troops. According to Gordon Reid, whose research on the events is extensive, 'at least 150 Aborigines died; the total may have been 300'.[54] As the reprisals against Aborigines in south-central Queensland dragged on through the early months of 1858, parallels with the 'Indian Mutiny' and the racial and religious logic that supported them were used to validate the continued and extensive killings. Thomas Murray-Prior would later call it 'eighteen months of warfare' and 'an anxious time for us'.[55] 'Business took me then a good deal from the station', he recalled; 'when I came home I used to canter pretty sharply to the top of the ridge from which the place was visible with my heart in my mouth, for there was always the fear that all hands might have been massacred'.[56]

Murray-Prior's own account of the reprisals, in which he participated, states that six weeks after the Fraser killings, when the Native Police response had not yet been large, Aboriginal people gathered in significant numbers in the Auburn range, near the station of a settler called Pigott. Word spread among the whites that Aboriginal people were planning further attacks. A travelling livestock-buyer called Horton visited Hawkwood, and claimed to have heard of such plans. Murray-Prior and Horton, along with a neighbouring settler, agreed that they should initiate a revenge attack, and sent messages to other stations. On a particular evening a group of local pastoralists and some of their 'black boys' gathered and camped at Hawkwood and, in a militarist gesture, named themselves the 'Browns'. It was shearing season, so there were white workers on the stations, but they were not involved. This vigilante squad headed for where they thought the Jiman were camped near Auburn, but the campsite had been vacated. They headed up the Auburn River, where they found tracks leading towards Redbank station; next morning they attacked the Aboriginal camp on horseback, opening fire as they rode, but most of the Aborigines fled into the scrub. At the Aboriginal campsite they found clothes, blankets, and books from the Hornet Bank station, some of which they kept and the rest they burned.

---

[54] Reid, *A Nest of Hornets*, p. ix.
[55] Murray-Prior, Serocold, McArthur, Pigott, Bungaban, 3 December 1857, to Col. Sec., 57/4995, in Oxley Library, COL, mfm, A2/39, quoted in Reid, *A Nest of Hornets*, p. 93.
[56] Thomas Murray-Prior memoir, p. 44.

From there they followed tracks to Redbank station where, in a planned and strategic attack involving two of their number going in first as a decoy, they shot and killed a number of Aborigines, though some escaped. Murray-Prior says the reprisal party put the women and the male captives into an old stable overnight and allowed the women to leave in the morning; seemingly the men not killed were kept as prisoners to await the police. The 'Browns' continued their reprisals in the region for three weeks, according to Murray-Prior, after which the Native Police arrived to take up the attacks and the settlers dispersed. Much of the haphazard reprisal killing (the 'at least 150' Aboriginal deaths) was conducted by the Native Police; there were other settler vigilante parties as well, including the surviving Fraser brothers and others, during the 'eighteen months of warfare'.[57] Murray-Prior is explicit in his recorded memories that these 'eighteen months' were indeed a time of war: 'The war was kept up for eighteen months, during which there were continually either one or more parties out.—& gradually a good many of the ringleaders were accounted for'. He is clear, too, that his own active involvement was limited:

> You will understand that only the first few weeks of warfare were carried on by us.— When the Native Police came to the front—we—(the Browns) dispersed & went to our homes.—& the Redbank slaughter was the only serious struggle of the kind that fell to our lot.[58]

Murray-Prior, no doubt aware that his scribbling daughter might well make use of his memoirs, seems to have been eager to show his own active participation as limited, yet in doing so he overtly characterizes that involvement as conducting a 'slaughter'.

Rosa Praed was a highly successful novelist of the turn of the twentieth century, producing over forty-five books, around half of which have Australian themes or settings. Interracial violence on the Australian frontier is a continuing theme, while the Hornet Bank killing of the Frasers and the reprisal vigilante killings of Aborigines that followed recur both in specific references (such as, 'the little war of my childhood, after the Fraser murder, between squatters and the Blacks'[59]) and as plot lines. They form a chapter in *My Australian Girlhood* (1902), a dramatic episode in *Australian Life: Black and White* (1885), and the plot setting for her supernatural novel *Fugitive Anne: A Romance of the Unexplored Bush* (1903).[60] Praed's writings of the mid-nineteenth-century Australian frontier depict the reciprocal violence and its horrors for both Aborigines and settlers, evincing sympathy for and a sense of outrage about the treatment of Aborigines while also

---

[57] Reid, *A Nest of Hornets*, pp. 86–95.
[58] Thomas Murray-Prior memoir, Rosa Praed Papers, OM64-1/3/1/1, State Library of Queensland.
[59] Campbell-Praed, *My Australian Girlhood*, p. 4.
[60] On Rosa Praed's life and work see Dale Spender, 'Rosa Praed: Original Australian Writer', in Debra Adelaide (ed.), *A Bright and Fiery Troop: Australian Women Writers of the Nineteenth Century* (Ringwood, Victoria: Penguin Books, 1988), and Patricia Clarke, *Rosa! Rosa!: A Life of Rosa Praed, Novelist and Spiritualist* (Carlton, Victoria: Melbourne University Press, 1999).

reflecting some of the racial thinking of her time. They show frontier life as harsh, especially for settler women and children.

In the 1850s Murray-Prior was one of a group of affluent pastoralists and investors who sought to diversify the Queensland economy, combining their finances to establish a pastoral and agricultural association, and hoping to develop a coalmining industry as well, to export coal to the other Australian colonies and around the Pacific.[61] In 1861 Murray-Prior joined the Queensland public service, first as postal inspector and then became postmaster-general, a position he held from 1862 to 1874. During his tenure, postmaster-general became a ministerial position, and Murray-Prior thus served in the Queensland Legislative Council from 1866 to 1874.[62]

Murray-Prior's career is significant because one would not, on the face of it, suspect a postmaster-general of having been a direct participant in frontier warfare. He represents the way in which—in the mid-nineteenth-century Australian colonies, like other settler societies—frontier violence became built into colonial culture and politics, including politics in the towns and cities even up to ministerial level. And his narrative of the particular reprisal party, which Praed reproduces at such length, reveals his own awareness of the direct connections between frontier violence and masculinity.

But that expedition was certainly not his only brush with frontier violence, nor the extent of his knowledge of it. One of Murray-Prior's habits as postmaster-general was to ride through the rural and frontier areas of the state, inspecting post offices and appointing postmasters. In this capacity, he learned about the state of race relations in outlying areas, building on what he already knew from his own experience and involvement. His private journal of 1863–64 records his journeys, observations, and conversations of those years in considerable detail. He became familiar with settlers and communities in various areas, knew the state of pastoral enterprises, and the personalities and fortunes of many individuals. He also heard about violent encounters between settlers and Aborigines.

And it was during such a trip that, in December 1863, he spent an afternoon in a post office in the vicinity of Bowen, north of Mackay, in deep conversation with 'Morrill who was 17 years among the Blacks'.[63] Jemmy Morrill was a shipwrecked sailor who eventually rejoined settler society after seventeen years of life with Aboriginal people, and who is familiar now to us as the historical figure upon whom David Malouf based his celebrated novel *Remembering Babylon*—the figure

---

[61] Bill Thorpe, *Colonial Queensland: Perspectives on a frontier society* (St Lucia, Queensland: University of Queensland Press, 1996), pp. 113–14.

[62] This information is from the *Australian Dictionary of Biography—Online Edition* entry on Murray-Prior, Thomas Lodge (1819–1892) by H. J. Gibbney. Desley Deacon has shown that Murray-Prior's assumption of the position of postmaster-general involved the displacement of the woman who had served ably in the job since 1855 (originally as the postmistress of Brisbane), a displacement in which he played an apparently zealous role. Desley Deacon, *Managing Gender: The State, the New Middle-Class and Women Workers 1830–1930* (Melbourne: Oxford University Press, 1989), pp. 38–40, 237–8.

[63] Mitchell Library, MSS 3117/4, CY Reel 495, Thomas Lodge Murray-Prior, 'Diaries' 1863–64, p. 18.

who wanders into a European settlement and declares himself to be a 'British object'.[64] Murray-Prior notes that Morrill was shipwrecked in 1846, only nine days' sail out of Sydney. Murray-Prior's long conversation with Morrill traversed the topics of frontier violence, Aboriginal perceptions of Europeans and their guns, sex between white men and Aboriginal women, and cannibalism.[65]

In his private journal Murray-Prior quotes Morrill at length, interweaving Morrill's recollections with his own judgements and speculations on him. On frontier violence, he paraphrases Morrill as saying:

> They are very frightened of the white man and his arms. he thinks that very frequently the Black is hunted, because the Squatter fears him. and not on account of the mischief already done—when they intend no harm. and that if they could only understand one another, that there would be less bloodshed—that if the natives knew that whenever they killed a white man that some 20 of theirs would be shot, that they then would be frightened and would be quiet.[66]

Murray-Prior is quite scathing in his opinions of Morrill, commenting that he seems to have had little positive influence 'over the Savage' and 'seems only to have excelled in snaring ducks which he gave to the Blacks'.[67] At one point in the conversation, he openly challenges Morrill. In a pamphlet that had been published in Brisbane on Morrill's experiences, after Morrill 'came in' as Murray-Prior calls his return to white society, Morrill had apparently claimed not to have had any sexual relations with Aboriginal women. Murray-Prior told Morrill point blank that he did not believe him on this, and Morrill readily recanted. He claimed that he had only meant that he had not had a 'regular wife'. Responding at some length to Murray-Prior's questioning, Morrill described young Aboriginal women as very good-looking, and apparently compared them favourably with white women. Rather immodestly, he boasted of his sexual successes: 'Chastity not being considered a virtue [by the Aborigines] he was a greater favourite than was good for his constitution'.[68] This marvellous line suggests that men of the 1860s took quite seriously the contemporary opinion that they should limit their sexual expenditures for the sake of their health.

Murray-Prior seemed to regard cannibalism as a more serious issue than either violence or sex. He laments to his diary: 'O. Mr. Morrill. I am truly afraid the temptation has been too strong and following the old precept—When at Rome ec. [sic] [you] have been tempted yourself, and know the taste of humanity'.[69] He also expresses scepticism about what Morrill admits to know in the way of details of frontier violence. '[H]e must have known more of the skirmishes between the Blacks and the Whites than he allows', Murray-Prior writes. Indeed, he suspected that Morrill knew that white people were in his vicinity for some time before he

---

[64] David Malouf, *Remembering Babylon* (New York: Pantheon Books, 1993).

[65] Thomas Lodge Murray-Prior, 'Diaries' 1863–64, MSS. 3117/4, CY Reel 495, Mitchell Library, pp. 18–21.

[66] Murray-Prior, 'Diaries', pp. 18–19.   [67] Murray-Prior, 'Diaries', p. 19.

[68] Murray-Prior, 'Diaries', p. 19.   [69] Murray-Prior, 'Diaries', p. 20.

presented himself, and that he 'only came in when he was afraid of being shot by his own countrymen'.[70]

While Jemmy Morrill's story was unusual (though not unique), Thomas Murray-Prior's was not. He may have been Queensland's first postmaster-general, but he was one of scores of early settlers and pastoralists on the Queensland frontier. Robert Hogg has studied the writings of white men on the nineteenth-century Queensland frontier, and the ways in which they discursively subordinated Aboriginal men, casting them as savage and uncivilized, while touting their own manly virtues—virtues that included '[i]ntegrity, honour, determination, courage, and competitive spirit'.[71] Frontier men celebrated their own and each other's toughness, endurance, and bravery—descriptions in which the use of violence could be implicit but was glossed over. The evidence presented by Thomas Murray-Prior and Rosa Praed shows the thorough imbrication of ideas of manhood and frontier violence—not only for settler men, but, importantly, also for the indigenous men who worked as Native Police and as stockmen on the pastoral stations.

We can glean further insight into Murray-Prior from the ledgers, journals, and diary he kept as a pastoralist, running Broomelton and Bungroopim stations on the Logan River (now on the southern edge of Brisbane) from 1844 to the early 1850s, and then Hawkwood Station in the Burnett district from 1854 to 1858. Across this period, Murray-Prior employed a mix of workers, including German indentured labourers, Aboriginal, and other non-white workers, a mix of Indian and Chinese labourers, whom he identified quite distinctly. The Indian labourers (perhaps Bengali or Sikh workers) he called 'Coolie' or 'Coolieman', while the Chinese workers are listed in his ledgers individually as 'Chinaman'. He used these terms seemingly in lieu of surnames, such that the workers are recorded for instance as 'Poki Coolieman' and 'Ubi Chinaman'.[72] Indeed, the detail he records in his ledgers includes the tasks assigned to these workers, their pay, and the length of the contract. For example, on 11 December 1849 he hired 'Tinko Chinaman' for five years at wages of £6 per year. 'Poki Coolieman' recurs in the ledgers, hired first in 1854 as a shepherd for twenty-one weeks at 30/- per week; in 1856 'to take charge of lambing at 30/- per week for 9 weeks and one day'; again in 1856 as a shepherd for thirty-eight days at 25/- per week; and in 1857 as shepherd and hutkeeper 'at 30/- per week for 16 weeks and two days' and again the same year as 'washer—16 days at 5/- per day'. Numerous other workers listed as 'Chinaman', 'Coolie', or 'Coolieman' are also shown with the details of their assignments, length of hire, and wages.[73] Diary entries also record Murray-Prior's awareness of his power over workers, such as his pleasure on 28 April 1855 in dismissing his

---

[70] Murray-Prior Diaries, p. 21.
[71] Robert Hogg, 'The Unmanly Savage: "Aboriginalism" and Subordinate Masculinities on the Queensland Frontier', *Crossings* Vol. 10.3/11.1 (March 2006).
[72] Thomas Lodge Murray-Prior, ML MSS 3117/6, CY Reel 1248, NLA mfm G28187, frames 485 and 440.
[73] Thomas Lodge Murray-Prior, ML MSS 3117/6, CY Reel 1248, NLA mfm G28187, frames 395–592.

shepherd 'Karim' and replacing him with 'Yager', apparently to Karim's surprise. Murray-Prior suggests Karim wanted higher wages: 'Slight mistake—bad man'.[74]

Amidst this specificity, there are references to 'Black Boys' with significantly less detail—such as one in 1857, with no names of the 'Black Boys' but a reference to the 'Stores account'.[75] After Murray-Prior sold Hawkwood and turned to being a banana planter, his private journals include casual references to his Aboriginal workers as 'blacks' or 'Black Boys'. On 4 February 1859, for example, he records: 'Paid the blacks the half crown apiece. I had provided them with some rations and let them go'.[76] Despite the relative anonymity of the Aboriginal workers, and much more casual methods of payment, some references to them are by name and reveal a continuity of employment and some level of personal relationship. On 10 May 1859 when he took a trip to Cleveland, Murray-Prior notes that he: 'Took Fred the Black Boy with me'.[77] These references to Aboriginal men by name in his private journal confirm Rosa Praed's recollections of 'Bean-Tree, Dick, Freddy, and Tombo', the Aboriginal station hands who worked for her father, and who wore white moleskins and 'Crimean shirts', 'rode among the cattle, looked for lost sheep, and brought up the horses'.[78] Murray-Prior's employment of Aboriginal workers, then, ran the gamut, from casual and relatively anonymous arrangements, to the continuing and personal relationships of squatter and station hand.

Not only was there a distinction between the specific, named, and detailed employment of Indian and Chinese labourers on the one hand, and the often casual and infantilized employment of Aboriginal workers on the other, but the employment of Aboriginal workers coexisted on a daily basis with relations of violence with Aboriginal people. Murray-Prior's diary from Hawkwood Station in 1855, for example, intersperses references to his Indian shepherds Bundoo, Poki, and Kasim, with a reference to 'the Black Boy Jimmy', and various references to violence by and against Aboriginal people. On 14 March 1855, he notes: 'I got Kean to let his Black Boy go with us to track the cattle at Hawkwood or the natives if bad'. On 4 April, he records: 'A good many young calves and they seem to have in great measure recovered from the fright the blacks gave them'. On 20 April, ominously, he records: 'the Black Boy Jimmy reported that he had seen smoke up Leichhardt's Gully and Sydney saying the cattle were much scattered and the

---

[74] Hawkwood Station, Wednesday 28 April, 1855, Diary, Thomas Lodge Murray-Prior, Murray-Prior Family Papers, Box 3, Folder 14, MS 7801, National Library of Australia.

[75] Scholarship on the employment of Aboriginal workers in the areas under discussion includes R. Evans, K. Saunders, and K. Cronin, *Exclusion, Exploitation and Extermination: Race Relations in Colonial Queensland* (Sydney: Australian and New Zealand Book Co., 1975) and Shirleene Robinson, *Something like Slavery? Queensland's Aboriginal child workers 1842–1945* (Melbourne: Australian Scholarly Publishing, 2008).

[76] Thomas Lodge Murray-Prior, ML MSS 3117/6, CY Reel 1248, NLA mfm G28187, Private Journal, entry for 4 February 1859.

[77] Thomas Lodge Murray-Prior, ML MSS 3117/6, CY Reel 1248, NLA mfm G28187, Private Journal, entry for 10 May 1859.

[78] Praed, *Australian Life*, p. 35.

moon full—supposed that they had come to kill the cattle so we resolved to go out and see'.[79] We can only imagine to what the phrase 'to go out and see' alluded.

In amongst these records of his employment of non-white workers, Murray-Prior's diary and journal evince his legal authority and political career. In April 1855, while a pastoralist at Hawkwood, Murray-Prior served as a local magistrate and noted in his diary his work at the Quarter Petty Sessions.[80] In 1859 and 1860 his journal records his failed candidature for the Lower House Queensland seat of East Moreton, a race he chose to run despite being offered a seat in the Upper House, the Legislative Council. Not surprisingly for a wealthy squatter in a frontier colony, he was well connected politically. His private journal for 5 January 1860, for example, notes that he 'called at Government House', and that the governor 'was very gracious and detained me talking of various colonial matters for some time', as well as introducing him to the incoming president of the 'Upper House'; Murray-Prior then '[l]unched with Roff who is to have a seat in the Upper House'.[81] He did join the Legislative Council in 1866, when his position as postmaster-general was turned into a political appointment. One of the surviving contemporary assessments we have of Murray-Prior is from the pen of Rachel Henning, a settler whose brother Biddulph was also an early squatter at Port Denison in Queensland. Rachel Henning met Murray-Prior during the years she spent helping to run her brother's household, when he visited their station on one of his tours. 'I suppose it does not require any great talent to be a "Postmaster-General"', Henning wrote scathingly. 'I hope not, for such a goose I have seldom seen. He talked incessantly, and all his conversation consisted of pointless stories of which he himself was the hero. The witty sayings that he had said and the clever things he had done'.[82]

Murray-Prior's political career was translated into fiction by his daughter Rosa Praed, particularly in her novel of political corruption, *Policy and Passion*, published in London in 1881, and based on her observations of Queensland politics. Praed had plenty of opportunity for first-hand observation of her father's political career, and the other politicians and officials of his day. Praed's mother Matilda died in 1868, and for the four years between then and 1872 when Rosa married Campbell Praed and Murray-Prior remarried, Rosa as his eldest daughter was mistress of his household. Murray-Prior had purchased a Brisbane home at Kangaroo Point, which with its expansive views over the Brisbane River recurs as a vivid setting in Praed's fiction. For example, one especially tense conversation between father and daughter in *Policy and Passion* occurs in 'the back room looking out upon the lawn, filled with Hansard's Parliamentary papers and standard tomes, where the Premier spent long hours in studying political precedents, and the principles

[79] National Library of Australia [NLA] MS 7801, Murray-Prior Family Papers, Box 3, Folder 14.
[80] NLA MS 7801, Murray-Prior Family Papers, Box 3, Folder 14, 15 April 1855.
[81] Private Journal 1858–1860, Papers of Thomas Lodge Murray-Prior, ML MSS 3117/7X, CY Reel 1248, NLA mfm G28187.
[82] David Adams (ed.), *The Letters of Rachel Henning* (Harmondsworth: Penguin Books, 1969), p. 144.

of representative government'.[83] In Brisbane, Rosa attended parliamentary debates and social gatherings of the political elite at Government House and other venues, and generally had an active social life.[84] She later recalled it as an exciting time of 'fantastic glamour', when she and the women relatives of other politicians attended debates but were especially anxious that political outcomes would allow them to stay in Brisbane: 'would the squatters' party have suffered defeat, and the ministerial women be condemned to a bush prison as a penalty for having miscalculated the views of the majority?'[85]

Policy and Passion's main character is Thomas Longleat, premier of the colony called Leichhardt's Land (Murray-Prior, soon after his arrival in Australia, had met the explorer Ludwig Leichhardt and accompanied him to Queensland). Longleat is the leader of the squatters' faction; he is campaigning to stay in office, and plans, after the election, to bring in bills for a railway and a large loan. His integrity is compromised through an affair with the wife of an opposing member of parliament, for whom he arranges a lucrative position in the north, so that Longleat (a widower) can spend uninterrupted time with the MP's wife. When the cuckolded husband learns of the affair, he joins forces with other political opponents to bring Longleat down: they expose him as a former convict and murderer, and Longleat commits suicide. Longleat is replaced as premier by Dyson Maddox, the novel's hero, an Australian-born former explorer who is disabled from being wounded by an Aboriginal spear. Honoria Longleat, the former premier's estranged daughter, having earlier eschewed Maddox as too Australian, not sufficiently an English gentleman, changes her mind and marries him. Thus Maddox, the Minister for Lands who becomes premier, bears the scar and disablement of frontier violence, yet represents moral integrity and political potency—the apotheosis of settler manhood. Whether or not Praed intended Longleat and/or Maddox to represent her father, the novel's portrait of a politically corrupt and morally bankrupt man, in conjunction with her memoirs of the vigilante violence in which her father engaged in the 1850s, connects frontier violence, moral lapses, and the early stages of settler self-government.[86]

Referring to the Burnett district in the late 1850s, Praed recalled: 'All the men we used to know in those days carried revolvers'.[87] Murray-Prior's own records, along with Praed's writing, suggest settler definitions of manhood that include frontier warfare, the euphemisms that surrounded it, and a cultural congruence between respectability, acts of violence, and political authority. Settlers' moral judgements extended to their use of vigilante violence, when it was or was not acceptable, and the incorporation of at least some forms of it into acceptable manly behaviour. As Robert Hogg has noted in his study of the gentleman squatter on the nineteenth-century Queensland frontier: 'violence was not only routine and

---

[83] Rosa Campbell-Praed, *Policy and Passion* (London: Richard Bentley and Son, 1881), p. 254.

[84] Dale Spender's introduction to Rosa Praed, *Outlaw and Lawmaker* (London: Pandora, 1988), p. ix.

[85] Campbell-Praed, *My Australian Girlhood*, pp. 253, 251.

[86] Campbell-Praed, *Policy and Passion*.

[87] Campbell-Praed, *My Australian Girlhood*, p. 58.

normal, but was often considered to be manly. Manly attributes such as courage, strength, rationality, and perseverance were distorted to justify atrocity'.[88]

CONCLUSION

The Australian settler frontier has significant implications for understanding the meanings of political maturation in the period from the 1830s to the 1860s, including how manhood was reconfigured through political enfranchisement and vice versa. The significance goes beyond Australia's shores. Representative and responsible government emerged in the Australian colonies as part of the interconnected nineteenth-century evolution of male suffrage in Britain, the settler colonies and beyond. Between 1832 and 1867 most of the settler colonies achieved responsible government—suggesting a global circulation of ideas of political authority, responsibility, and citizenship that were constitutive of full manhood as it was understood in British imperial culture.

Histories of the emergence of responsible government in the Australian colonies have often cast the political struggles as between elite free settlers and the emancipated people they disdained, and between Tories and radicals. The political stage has frequently been limited to urban movements and the relations between Sydney and London. But we need to see the establishment by settler men of their own authority as extending beyond an aspiration to Edmund Burke's vision of 'a manly, moral, regulated liberty'.[89] That claimed political authority, which was to become the basis for more democratic rights than in Britain, had its roots also in the race relations of the frontier, and the status of white-settler master of non-white labour—the master who judged types of employment arrangement, and asserted the moral authority to make such judgements, and to resort to the use of violence when supposedly necessary.

Connecting the dots between frontier history, political history, and gender history suggests that we need to consider the ways in which violence may have shaped ideas of masculinity, conceptions of political authority in the Australian colonies, and hence settler colonialism on a larger scale. Several scholars have already pointed out that knowledge of frontier violence was more matter-of-fact in the nineteenth century than mid-twentieth-century histories, or the political controversies of the late twentieth century, would suggest.[90] Eminent novelist David Malouf has made the same point eloquently in his short story 'The Valley of Lagoons'. The descendants of frontier settlers, he suggests, speak of their

[88] Robert Hogg, ' "The Most Manly Class that Exists": British Gentlemen on the Queensland Frontier', *Journal of Australian Colonial History* Vol. 13 (2011): 70.

[89] Peter Cochrane, *Colonial Ambition: Foundations of Australian Democracy* (Carlton, Victoria: Melbourne University Press, 2006), p. 2.

[90] Ann Curthoys, 'Mythologies', in Richard Nile (ed.), *The Australian Legend and Its Discontents* (St Lucia, Queensland: University of Queensland Press, 2000), pp. 29–30; Robert Foster, Rick Hosking, and Amanda Nettelbeck, *Fatal Collisions: The South Australian Frontier and the Violence of Memory* (Kent Town, South Australia: Wakefield Press, 2001).

connections to land by referring to their 'grandmother's country'. It was 'grandmother's country' because people preferred to be silent about the grandfathers—the 'men who, in defiance of conditions so hard that to survive at all a man had to be equally hard in return (in defiance too of the niceties of law as it might be established fifteen hundred miles away, in Brisbane)'. Malouf continues:

> No one would ever have spoken of Matt Riley's 'grandfather'. That would have given something away that in those days was still buried where family history meant it to stay, in the realm of the unspoken. 'His grandmother's country' was a phrase that referred, without raising too precisely the question of blood, to the relationship a man might stand in to a particular tract of land, that went deeper and further back than legal possession. When used in town it had 'implications', easy to pick up but not to be articulated. A nod to the knowing.[91]

Malouf's formulation of implications that were easy to pick up, but not to be articulated, is an important insight into settler relationships with the land, and the ways in which silence and knowledge have reinforced each other. His notion that grandfathers are a subject to be avoided in rural discourse is highly relevant here, because he suggests that manhood—perhaps especially older definitions of manhood—has been linked to frontier violence.

The evidence of the Australian settler frontier casts light on the limited and gradual evolution of democracy, imperially and globally, in the period from the 1830s to the 1860s. Catherine Hall has pointed to the significance of gendered political connections between Jamaica and Britain in this period,[92] and I suggest that we need to do the same for the white settler colonies—as well as connections *among* the latter. Definitions of manhood forged on imperial frontiers circulated from colony to colony, bush to city, and colony to metropole, underscoring the need to recognize the existence of the more violent definitions, not least in the early to middle decades of the nineteenth century.

Historian Jock McCulloch has delineated the systematic use of violence within the labour system in southern Africa in the early twentieth century, and suggested that it was integral to definitions of masculinity and to colonial state formation. McCulloch makes the further point that, under colonialism, violent behaviour by white men was often sanctioned at least tacitly, and permitted by colonial officials and courts. Violence, he suggests, could coexist with concepts of civility.[93] I would add, linked to civility, that under colonialism, violence could be accepted as part of respectable manhood, especially if it remained understood but not articulated. In settler society, frontier violence was accepted within evolving definitions of manhood and hence political responsibility.

Nineteenth-century respectable manhood has typically been defined in terms of responsibility, self-discipline, independence, and reason. Moreover, responsible

---

[91] David Malouf, *Every Move You Make* (London: Chatto & Windus, 2006), pp. 39–40.

[92] Catherine Hall, *Civilizing Subjects: Metropole and Colony in the English Imagination, 1830–1867* (Chicago: University of Chicago Press, 2002).

[93] Jock McCulloch, 'Empire and Violence, 1900–1939', in Philippa Levine (ed.), *Gender and Empire* (Oxford: Oxford University Press, 2004), pp. 220–39.

government in the Australian colonies has not usually been considered in terms of gendered definitions. The evidence canvassed here suggests that perhaps we *should* think about the gendering of political responsibility, and how that was connected to social understandings forged in the bush. By the late 1850s in the Australian colonies, politically enfranchised manhood was a gendered status that cut across other distinctions, such as emancipated convict versus free immigrant, and squatter versus selector or labourer. Adult male suffrage occurred in the Australian colonies fully six decades before it was introduced in Britain in 1918, thus making colonial manhood an imperial benchmark to which the metropole had to aspire. Yet when we link frontier violence to gendered authority, perhaps political manhood itself needs to be seen as less about disciplined reason and more about colonial conquest.

7

The Australian Colonies and Imperial Crises: The Indian 'Mutiny' and the 'Maori Wars'

Australian settlers were interested in the world around them, an interest that extended well beyond economic matters of trade and labour. Many keenly followed imperial and global events through newspapers and personal correspondence. From such sources, we can reconstruct their sense of themselves as part of wider British imperialism, a shared enterprise in which the dispersed but determined British supported each other, not least against the empire's enemies. British colonies in the Indian Ocean and South East Asian region were connected through trade, the movement of troops and officials, charitable relief efforts, religious commonality, moral support, and—for the colonizers—racial solidarity. Settlers viewed the prosperity of the Australian colonies as dependent on British success elsewhere, even in the very years when they sought to gain greater autonomy through self-government. And even after they became self-governing, Australians saw a range of racial, religious, military, and economic reasons to participate actively in the empire's fights, perhaps especially those in their region.

By considering contemporary colonial press coverage of the 1857–58 war in India (the 'Mutiny') and the New Zealand Wars of the 1860s, we can glean evidence of how settlers understood imperial crises in their region, and how such coverage refracted views of their own actions in their newly matured self-governing colonies. In both cases, some detail of prior traffic and relations between colonies helps to set the context.

While the rebellious sepoys in India and the warlike Maori in New Zealand were undoubtedly the enemies in these nearly consecutive imperial battles, the language used to evaluate and condemn them differed. The Maori may have been 'savages' and only part of the way along the path towards civilization, and moreover probably headed towards extinction, but they did not excite the same religious vehemence and accusations of moral depravity as Indians. It was the Indians who were repeatedly condemned in the Australian press as fiends, monsters, scoundrels, idolators, and brutes. In part, this was because of the religious freight these accusations carried, the long-held Christian antagonism towards Muslims, as well as the more recent British aversion towards Hinduism. Christianity was foundational to British settler colonies in this period: Christian faith was openly assumed among settlers and a constant reference point. The nature of the wars was different, too. In India, the rebellious sepoys and their supporters were considered viciously ungrateful for all of the benefits of Christianity and civilization the British considered they had brought to the subcontinent, and the wisdom with which they thought they ruled. British conquest of India, it seemed, had been settled long before. In New Zealand, it was the land itself that was at stake—a frontier war for land and sovereignty that Australian settlers understood all too well, for all of their refusal to see Aboriginal fighters as comparable to the martial Maori. And New Zealand was essentially one of the Australian colonies, territory that had to be defended and the British rights to which had to be firmly established. New Zealand's fate seemed to be connected to that of the other Australasian colonies, even beyond its economic prosperity.

'A TAINT OF BLOOD IS ON THE BLAST': REACTIONS IN THE AUSTRALIAN COLONIES TO THE 'INDIAN MUTINY' OF 1857–58

In 1870, Adelaide settlers Nora Burney Young and her mother Lady Charlotte Bacon were much preoccupied with the possibilities and pitfalls of trading with India and Ceylon, through the ill-fated business enterprise of their brother and son Anthony, also known as Harley. In her youth Lady Charlotte had been immortalized as the 'Ianthe' to whom Byron dedicated his poem *Childe Harold's Pilgrimage*. Lady Charlotte's husband, the elder Anthony Bacon, had fought as an army officer at Waterloo, as well as serving in Spain, France, Gibraltar, and India. Despite his imperial service, Anthony Bacon landed in debtors' prison for a time, where he met fellow inmate Robert Gouger, and became an enthusiast for the planned colony of South Australia. Anthony Bacon himself never made it to South Australia, but three of their children and Lady Charlotte eventually did. The Bacons' son Anthony, or Harley, seems to have inherited his father's spendthrift tendencies.[1] In April 1870 Lady Charlotte wrote: '[Anthony] is gone to Ceylon, he sailed on the 19th with 52 horses, most of them his own, cows, flour, potatoes and fruit. If he arrives with his cargo safe I hope he will make a good thing of it'.[2] Nora, however, gave her sister in England a much less sanguine account of the same undertaking:

> Harley . . . has gone to India with horses. I am sure I hope he will succeed, but I very much fear because somehow he always makes a mistake in everything he undertakes and he's lost so much money, it must be acknowledged that Harley is not clever and he has no head for business transactions . . . [Mama] is in very good spirits just now,

---

[1] This detail of Lady Charlotte's early life, her marriage to Anthony Bacon, and a story of the coach she inherited from Lord Byron ending up in a chicken shed on Eyre Peninsula is from a paper by Jeff Nicholas, 'From Elinor to Ianthe: Byron's Barouche and an Outback Aussie Chook House', presented at the 'Robert Southey, Romantic Renaissances and Contexts' conference at Keswick, April 2010. I thank Jeff for allowing me to read and quote from this paper.

[2] State Library of South Australia, PRG 541/1/2 [this folder is letters from Lady Charlotte Bacon to her daughter Luz (Mrs Hext Boger) in Plymouth], letter 23 April 1870.

I think she anticipates a certain success with regard to the horses, but I am afraid she will be disappointed.[3]

In July Nora wrote again to her sister, now concerned that her brother's folly may have implicated the new governor of South Australia, Sir James Fergusson, who had arrived the year before:

We have heard from Harley, & I am afraid he has [not] done very well, he <u>says</u> he has made enough to pay expenses only, so I hope and trust Sir James will not be let in, his kindness was beyond that of even a brother, but I quite tremble for altho' Harley means well and would intend to repay he is so weak and foolish that he is led into all sorts of extravagances & all his money goes in rioting in the Town, if the Governor knew it I am sure he would be very vexed, for he is so particular and Harley does not even riot in a gentlemanlike way but goes about with such a low set. Pray don't mention this, burn my letter . . . People see Mama's weak points and to please her they praise Harley and she believes it all, and a man who is a known liar told her the other day that nothing could have exceeded the manner in which he transacted his business in Ceylon, the energy and knowledge of business he showed was surprising and dear Mama tells this to everybody and I feel so sorry to hear her because I know people smile at it afterwards, for Harley has no notion of business . . .[4]

By September, Nora's anxiety was focused on whether and how much of the governor's money Harley had lost in his failed trade speculation:

I have not been able to find out from Mama whether Harley was able to return <u>all</u> Sir James' money, she will not say a word except that he did <u>himself</u> very little good. I want so much to know, but she is so touchy about him, I dare not say anything, if he has lost any of the money and I knew it, I would never show my face at Government House again. I think with such advantages he might have done better, but you know Harley <u>is not</u> clever.[5]

If Nora was worried about her own social acceptance at Government House, Sir James's involvement in the speculation was not based on ignorance of colonial mercantile relations: he had served in London as under-secretary for India from 1866 to 1867.

Harley Bacon's undertaking was only one instance of trading ventures between India and the Australian colonies. Beside merchants like Harley, and officials such as Sir James Fergusson, there were many other connections between the Australian colonies and India in the nineteenth century. We are steadily learning about the nature and extent of colonial traffic between them, what has been called the

[3] State Library of South Australia, PRG 541/2/2, Letters from Mrs Nora Burney Young (wife of Charles Burney Young and daughter of Lady Charlotte Bacon) to her sister Luz (Mrs Hext Boger who lived at Plymouth, Devon), 1866–1872, letter 24 April 1870.

[4] State Library of South Australia, PRG 541/2/4, Letter from Mrs Nora Burney Young, Walkerville, 17 July 1870.

[5] State Library of South Australia, PRG 541/2/5, Letter from Mrs Nora Burney Young, Walkerville, 10 September [1870?].

'surprising history of connections between India and Australia'.[6] Numerous Australian settlers had direct experience of India, such as Captain Charles Bagot, whose prior military career included South America, the Cape of Good Hope, Mauritius, and India.[7] In late 1830 a Hobart settler, Captain Bamber, was described as having 'been much in both Indies'.[8] As noted in Chapter 5, while the mid-nineteenth-century migration advocate Caroline Chisholm is enshrined in Australian popular memory and her image has graced the nation's currency, the familiar story omits the fact that her husband Archibald served in the East India Company army and that they spent six years in India before moving to Australia. Another example is John Hutt, one of the early governors of Western Australia (1839–46), who had previously spent thirteen years in India working for the East India Company.

Others knew indirectly about connections between the Australian colonies and India, such as trade and the importation of Indian labourers. Some Indians (as well as Malagasy and people from other parts of the Indian Ocean region as well as further afield) arrived as convicts; and from 1816 onwards groups of labourers were brought from India under indenture. Chapter 3 in this volume shows how widespread by the 1840s were schemes that brought Indian indentured labourers to the Australian colonies.

There were organizational connections too, such as the short-lived Australian Association of Bengal, established in 1837 by Charles Prinsep to stimulate trade and migration between Australia and India, which had its head office in Calcutta and branches in the Australian colonies.[9] From the eighteenth century, generations of the Prinsep family were involved in the East India Company and the British Raj. Subsequently, various family members visited the Australian colonies, established pastoral properties in Western Australia and Van Diemen's Land, and some settled.[10] Like Harley Bacon in South Australia, horses were a key part of the Prinsep trade between Australia and India.

While Harley Bacon's trade with India occurred after the 'Mutiny' or war of 1857–58, many connections preceded it, so it is not surprising that the Australian colonial press followed the events closely and in growing detail. In the 1840s, the *South Australian Register*'s interest in India, for example, had extended to occasional articles on political and military events. In 1857 the frequency and extent of Australian press coverage of India escalated suddenly and dramatically.

---

[6] For example, Margaret Allen, '"A fine type of Hindoo" meets "the Australian type": British Indians in Australia and diverse masculinities', in Desley Deacon, Penny Russell, and Angela Woollacott (eds), *Transnational Ties: Australian Lives in the World* (Canberra: Australia National University E-Press, 2008), pp. 41–56; Joyce Westrip and Peggy Holroyde, *Colonial Cousins: A Surprising History of Connections Between India and Australia* (Kent Town, South Australia: Wakefield Press, 2010).

[7] *A holograph memoir of captain Charles Hervey Bagot of the 87th. Regiment* (Adelaide, 1942).

[8] Canon Burton, 'The Diary of Anne Whatley', *The Western Australian Historical Society Journal and Proceedings* Vol. 1, Part VII (1930): 33.

[9] Westrip and Holroyde, *Colonial Cousins*, p. 254.

[10] Malcolm Allbrook, '"A triple Empire...united under one dominion": Charles Prinsep's Schemes for Exporting Indian Labour to Australia', *South Asia: Journal of South Asian Studies* (2012), DOI:10.1080/00856401.2011.649676, pp. 1–23.

In May 1857, Indian soldiers stationed at Meerut near Delhi mutinied, killing their officers, and all the other Britons they could find. They set fire to their cantonment, and then marched to Delhi to proclaim the Mughal ruler the head of Hindostan (or India). When word spread, similar uprisings were staged by sepoys (Indian soldiers) in other parts of northern India. The rebellion was a protest against the British presence and rule in India, and was largely sparked by the way that the British were running their army. While problems in the army were the specific cause of unrest, it was fuelled by deep resentment about British power, British intervention, and British economic and political control in India—in short, resentment against British imperialism. It took the British two years to quash completely the uprising and the ensuing rebellions. In those two years, the British fought hard to regain control, even though the spate of rebellions was limited to parts of northern India. A number of peasants rebelled in support of the sepoys, and in the cities of Delhi and Lucknow support for the uprising was such that there was extensive fighting and destruction.

In the wake of the uprising, the *South Australian Register* printed stories arriving from Calcutta newspapers, the *Lahore Chronicle*, Singapore newspapers, the *Friend of India*, and the *Bombay Telegraph*. When the news of the uprising first reached the Australian colonies, initial reactions were to downplay its significance. By July 1857 the *Register* editorialized on the crisis, considering that although 'the disaffection appears to be more widespread than was at first imagined', the likely outcome would mostly consist of punishment of the Indian troops involved, which it hoped would not be too extremely severe—a merciful attitude that later evaporated.[11] In September 1857, its tone had shifted: the Indian troops involved were now called 'the monsters engaged in the recent inhuman butcheries', yet the paper pointed to the vast size of the British colonies in India, the small proportion of Englishmen compared to Indians, and corruption in the British administration. 'The extension of our Indian frontier, like the extension of our African frontier, has involved the British Empire in accumulated expenses, and has rendered the administration of its colonial government infinitely more difficult than before', it opined.[12]

As the events wore on, and the fighting and bloodshed continued, the Australian press grew more critical of the sepoys. By October 1857, the *Register*'s tone was irate.

> It may, indeed, be useless to dwell upon these horrors, but is it right to dismiss from our minds the consideration of the unutterable sufferings of our fellow-subjects? Ought we not, even in these remote dependencies of the British Crown, to evince some measure of sympathy with the unhappy victims of this most fiendish rebellion? Had the sepoys merely united to exterminate the European population, brutal as it would have been to murder inoffensive women and children, our feelings of indigna-tion would have been less intense than they now are; but to practise every conceivable refinement of slow torture upon shrinking women and harmless babes is so utterly inhuman that its perpetrators have no claim to any other treatment than would be awarded to wolves and tigers.

[11] 'India and Persia', *South Australian Register* 14 July 1857, p. 2.
[12] 'The Indian Mutiny', *South Australian Register* 10 September 1857, p. 2.

The paper continued with a lurid account of the violence at Kanpur/Cawnpore, with highly detailed stories of extreme violence supposedly inflicted by sepoys on British children, and the rape and mutilation of British women, before admitting that 'a great degree of uncertainty characterizes all the accounts received from India'.[13]

Colonial reporting reflected a sense of direct involvement. In the Sydney press there was a detailed accounting of 'our' actions and 'our' losses and victories:

> the mutinous and rebellious spirit is confined to the pampered and Brahminised Bengal Army and to some few of the Mahomedans. The people of India, those of the Punjaub, and the armies of Madras, Bombay, and the Punjaub, seem to appreciate the benefits of our rule and remain loyal. We firmly believe that this outbreak will but consolidate our power.

The settlers' willingness and ability to identify with the imperial cause in India to the extent of calling it 'ours' derived in good part from their birth in or close familial connections to Britain, as well as their colonial belonging to the wider entity of the empire. Moreover, their sense of military, political, and cultural participation in the empire was the product of earlier wars, which they had also followed with interest. In the years 1839–42, settlers in Australia were well aware of Britain's war with China, the 'Opium War' that resulted in Britain's annexation of Hong Kong, and during which some British troops were diverted from elsewhere in the region. As well, there were Britain's unsuccessful military campaigns in Afghanistan in 1838–42, the 1830s, 1840s, and 1850s wars in southern Africa, and, of course, in 1854–56, along with the rest of the empire, settlers were engrossed by the events of the Crimean War against Russia. Around the same time as they became captivated by news of the events in India, Sydney's citizens welcomed the 77th British Regiment, which had distinguished itself and suffered heavy losses in fighting in Crimea. In late September 1857 the regiment was warmly welcomed when it arrived at Circular Quay and marched through the city, and a few days later thrilled a crowd of eight thousand on the Domain by parading, firing volleys, and repelling imaginary foes.[14]

These wars of empire, the comings and goings of the troops stationed in Australia, and the newspaper coverage of Britain's victories, defeats and, in some instances, hostages of war, built a shared sense of investment in the expanding empire and the necessity of the military force on which territorial conquest depended. Residents in the Australian colonies absorbed lessons of the hostilities inherent to colonialism, and thus could be philosophical about the loyalty or otherwise of colonial subjects elsewhere, such as in 1857 India:

> If we have painful proof that disaffection and hatred of our rule are widely spread in some quarters, we are not without evidence that in others a loyal and intense abhorrence is felt of the treasonable and murderous outbreaks which have occurred.[15]

---

[13] 'The Indian Mutiny', *South Australian Register* 24 October 1857, p. 2.

[14] Craig Wilcox, *Red Coat Dreaming: How colonial Australia embraced the British Army* (Cambridge: Cambridge University Press, 2009), pp. 53–4.

[15] 'India. More About the Mutiny', *Sydney Morning Herald* 14 July 1857.

For settlers in the Australian colonies, the belief that British military supremacy in India constituted 'our rule' shows at once their identification with imperial rule by force, and a sense that such enforcement was morally justified in Australia and India.

As the war in India continued, the tone in the colonial press shifted to vengeance and bloodthirstiness, initially reflected in the following excerpt from the *Age* in Melbourne, which was billed as 'Extract of a letter from an officer in India to his family residing at Sydney, dated Masuliptam, 3rd and 17th July, 1857':

> At Lucknow the Commissioner is hanging the mutineers by dozens. He has a brigade of guns at the bottom of the gallows; he has a few Europeans, and he is keeping some thirty or forty thousands of them in awe . . . The number of Europeans the mutineers have murdered is enormous, and the poor ladies, the scoundrels first dishonoured and then put to a painful death; but the Madras European Regiment now in Bengal is avenging them, they are styled the 'English Bull Dogs,' and well they deserve the name. There were only 140 of them, and 40 Bengal Artillery, against two regiments of infantry, and one of cavalry, and they scarcely left a man of them alive; it was a dreadful slaughter . . .[16]

Exaggerated and false stories of the rape and torture of British girls and women became integral to British narratives of the war. Stories of interracial sexual assault were told and retold to justify harsh revenge in terms of defending British honour and virtue, and to deflect attention away from British military setbacks, losses, and vulnerability.[17]

Religious bigotry came to the fore, showing the tight interlinkage between colonial security anxieties, Christian hostility towards Hinduism and Islam, and Australia's geographical location. By July 1858, the *South Australian Register* openly displayed racial and religious bias, alleging that even the most horrific stories from India gained credibility from 'our knowledge of Asiatic cruelty', and the way power is 'wielded by depraved idolators and the sensual disciples of Mahomet'.[18] Press coverage from Victoria also highlights the role of religion in Australian reactions. The *Age* on 8 July 1857 printed a letter from a Dr D. C. Mackie whom it described as 'a gentleman well known in commercial circles'. Writing from Calcutta on 3 June 1857, Mackie asserted that when the 'three native regiments at Meerut' first revolted, a 'general massacre of the Christians took place'. '[N]o less than nine other regiments at other stations have likewise mutinied, and are on their way to join the main body', Mackie continued:

> Many causes have been assigned for the revolt, but I believe it may be traced to the religious fanaticism of both Mussulman and Hindoo, acted upon by intriguing and vindictive ministers and emissaries of the fallen states that have of late years been taken possession of by the East India Company.

---

[16] The *Age* 24 September 1857.

[17] On this, see Nancy L. Paxton, *Writing Under the Raj: Gender, Race, and Rape in the British Colonial Imagination, 1830–1947* (New Brunswick, NJ: Rutgers University Press, 1999) and Jenny Sharpe, *Allegories of Empire: The Figure of Woman in the Colonial Text* (Minneapolis: University of Minnesota Press, 1993).

[18] 'Sepoy Atrocities and the Indian Relief Fund', *South Australian Register* 2 July 1858, p. 2.

And in September the Sydney press agreed:

> The late insurrection is said to be connected with religious revenge. The Mahometan population are in India, as everywhere else, fanatics, and are capable of enormous treachery and cruelty: the Hindoos are scarcely less so. The British Government has been tender to their prejudices—quite as much as any Christian Power can be without infamy.[19]

A further issue was that of the Australian colonies' own military security and defence. Imperial troops were despatched from the Australian colonies to fight in India; some colonial press reports reveal a feeling of vulnerability when the British troops stationed there left. In October 1857 the *Age* expressed nervous acquiescence: 'The troops, it is said, are going to leave us; and we shall be "utterly unprotected." We are going to be forsaken by our armed defenders... Her Majesty's troops are wanted in India. It is proper and imperative that they should go there without delay'. Though imperial troops would return, they would leave for good in 1870. The anxiety expressed in 1857 was thus a harbinger of what would become a larger concern.

> Why, unorganised, unarmed, and in great part ignorant of the use of arms, as we are now when the soldiery are withdrawn, a fleet or two of Malay desperadoes or Chinese pirates could burn our outports, and carry off the shipping in Portland Bay, or Warrnambool, or even in Hobson's Bay itself, if the steam sloop were away. At any rate, it will not do, in the future, to be dependent on the few companies of soldiery the mother country can spare us. There is no saying what eventualities may come about from the progress of the Russians in Asia; or from these doings in India; and it will be every way judicious to establish a national militia in time, for it is a thing which cannot be organised in a day. There is, indeed, a want of dignity and self-respect in a free people not having done so before now.[20]

On 2 August 1858 the British Parliament passed the Government of India Act, transferring all the rights the East India Company had previously enjoyed in India to the Crown, that is, to Queen Victoria and the British government. A cabinet-level position was created: the Secretary of State for India. Perhaps the most pervasive impact of the war was in the increasingly bitter and tense race relations that would characterize the British Raj for the rest of its existence. On both sides, memories and stories of the acts of violence during 1857–58 were constantly replayed. On the British side, lurid stories circulated from the beginning, so that events such as the killings at Kanpur/Cawnpore were told in highly melodramatic and untrue ways, that exaggerated the numbers dead and the way they were treated. Memoirs, fiction, and plays that recycled such stories were produced by the British for the rest of the nineteenth century, replete with the hyperbolic narratives of interracial sexual assault.[21] 'Mutiny' stories and representations continued to

---

[19] *Sydney Morning Herald* 12 September 1857.
[20] The *Age* [Melbourne], 17 October 1857.
[21] Paxton, *Writing Under the Raj* and Sharpe, *Allegories of Empire*.

circulate around the empire, proving a touchstone of imperial culture to which settlers in the Australian colonies related.

IMPERIAL LOYALTY: CAROLINE CARLETON

One kind of response to the bloodshed in India was overt demonstrations of imperial loyalty and British fealty. Caroline Carleton (1819–74) arrived as a settler in Adelaide in 1839 with her husband Charles, who had served as ship's surgeon on their vessel the *Prince Regent*. Caroline Carleton undertook projects such as setting up schools, but she is famous as the author of the lyrics of 'The Song of Australia' (see Fig. 7.1). Carleton wrote the lyrics for an 1859 competition run by the Gawler Institute; the music was written by German immigrant Carl Linger. In 1977 'The Song of Australia' was one of the four shortlisted choices for a new national anthem, to replace 'God Save the Queen'; it did not win, but apparently it was the most popular choice in South Australia where even then children learnt it at school. Its highly patriotic stanzas run:

Fig. 7.1 Caroline Carleton, *c.*1830, portrait.
Courtesy of the State Library of South Australia. SLSA: B 6675.

There is a land where summer skies
Are gleaming with a thousand dyes,
Blending in witching harmonies, in harmonies;
And grassy knoll, and forest height,
Are flushing in the rosy light,
And all above is azure bright—
Australia! Australia! Australia!

There is a land where, floating free,
From mountain top to girdling sea,
A proud flag waves exultingly, exultingly;
And Freedom's sons the banners bear,
No shackled slave can breathe the air,
Fairest of Britain's daughters fair—
Australia!

There is a land where honey flows,
Where laughing corn luxuriant grows,
Land of the myrtle and the rose, land of the rose;
On hill and plain the clust'ring vine
Is gushing out with purple wine,
And cups are quaffed to thee and thine—
Australia!

While some Australians today may know the first verse of the song, perhaps particularly the lines 'There is a land where summer skies/ Are gleaming with a thousand dyes', few would know the words of all five verses. Even fewer would know that Carleton's patriotic and pro-imperial poems included at least two 1850s poems about the 'Indian Mutiny'. One, entitled 'The Cawnpore Massacre' (about events in Kanpur), includes the lines:

The music of the sunlit wave.
With its crest of rainbow light,
Sounds like the footfalls of the past,
On memory's tablet bright.

This sadden's heart can only hear,
In the music of the sea,
A wailing from a far-off land,
A dirge like melody.

To fancy's ear the murm'ring waves
Echo a funeral strain,
And chant a requiem for the souls
Of the Cawnpore victims slain –

The fresh'ning winds fan the glad brow;
Sweet is the evening breeze,
That gently stirs the pensile leaves
Of the silvery wattle trees.

But a taint of blood is on the blast,
A death-shriek fills the ear,
A tortured mother's bitter cry
Of agonized despair! –

In February 1858 an 'Indian Relief Fund' was set up in South Australia at the request of the Governor. Carleton wrote another poem, simply entitled 'Lines', in support of the 'Appeal of the Committee of the Indian Relief Fund to the Australian Colonies'. Its first stanzas ran:

> Tho' we must tread the circling earth
> Till half its space be traversed o'er,
> Before our longing eyes can greet
> The white cliff of Britannia's shore.

> And tho' beneath Australian skies,
> Our children pluck the clust'ring vine
> With throbbing hearts we proudly own –
> Britain, our fealty is thine!

> And when the quivering needle points
> To woe and danger, threat'ning thee –
> The answering chord responsive owns
> Th' electric touch of sympathy.[22]

These lines, and Carleton's desire to help the Indian Relief Fund, speak to the connection at least some Australians felt to the imperial effort to put down the uprising in India. The South Australian fund to help victims of the 'Mutiny' had similar counterparts in the other Australian colonies. Such relief fundraising efforts were widespread in the nineteenth century; as Christina Twomey and Andrew May have shown in their work on fundraising for the 1870s Indian famine, while these campaigns invoked Christian philanthropy, in Australia they also depended on racially nuanced articulations of empire loyalty and compassion.[23]

FROM INDIA TO HORNET BANK, QUEENSLAND: RACIAL CONNECTIONS AND RELIGIOUS DIMENSIONS

Perhaps not surprisingly given the timing, when one of the worst massacres of white settlers by Aborigines occurred in southern Queensland in October 1857, Queensland settlers drew parallels with the Indian uprising. As discussed in Chapter 6 in this volume, on 27 October 1857 a large group of Aborigines attacked the Hornet Bank Station homestead of the Fraser family on the Dawson River in south-central Queensland, killed all the males except one who survived, raped the mother and two of her daughters, and then killed the women and children. In sum, eleven white people, including several of the Fraser family's employees, were killed.

---

[22] Rae Webling, *A Song for Australia: Caroline Carleton—her Poems and Biography 1820–1874* (Privately published, 1977).
[23] Christina Twomey and Andrew J. May, 'Australian Responses to the Indian Famine, 1876–78: Sympathy, Photography and the British Empire', *Australian Historical Studies* Vol. 43, Issue 2 (June 2012): 233–52.

Thomas Murray-Prior, the neighbouring station-owner, was involved in the reprisals. A good portion of the surviving evidence of the extensive reprisals conducted by settlers and the Native Police comes from Murray-Prior's papers and the published memoirs of his daughter Rosa Campbell Praed. Gordon Reid has suggested, based on his research, that 'at least 150 Aborigines died; the total may have been 300'.[24]

Connections drawn by settlers between the actions of the Aboriginal people in the Dawson River area, and the sepoys in India, served to justify brutal reprisals. The Jiman [Yee-man] and other Aboriginal people in the region had been under pressure for some time from the settlers encroaching on their lands and taking them as pastoral properties. There had been widespread rape, assault, and abuse of Aboriginal women, and numerous instances of unprovoked violence by the white settlers. Yet the settlers cast the attack on Hornet Bank Station as murderous and treacherous, in similar terms to those used about the sepoys. While the Queensland press was divided in their responses to the killing of the Frasers, with at least one paper calling for fairness towards the Aborigines, the *Moreton Bay Free Press* commented:

> Little did we imagine that when reading the horrible indecencies inflicted upon, and the subsequent butchery of, one-hundred-and-seventy-nine women and children at Cawnpore, that a tragedy of similar nature was being enacted at our very doors.[25]

In November 1857 after Delhi was taken by the sepoys and their supporters in the Indian rebellion, the paper *Bell's Life in Sydney* drew parallels, saying that 'in dealing with the present race of ruthless barbarians belonging to the Upper Dawson, we must adopt the motto of "an eye for an eye, and a tooth for a tooth"'.[26] In December 1857 a settler in a neighbouring Queensland region wrote to his brother in Sydney 'that the blacks in his district were harbouring the Dawson tribe who had been committing atrocities equalled only by those of the Sepoys in India'.[27] In early 1858, as news reached the Australian colonies of the events in Kanpur that became known as the 'Cawnpore massacre' in which British men, women and children were killed, parallels continued to be drawn between the events in India and the events at Hornet Bank Station.[28] As the reprisals against Aborigines in southern Queensland dragged on through those months, these parallels and the racial and religious logic that supported them were used to validate the continued and extensive killings. Thomas Murray-Prior, who as noted earlier was a participant in the reprisals, would later call it 'eighteen months of warfare' and 'an anxious time for us'.[29]

[24] Gordon Reid, *A Nest of Hornets: The Massacre of the Fraser Family at Hornet Bank Station, Central Queensland, 1857, and Related Events* (Melbourne: Oxford University Press, 1982), p. ix.
[25] *Moreton Bay Free Press* 18 November 1857, quoted in Reid, *A Nest of Hornets*, p. 74.
[26] *Bell's Life in Sydney*, 5 December 1857, quoted in Reid, *A Nest of Hornets*, p. 74.
[27] Walter Lamb, Sydney, 14 December 1857, to Col. Sec., NSA Col. Sec. Special Bundle 4/719.2, 57/5004, quoted in Reid, *A Nest of Hornets*, p. 75.
[28] Reid, *A Nest of Hornets*, p. 94.
[29] Murray-Prior, Serocold, McArthur, Pigott, Bungaban, 3 December 1857, to Col. Sec., 57/4995, in Oxley Library, COL, mfm, A2/39, quoted in Reid, *A Nest of Hornets*, p. 93.

For settlers in Queensland, the primary reason for their protracted vigilante violence was to establish their hold over the land. They told colonial officials that as a recently and sparsely settled region they were vulnerable to Aboriginal attack, and complained about the inadequate numbers and inefficiency of the Native Police forces. They believed, with some reason, that had they not acted in reprisal, comparable subsequent attacks would have been made on other stations. Racial reasoning, too, was invoked to justify the disproportionate killing of Aborigines. Gender and sexuality were part of the mix, with the rape of the Fraser females considered a horrific part of the attacks, and this, too, was a link to the greatly exaggerated stories of the sexual assault of British women emanating from India. As Jessie Mitchell has contended, Queensland newspaper reports linking Aboriginal attacks to India show 'how gory tales from Kanpur and Delhi had become part of an Australian vernacular'.[30] Interestingly, Thomas Murray-Prior made an issue in his reprisal party that Aboriginal women and children must be spared as far as possible—though overall in the reprisals they were not spared.

The connections drawn between Queensland and India also underscore the significance of religion, as do the press reports of events in India quoted earlier. Major General Sir Henry Havelock was cast as a virtuous British hero in the events of the Indian war of 1857–58, particularly the fighting at Lucknow. Graham Dawson suggests that the war did much to promote the idea of the 'Christian soldier' in British imperial culture, linking religion and imperial militarism in a way that they had not been linked in the preceding period—such as during the decades of the 1820s to 1840s when religion was more overtly connected to the humanitarian circles of the empire. Such a connection had not been possible in the Crimean War earlier in the 1850s, because the enemy was Christian. Dawson argues that: 'A 62-year-old man on the brink of retirement after thirty years as a career officer, and a practising Baptist who proselytized among the rank-and-file in the Indian Army, Henry Havelock was an unlikely hero'.[31] Havelock's death not long after his troops entered Lucknow contributed to his heroic status, despite the fact that he died of dysentery. This popular shaping of the evangelizing Havelock as the Christian hero of the 'Mutiny' underscores the extent to which Christian hatred of Hindus and Muslims fuelled British sentiments. And the role of religion in justifying the bloody suppression of the 'Mutineers' in India needs to be taken into account in the links drawn with Queensland.

POLITICAL MEANINGS AND LEGACIES

The timing of the 'Mutiny' was significant, just after four of the Australian colonies became self-governing, a maturation that Queensland would also soon attain.

---

[30] Jessie Mitchell, ' "Great difficulty in knowing where the frontier ceases": Violence, governance, and the spectre of India in early Queensland', *Journal of Australian Colonial History* Vol. 15 (2013), p. 59.

[31] Graham Dawson, *Soldier Heroes: British Adventure, Empire and the Imagining of Masculinities* (London: Routledge, 1994), p. 80.

As discussed earlier, the British Parliament enacted constitutions for responsible government in the Australian colonies as follows: New South Wales, Victoria, and Tasmania all in 1855, South Australia in 1856, and Queensland in 1859. While Western Australia was not given responsible government until 1890, this clustering of the achievement of self-government in the other colonies, with male suffrage also achieved in most colonies during these years, shows the 1850s as an important time of transition in the Australian colonies. With self-government, Australian settlers asserted their direct authority over much of the continent, diminishing the control of the British imperial government. The events at Hornet Bank brought home to the new government in New South Wales and those looking towards political separation for Queensland, the resistance they faced from Aboriginal people. Just as the reaction in British India was one of astonishment that Indian subjects could 'mutiny' against their imperial rulers, the use of similar terms in Queensland—such as atrocity, outrage, and murder—shows a comparable sense of authority challenged, just when it had been constitutionally established.

Various scholars have pointed to the mid-nineteenth century decades as a time when the empire was envisaged as an interconnected body politic. Kirsty Reid shows how visions of imperial unity combined with metaphors of bodily and familial health in the movement to end convict transportation.[32] And Catherine Hall has traced imperial interconnections in the shift she asserts occurred, shown in relations between Britain and Jamaica, from 1830s humanitarian concerns to the 1860s dominance of racial thinking and hierarchies.[33]

Australian reactions to the Indian Rebellion of 1857–58 reveal the strength of imperial identity among settlers, as well as the significance of religion as much as race to that identity. Approval of the violent suppression of the uprising in India coalesced with approval, tacit or otherwise, of the violent dispossession of Aboriginal people. Racial and religious hatreds, seemingly, could be directed simultaneously within and without, perhaps thus reinforcing each other. Passionate condemnation of the sepoys in India was fuelled by settler fears: at some level, the threat to the British Raj and the departure of troops for India may have implicitly challenged the stability and prospects of the British colonies in Australia. Yet the virulent expression of imperial identity also showed a confidence in imperial strength and its martial character that underpinned the settler hold on the Australian continent.

The lessons Australians drew from the 'Mutiny' were long-lived and influential. Decades later, in the prelude to Federation, Alfred Deakin, one of its major advocates and future prime minister, continued to write about the events of 1857–58 as a time of dramatic imperial crisis that bore directly on the Australian colonies. Deakin, who visited India for several months from November 1890 to February 1891, wrote a series of newspaper articles and two books about the

---

[32] Kirsty Reid, *Gender, Crime and Empire: Convicts, Settlers and the State in Early Colonial Australia* (Manchester: Manchester University Press, 2007), esp. Ch. 5.

[33] Catherine Hall, *Civilising Subjects: Metropole and Colony in the English Imagination, 1830–1867* (Chicago: University of Chicago Press, 2002).

subcontinent. His second volume *Temple and Tomb in India* (1893) dealt largely with Indian architecture, religion, and monuments, yet its final and longest chapter was devoted to 'The Mutiny'. In this chapter, Deakin expatiates on the nature of British rule in India, the causes of the 'Mutiny', its events, and responsibilities on both sides. At one point he acknowledges that, while the British version of events recounted in several well-known histories will be familiar to his readers, there was another version, that was 'repeated by groups under the banyans, hissed in anger at secret meetings of savage sectaries, or whispered under the breath in the recesses of the bazaar'.[34] He contends that the events of 1857–58 shaped the Raj: 'To comprehend the mutiny one must realize modern India. To comprehend British India one must realize the mutiny'.[35] Despite his recognition that Indians have their own versions of the events, Deakin's summary is that the war was an inexorable assertion of British might and rule in India, a rule that should continue: 'the country has been won by the sword, is still held by the sword, and can only be retained by the sword . . . [W]hat is certain is not only that there must always be a supremacy in India, but that it must be the supremacy of arms'.[36]

He cast the British in India at the time of his writing in the 1890s as imperial heroes: 'a handful of daring whites, with their backs to the sea, the source of their supplies, and their faces set stedfastly [sic] inland, determined by indomitable courage, inexhaustible resource, and superhuman energy to dominate the mighty empire and master its innumerable hordes'.[37] Those who fought the 'Mutiny' in the 1850s had been perhaps even more gloriously heroic: 'The days of chivalry could not furnish a longer list of glorious achievements than the mutiny, nor the Crusades a more brilliant episode in the conflict between East and West'.[38] Yet Deakin concludes the book by arguing that the British in Australia will be strengthened by contact with 'the great nations of the East' as well as 'abler rivals'. Australians must be open to such contact: 'Far away as at first the Hindus appear in origin, foreign in blood, strange in practices, and remote in aims, they are not in reality without kinship to us. Politically and intellectually, as well as geographically, we are already allied'.[39] But, in Deakin's view, kinship and contact was as far as things should go: immigration was out of the question. As Ipsita Sengupta has suggested, Deakin's narrative cast heroic Anglo-Saxon imperial men against treacherous Hindu and Muhammadan natives in such a way as to make the story of the 'Mutiny' part of the reasoning for the exclusively white Australia that was then his major objective.[40]

[34] Alfred Deakin, *Temple and Tomb in India* (Melbourne: Melville, Mullen and Slade, 1893), p. 131.

[35] Deakin, *Temple and Tomb*, p. 131.   [36] Deakin, *Temple and Tomb*, pp. 129–30.

[37] Deakin, *Temple and Tomb*, p. 130.   [38] Deakin, *Temple and Tomb*, p. 145.

[39] Deakin, *Temple and Tomb*, pp. 150–1.

[40] Ipsita Sengupta, 'Entangled: Deakin in India', in David Walker and Agnieszka Sobocinska (eds), *Australia's Asia: From Yellow Peril to Asian Century* (Crawley, Western Australia: UWA Publishing, 2012), p. 67.

THE NEW ZEALAND WARS OR 'THE MAORI WARS'

The war of 1857–58 in India was far from the only imperial event covered by colonial papers such as the *South Australian Register*. The paper had earlier covered the so-called 'Kaffir wars' in South Africa in the 1840s and early 1850s with unambiguous bias against the indigenous Africans and the Dutch-descended Afrikaners. In 1846 as well as later in 1860, the *Register* followed in detail the wars over land and sovereignty in New Zealand, frequently expressing great respect and sympathy for Maori, while ultimately supporting British right and British might. In these ways, the *South Australian Register* was representative of the Australian colonial press, whose coverage of the 1860s New Zealand Wars provides us with insight into how settlers viewed the colony across the Tasman Sea, its relationship to the Australian colonies, and the difficult shared questions surrounding land possession, sovereignty, and the indigenous inhabitants.

Traffic between the Australian and New Zealand ports and settlements was integral to colonial life in the early to mid-nineteenth century. It is salient now to recall that colonial residents did not conceive of Australia and New Zealand in their current national forms until significantly later. In this period, British settlements on the Australian continent, and on the islands of Van Diemen's Land and New Zealand, shared their regional location as well as their status as burgeoning British colonies. In terms of geography and trade, at least, New Zealand was not unlike Van Diemen's Land. Indeed, in the early years of the century, colonial inhabitants would have conceptualized their region mostly in terms of ports, sailing routes, and connections that could be made for trade, or as stops en route to destinations further afield. By the mid-nineteenth century more fully developed colonies with hinterlands formed their regional world. In the mid-nineteenth century and later, New Zealand was commonly represented as one of the Australian or Australasian colonies; in fact, when it was first officially established in 1840 it was briefly part of New South Wales. British settlers in Australia were also aware of the Dutch East Indies colonies to their northwest, and that Batavia (now Jakarta) was an important regional entrepôt, as well as the various colonial ports elsewhere in South East Asia. The British colonies in the area were bound by ties of imperial loyalty, language, and culture that separated them from the Dutch and French colonies in the region.

New Zealand's first European settlements sprang from the Australian colonies as trading bases, Christian evangelical expeditions, and as safe havens for escaped or former convicts, some of whom survived as beachcombers. Traffic back and forth across the Tasman began shortly after the arrival of the First Fleet; by 1793 Australia had its first Maori visitors.[41] The first missionaries to establish their presence in New Zealand were Anglican, particularly the Rev. Samuel Marsden who was based at Parramatta. As early as 1814 Marsden developed relationships with Maori from the Bay of Islands in the North Island, hosting a group at

---

[41] Philippa Mein Smith, *A Concise History of New Zealand* (Cambridge: Cambridge University Press, 2005), p. 29.

Parramatta, and then in turn establishing a new mission settlement at Kerikeri from December that year.[42]

The islands of New Zealand, including the many smaller ones, such as those around Van Diemen's Land, in Bass Strait and Kangaroo Island, were all enmeshed in the sealing and whaling trades that plied the southern seas in these decades, from as early as the 1790s. Whaling ships were global enterprises, often run by captains whose home bases could be in America or Europe. The sailors who crewed the ships and performed the arduous and dangerous work of whaling and sealing were a polyglot mix of ethnicities from Europe, the Americas, and around the Indian and Pacific oceans. Within this global mix of mariners, Aboriginal and Maori sailors worked and travelled between the Australian and New Zealand ports as well as back and forth further around the region.

We know, for example, of the story of Tommy Chaseland, a mixed-race man born on the Hawkesbury River of New South Wales in the late 1790s to an Aboriginal mother and ex-convict English father. Tommy Chaseland grew up among the shipbuilding and boating industries on the Hawkesbury, and by 1817 joined a ship's crew headed for Bass Strait and Van Diemen's Land on a sealing voyage. Later voyages took him to Kangaroo Island, the Marquesas, Tonga, New Caledonia, and elsewhere in the Pacific. Chaseland was apparently famous for his physical strength, extraordinary long-sightedness, and abilities as a sailor and whaler. Around 1824 Chaseland decided to settle on Stewart Island at the southern tip of New Zealand's South Island, and spent the rest of his life in this vicinity, working as a whaler and sealer, ship's pilot, and interpreter, and managing whaling stations. He married, sequentially, two local Maori women.[43] Chaseland's story exemplifies the mobility among the Australian and New Zealand settlements in this early period, and the culturally rich fabric of their interconnections.

In the 1840s and 1850s, residents in the Australian colonies, perhaps especially those in South Australia and at Australind, would have been aware of the systematic colonization schemes of the New Zealand Company, and its ventures at Port Nicholson (Wellington), Wanganui, New Plymouth, Nelson, Canterbury, and Otago. The success or otherwise of the Wakefieldian colonial experiment was a tie that joined these scattered Antipodean settlements. Even for those in the non-Wakefieldian colonies, these organized schemes partly represented the prospects for settler society in the region and to that extent would have been of interest.

British settlers frequently crossed the Tasman Sea back and forth in the middle decades of the nineteenth century. Despite their name, 'settlers' were often peripatetic, following leads, opportunities, or family members from place to place, or hoping to do better in a new locale than they had in the last. In the 1850s and 1860s British, European, Chinese, and other men traversed the Pacific and the Tasman pursuing the serial gold rushes in California, New South Wales, Victoria, and Otago. When gold digging and panning proved unrewarding, men set up in

---

[42] Mein Smith, *A Concise History*, p. 32.
[43] Lynette Russell, *Roving Mariners: Australian Aboriginal Whalers and Sealers in the Southern Oceans, 1790–1870* (Albany: State University of New York Press, 2012), pp. 47–63.

trade or business, or sought jobs in the various Antipodean settlements; or they moved on, or went home.

Settler women were more enterprising and more mobile than historians have generally realized. They, too, moved back and forth across the Tasman, not only with husbands and other family members but on their own account, a mobility made possible by their trade skills and entrepreneurialism. Catherine Bishop's recent research on women in business in nineteenth-century Sydney and New Zealand has shown the extent of women's undertakings and their movements. We know, for example, about Helen Uther Welch who moved in 1854 with her doctor husband from New South Wales to New Zealand, where she established her own girls' school in Wellington. Welch subsequently separated from her husband and moved between Wellington, Napier, Hamilton, and Auckland, running schools and offering music lessons.[44]

Piecing together evidence from a wide range of sources, Bishop has carefully reconstructed the remarkable story of Mrs W. H. Foley, who made her name as an actor in the theatre and a circus performer in Australia and New Zealand in the 1850s and 1860s. Foley may have crossed oceans more than most, in the pursuit of a business that required travelling circuits. Foley was born into a theatrical family in England around 1820 as Catherine Huggins. In 1845 she married Daniel Caparn, a chemist and pharmacist. In 1847 Catherine and Daniel Caparn left England and sailed to Hobart, where she went into business as a milliner and dressmaker. In 1849 Catherine left by herself for San Francisco, among the throngs attracted by the California gold rush. In California Catherine met American circus impresario William H. Foley, whom she married after learning of Daniel Caparn's death in 1851. Mrs Foley then became an actress and performer, and in 1854 the Foleys took their circus and theatre performances on tour in Australia and New Zealand. Having briefly run a boarding house in Christchurch in 1857, in 1858 the Foleys separated. Mrs Foley performed again in Sydney in 1859, prior to establishing her own theatrical company in New Zealand, which apparently survived for several years. In 1867 Mrs Foley, with her new companion, left New Zealand for Valparaiso, Chile, where they established a theatrical company. By the 1880s, Mrs Foley (now also Mrs Lowten) was back in New Zealand, living and performing, and running a hotel in Napier.[45]

While Mrs Foley's mobility was probably greater than most, the extent of settler movement as well as trade between the Australian colonies and New Zealand was one reason that 'Australians' took great interest in events across the Tasman. Certainly, the contemporary Australian colonial press suggests that political and military developments in New Zealand were keenly followed. The first 'New Zealand War' broke out in the 1840s. First there were violent disputes over land in the Wairau region on the South Island in 1843, then in 1844 and 1845 there were hostilities in the Bay of Islands on the North Island resulting from different

---

[44] Catherine E. Bishop, 'Commerce Was a Woman: Women in Business in Colonial Sydney and Wellington', PhD thesis, Australian National University, 2012, pp. 269–71.
[45] Bishop, 'Commerce Was a Woman', pp. 271–7.

interpretations of the sovereignty established by the 1840 Treaty of Waitangi. There was further violence between 1845 and 1847, during which the Australian colonies provided arms, soldiers, and sailors to help the British put down Maori resistance.[46]

The war that broke out in 1860 in the Taranaki region, and later in the Waikato region in the west of the North Island, was fought over land, sovereignty, and, ultimately, control of New Zealand. It extended until 1872 and included pitched battles, extensive fortifications, the use of gunboats, and the intensive deployment of British troops and volunteers, including 'military settlers' from the Australian colonies.

In a 2009 book on the contributions of the Australian colonies to the New Zealand Wars, Jeff Hopkins-Weise goes so far as to argue that the close involvement of settlers from Australia needs to be seen as the origin of the twentieth-century 'Anzac' relationship between Australia and New Zealand. The term 'Anzac', still used to connote Australian and New Zealand military bonds and shared wartime legends, comes from the Australian and New Zealand Army Corps of the First World War. Hopkins-Weise contends that the 'Anzac legend' had its 'genesis' in 'this bond as "blood brothers" derived from the nineteenth-century conflicts, when colonists and imperial representatives on both sides of the Tasman united in a resolve to settle New Zealand's wars'.[47] This is a contentious argument, because the Anzac mythology was actively constructed from 1915 onwards based on the specific events at Gallipoli and elsewhere during the 'Great War', and has since been spurred at different points for a variety of ideological and cultural reasons. It is historically confusing to read this specific set of ideas back into the history of the 1840s and 1860s wars of British conquest when both colonial and military exigencies were quite different.

Nevertheless, Hopkins-Weise demonstrates the extent and significance of Australian colonial involvement in the New Zealand Wars. He points out that many of those recruited from the Australian colonies were 'military settlers'—a specific kind of settler, recruited in various places to go to fight the territorial wars of British colonialism, with the expectation that they would stay, receive land grants, and settle once the indigenous people were defeated and dispossessed. The recruitment of military settlers began in the Australian colonies in 1863, and was condoned by Australian colonial governments as well as imperial officials. Some of the contingents in which these militias served bore Australian identification, such as the Victorian and New South Wales Contingents of the Waikato Military Settlers in 1863, and the Melbourne Contingent of the Taranaki Military Settlers in 1864. These military settlers were not mercenaries (though perhaps economic incentives played a part), because they were a formally constituted British military force, organized at the behest of the New Zealand government.[48] About 2,500 men were recruited as military settlers, some of whom went on to serve in various New

---

[46] Mein Smith, *A Concise History*, pp. 63–5.
[47] Jeff Hopkins-Weise, *Blood Brothers: The Anzac Genesis* (Kent Town: Wakefield Press, 2009), p. 10.
[48] Hopkins-Weise, *Blood Brothers*, pp. 12–13.

Zealand military units. In total, thousands of those who fought on the British settler side of the conflict were Australian born, or enlisted in Australia, or departed from an Australian port. Hopkins-Weise notes that many of these men would have identified primarily as British, whether they were born in the Australian colonies or not. The Australian men who fought may have believed in the imperial cause—what Hopkins-Weise terms the 'crimson thread of kinship'; they may also just have wanted the army pay—or perhaps both.

The Australian colonies supported the settlers in New Zealand in other ways, too. Some families accompanied the military settler troops, and stayed long-term. Australian businesses manufactured or were the supply source of many of the provisions of the war—from arms, ammunition, heavy weapons, riverboats, and gunboats, to food, horses, cattle, coal, and other goods.[49] Moreover, like the Relief Fund for the British in India mentioned in relation to Caroline Carleton's imperially patriotic poems, in the 1860s residents in the Australian colonies raised charitable funds for the relief of Taranaki settlers, and for the relief of the families of British soldiers and sailors killed or incapacitated in New Zealand. Just as in the case of India in the 1850s, in the following decade Australians demonstrated an active sense of imperial identity, loyalty, and support.

AUSTRALIAN PRESS REPORTS AND COMMENTARY ON THE 1860s NEW ZEALAND WARS

The Australian colonial press was full of stories about the wars, not least because Australian newspapers sent their own correspondents to cover them.[50] On 26 March 1860, the *South Australian Register* set out to explain developments in New Zealand to its readers, as gleaned from the New Zealand newspapers. The paper sought to explain the outbreak of hostilities over a land sale in Taranaki in terms of problems with which South Australian settlers would be familiar, as well as the peculiar exigencies of the New Zealand colony—including what they saw as the greater bellicosity of Maori compared with Aborigines.

> Difficult a subject as the 'land question' is in this and the adjacent colonies, we have fortunately no experience of the troubles which surround it in the provinces of New Zealand. There that question is one with which is involved, not merely the raising of revenue and the settlement of immigrants, but the claims of a warlike people who look with jealousy on the alienation of their soil by foreigners, and who have more than once made fierce appeals to arms in what they consider to be a defence of their rights. Nor have the New Zealanders [Maori] on those occasions been found in any respect a despicable foe.[51]

The paper went on to remind its readers of the 1840s hostilities on the North Island, and the poor military performance and losses on the part of the British,

[49] Hopkins-Weise, *Blood Brothers*, p. 235.   [50] Hopkins-Weise, *Blood Brothers*, p. 236.
[51] 'The Revolt in New Zealand', *South Australian Register* 26 March 1860, p. 2.

indeed, the questionable fairness of British military strategy in putting down one uprising. Nevertheless, the *Register* contended that the British had right on their side in this fresh outbreak of war: 'In the present dispute . . . the purchase of land sought for by the Government was altogether in accordance with a system which the native population have subscribed to and acted upon over and over again', that of the government only buying land with the consent of its owner. Further, according to the Adelaide paper, in the land sale that was the cause of the new uprising, its leader was inconsistent in not following earlier precedent: Wiremu Kingi 'no sooner finds the Government Surveyors about to enter upon the land, than he appears with a large armed force, expels the Surveyors, and sets the authority of the Government at defiance, though he himself does not even pretend to have any right to the property'.[52] These events led the governor of New Zealand to sail from Auckland to the Taranaki (New Plymouth) region with a war steamer and a large armed force.

In July 1860, the *Age* similarly sought to explain the causes of the war to its Victorian readers, quoting from a September 1859 letter from settlers in Auckland to the Duke of Newcastle, and pointing out that in theory the Treaty of Waitangi had promised the Maori equal rights and privileges to those of other subjects of the British Crown. Yet the Maori did not believe they received equal treatment in relation to the sale of land, demanding to know: 'Why is there one law for the white man and another law for the Maori? Why are we not all treated alike if we are all the subjects of Queen Victoria?'[53] This attempt to explain Maori grievances, even as the war was being fought, is striking not only because the *Age* did not oppose settler support for the war, but also because of the absence of any comparable attempts on its part to explain Aboriginal grievances in its own colony.

Despite such preparedness to try to understand the Maori perspective on the struggle, the Australian press expressed firm support for British military efforts and the troops leaving to fight. Perhaps it is not surprising that, by March 1866, the *Brisbane Courier* was heated in its defence of the British cause and scathing of humanitarian views. By then the war had stretched on for years; and for Queenslanders in the 1860s, frontier war was a subject close to home. The *Courier* excoriated the Aborigines Protection Society as well as writers in the *Saturday Review*, *The Times*, and 'other London journals' for suggesting 'that the recent war in New Zealand was undertaken merely to satisfy the colonists' greed for land and the other relative pecuniary advantages of it'. The Aborigines Protection Society were noted 'for their maudlin sympathy for the natives, and the absolute untruthfulness of the information they have disseminated on New Zealand affairs'. To the contrary, in the *Courier*'s view:

[T]here does not appear to be the shadow of a doubt that the natives have been the aggressors; and that it was necessary if the northern island of New Zealand should remain a dependency of the British Crown that this constantly recurring tendency to

---

[52] 'The Revolt in New Zealand', *South Australian Register* 26 March 1860, p. 2.
[53] The *Age* 30 July 1860, p. 5.

rebellion should be destroyed root and branch; that the natives should, once for all, be taught to feel that resistance was hopeless, and that subjection to the Queen of England did not mean slavery, or any relinquishment of their just rights as subjects.[54]

If the *Courier* was particularly strident in its tone, other Australian papers were clear in their support for the war, too.

Reports commonly noted the numbers of troops going, the supplies being sent with them, and the level of popular support for the settler war effort. On 11 April 1860, for example, the *Sydney Morning Herald* reported that: 'Yesterday, one hundred and seventy-three men, rank and file, from the Royal Artillery and Twelfth Infantry Regiments, embarked at the Circular Quay, near the Military Stores, on board the *City of Sydney, en route* to New Zealand, where their presence has been required on account of the Maori insurrection'. The paper went on to enumerate by size the guns accompanying the troops to 'the scene of the much-to-be-regretted conflict between the Queen's subjects and the insurgents', and the number of members of both the artillery and infantry detachments of each rank. Moreover, it noted the size and cheerfulness of the crowd that had come to the Quay to farewell the troops: 'At twenty-five minutes past four o'clock in the afternoon the Artillery came down to the ship, their band playing "Auld Lang Syne," and other appropriate airs. They were received with cheers by the people, already congregated on the spot to the number of at least a thousand persons'.[55] (See Fig. 7.2.)

This large, exuberant send-off was typical of such troop departures for imperial conflicts. Australian society thoroughly embraced the British redcoat soldiers who were stationed in the colonies, from the landing of the First Fleet in 1788 until 1870 when British troops left for good and the colonies were compelled to take over their own defence. As Craig Wilcox has shown, some redcoats settled in the colonies when their terms expired, and even those who only sojourned for the duration of their service contributed to the local economy, entertained people with parades and military bands, and were often the objects of social and other attentions. They were also celebrated for their contributions to imperial wars. The troops who went to serve in New Zealand were a mix of regulars and volunteers. Public interest in the troops' departure for New Zealand was such that, when two companies of the 40th regiment left Melbourne in July 1860, a crowd of between six and eight thousand well-wishers watched and cheered as they marched onto the wharf.[56] Similar scenes occurred at other moments in Melbourne, and on multiple occasions in Sydney, as contingents of troops left to sail across the Tasman.

As with India in the 1850s, one issue aired in the press was whether the troops being sent to New Zealand would leave the Australian colonies vulnerable in terms of their own defence and security. This anxiety surfaced immediately, as shown in the *Sydney Morning Herald*'s report on 6 April 1860 of discussion in the New South Wales Lower House of Parliament following its receipt of a proposal from the

---

[54] *Brisbane Courier* 15 March 1866, p. 2.
[55] 'Departure of Troops for New Zealand', *Sydney Morning Herald* 11 April 1860.
[56] Wilcox, *Red Coat Dreaming*, p. 60.

Fig. 7.2 John Skinner Prout, 'Port Jackson from Dawes' Battery', oil.
State Library of New South Wales ML 625.

governor-general 'to despatch 120 men of the 12th Regiment, forty Artillery, and six Sappers' in response to a request from the governor of New Zealand. Henry Parkes immediately demanded of the government:

> whether these troops could be spared from the colony, and also what condition the colony would be left in when they were gone. The disturbances that had arisen in New Zealand were likely to continue for some time, and he presumed that the troops now in the colony were of the smallest number necessary for the requirements of the colony, and the Government should explain how these troops could be spared.

Parkes had touched a nerve, causing Mr Robertson to respond defensively for the government that 'there was a vast difference between the removal of troops to India and the removal to one of the Australian colonies [meaning New Zealand], wherever that might be'.[57] The same day a separate report in the same paper noted that a 'detachment of 100 rank and file of the 12th Regiment are under orders for immediate despatch to New Zealand'.[58]

Another parallel with the Indian war of 1857–58 was that settlers in the Australian colonies raised funds for the relief of the British in New Zealand who were most affected by the war. In September 1860 a fund was established in Melbourne, for example, 'in aid of the sufferers at Taranaki'. The committee set up to raise funds for this purpose resolved at its first meeting that 'the privations

---

[57] 'Disturbances in New Zealand', *Sydney Morning Herald* 6 April 1860.
[58] 'New Zealand', *Sydney Morning Herald* 6 April 1860, p. 7.

now being endured by the Volunteers militia, and their families, and the destitution of other colonists in New Plymouth, caused by the rebellion of the Maori's [sic] in that province, loudly call for prompt sympathy and aid'.[59] The governor of Victoria personally chaired a meeting at the Melbourne Town Hall in aid of the relief fund, noting in his speech that:

> The greatest amount of hardship, and he might say all the horrors of war had been realised by the colonists at Taranaki during the past few months, and to such an extent but that they had no alternative but to leave their homes, or be ruthlessly murdered. They had seen their homesteads destroyed; their land overrun by savages; and . . . the entire fruits of their industry in cultivation utterly lost. . . . [T]here were no less than 1700 women and children huddled together in a straggling village . . . and destitute of proper places for shelter.[60]

The efforts put in to raising such charitable funds, and the donations given by ordinary settlers, speak perhaps more loudly than any other evidence of the ties that those in the Australian colonies felt for their counterparts in India and New Zealand faced with violence or the threat of violence, and the loss of property and life. Knowing that frontier warfare had been and continued to be inherent to British colonialism in Australia must have stirred their empathy and their ability to imagine settlers' suffering in New Zealand.

Nevertheless, colonial press attitudes towards Maori continued to be a mix of admiration and racist disdain, and the rights and wrongs of the war continued to be rehearsed, at times quite defensively—even while writers repeatedly referred to Maori as 'savages'. In December 1860 the *South Australian Register* admitted to lingering doubts about the justice of the British cause, while concluding that British conquest was inevitable.[61] Even from the first outbreak of war in April 1860, the *Sydney Morning Herald* contended that the Maori were going to be tough to defeat:

> No one doubts the fate of the war, or the hopelessness of the struggle to which the natives have committed themselves, but they are an enemy not to be despised. Considering their recent civilization, they possess great wealth. They are courageous, alert and persevering . . . No mistake would be greater than to underrate their resources and their prowess.[62]

James Belich has shown the ways in which a range of British commentators on the war overstated British victories and under-represented the military success of the Maori, systematically refusing to acknowledge how well-engineered Maori fortifications were, and how tactically astute Maori were in military strategy. Confidence in British military superiority, Belich argues, predated the mid-nineteenth-century ascendancy in racial thinking but 'lent itself easily to fusion with ideas of racial superiority'.[63]

---

[59] 'Taranaki Relief Fund', *Age* 22 September 1860, p. 5.
[60] 'The War in New Zealand', *Age* 8 September 1860, p. 5.
[61] 'The Origin of the New Zealand War', *South Australian Register* 6 December 1860, p. 2.
[62] *Sydney Morning Herald* 9 April 1860.
[63] James Belich, *The Victorian Interpretation of Racial Conflict: The Maori, the British, and the New Zealand Wars* (Montreal: McGill-Queen's University Press, 1989), p. 322.

Around the same time the Melbourne *Age* paid grudging respect to the Maori, and predicted that the war would drag on.

> They believe, and with some truth too, that their lands will eventually pass into the hands of the Pakeha, and that their people will melt away or become the servants of the white man, an alternative more painful to the Maori than the prospect of extinction ... They may be beaten now, but they will rise again and again. What they demand is a Government of their own.[64]

Seven years later, the *Sydney Morning Herald* conceded that: 'It is out of the fertile subject—land—that all future Maori quarrels will arise; and it is impossible to see any term to them so long as there are any Maories [sic] left in New Zealand'. Ultimately, the paper contended, population decline among Maori would solve the problem:

> The Maories [sic], numbering barely 60,000 of all ages and sexes, who are yearly diminishing, hold, even after the late confiscations, perhaps three-fourths of the soil of the island. The English settlement is nearly double in numbers, and is increasing. How can it be supposed that the two races can continue in amity if the inferior persists in excluding its masters from extending their borders? ... The best, if not the only, assurance of ultimate peace in New Zealand is furnished by the census returns lately published, which prove that, in spite of all impediments, the British population of the island is steadily advancing and the Maories [sic] rapidly decreasing. Of the ultimate solution of the problem it is nature which has taken charge.[65]

'Nature' thus seemed to absolve the settlers from any undue guilt. For all of their bravery and martial abilities, the Maori were condemned as inferior 'savages' who were heading towards extinction and would thus inevitably make way for their imperial 'masters' to acquire full control of the desirable New Zealand land. Maori were acknowledged as having progressed some way toward civilization, to have understood the desirability of cultural autonomy and self-government, to have succeeded in acquiring some capital, and to have used it to arm themselves. But they could not and should not withstand British might. Even if they were more advanced than Aborigines, nevertheless, like the indigenous people in Australia, they were bound to die out.

White Australians' ambivalence toward Maori, and their categorization of them as superior to Aborigines, would be strikingly represented in the Commonwealth Franchise Act of 1902, which stipulated who could vote for the Federal Parliament in the new nation born in 1901. The Act enfranchised white women, making Australia only the second country in the world, after New Zealand, to give voting rights to women. At the same time it explicitly excluded Aboriginal people, men and women, from the suffrage, while explicitly including Maori resident in Australia, male and female, the only non-white people to be so included. This extraordinary singling out of Maori residents, and the distinction between Maori and Aborigines—the actual indigenous inhabitants of the nation—was for a

---

[64] 'The War in New Zealand', *Age* 25 May 1860.
[65] 'The New Zealand War', *Sydney Morning Herald* 27 March 1867, p. 3.

combination of reasons. Partly it was because Australia's founding fathers had not quite given up the hope that New Zealand might yet join the federation, which it had earlier contemplated. New Zealand representatives who had attended the early Federation conventions made it clear that Maori inclusion in citizenship would be a condition of their joining; Maori men and women were enfranchised in New Zealand, and that enfranchisement would have to extend to the larger parliament. However, that was not the only reason. Statements made by Australian politicians during the franchise debate evinced the view, widespread in the nineteenth century, that Maori were racially superior to Aborigines, that they were more 'civilised', a 'better type of native'.[66] This view was founded on the slightly different legal position of the Maori, due to the 1840 Treaty of Waitangi that acknowledged their claims to the land, as well as racial ideology and the finely gradated racial hierarchies of contemporary thought.[67]

CONCLUSION

By the 1850s, the Australian colonies were burgeoning, respectable, self-governing British societies occupying the region between South East Asia and the southern seas. Settlers in Australia tracked events in other colonies in their region, as well as the world further afield, through their newspapers and personal correspondence, as their predecessors had from the 1820s, as discussed in Chapter 1 of this volume through the example of the interconnected familial networks of the Dumaresqs, Darlings, and Macleays. They knew that their trading relationships, supplies of food and other goods, and general prosperity were linked to the stability of other British colonies and the region more generally. They also understood quite well the extent to which the British Empire's grasp of its numerous colonies hinged on military force, through its continued presence and implied threat, and sometimes the quashing of actual violence. Up until 1870 residents in the Australian colonies relied on the British soldiers and sailors in their midst for their own sense of military security, and felt vulnerable when those forces were depleted when sent elsewhere. British imperial and military ascendancy, especially in their region, was very much in their own interests.

For all of these reasons, their attention was captured when the Indian Rebellion erupted in 1857 and took two years of bloody fighting to quell, and a mere three years later war erupted in New Zealand, a sequel to the 1840s hostilities of which the Australian colonies had been well aware. Tracing attitudes to these conflicts evinced in the Australian colonial press, and through poetry, relief fund-raising, and politicians' visions, allows us to see the complexities of settlers' imperial and racial

---

[66] Patricia Grimshaw, 'A White Woman's Suffrage', in Helen Irving (ed.), *A Woman's Constitution? Gender and History in the Australian Commonwealth* (Sydney: Hale and Iremonger, 1996), pp. 77–97, esp. p. 85.

[67] See, for example, Tony Ballantyne's study of the ethnology of Aryanism moving from British India to New Zealand in the second half of the nineteenth century. Ballantyne, *Orientalism and Race: Aryanism in the British Empire* (New York: Palgrave Macmillan, 2002).

thinking. In a fight that pitted the imperial British against their rebellious Indian subjects, settlers' support for the war became increasingly sure, vociferous, and vindictive, expressed in racialized religious terms that cast the war as a heroic Christian crusade against Muslims and Hindus. In the case of 1860s New Zealand, Christianity was a factor in that the warring Maori were routinely condemned as half-civilized 'savages', but it was less central. Instead, the imagined inevitability of Maori defeat was conveniently ascribed to their inherent racial inferiority, despite their admitted virtues, in a glossing over of settlers' rights to the land through confidence in imperial might.

Settlers in Australia saw their own role as supportive of the British cause in both crises, to the extent of sending troops off with emotional farewells (if not actually volunteering themselves), following events closely and in detail, and raising charitable funds for the relief of the British caught up in the fighting. Their affective engagement with these imperial wars nearby may also have been driven by a sense that, by extension, they became part of the justification for settlers' own violence towards Aborigines. In the 1850s and 1860s, frontier warfare was rife in Queensland particularly, if perhaps past its peak in the more southerly colonies. If violent suppression of indigenous inhabitants was a common aspect of British colonialism in this period, then frontier violence in the Australian colonies, even if not openly discussed, was all the more normative and justifiable.

In Conclusion: Staking Claims to Land, Labour, and Self-Government

Desire for land was at the very core of settler society in the expanding Australian colonies. As Caroline Chisholm articulated it in 1859, echoing Henry Dumaresq in the 1820s, it was a fundamental longing:

> In regard to that love of land with which all men were so generally actuated every-where, it was not to be supposed that the feeling took its origin in the mere desire of becoming agriculturists. Far from it. It arose in that instinctive longing to possess a piece of land upon which a man might set his foot as owner, and on which he might make a home.[1]

Possession for settlers, as they well knew, was predicated on dispossession of the Indigenous people. Unlike the fictional Mrs Jellyby's concern to 'educate the natives of Borrioboola-Gha', Mrs Chisholm was silent on the subjects of frontier violence and Aboriginal people—other than tacitly alluding to their presence through 'stories about blacks and robbers', and her claims to have travelled where very few white women had ever been. The widely varied stories of settlers from the influentially connected, land-hungry Dumaresqs in the 1820s and 1830s, to the more modestly affluent and social-reforming Chisholms in the 1840s to 1850s, allow us to realize the broader pattern that constituted what can be called 'settler society'. Looking across these decades and around the Australian continent to assess the settlements' commonalities makes it possible to apprehend something of the connections between cultural values, land possession and dispossession, labour systems, and the development of colonial self-government. In turn, this broader lens reveals the imperial significance of a fully articulated and continent-wide settler society rising above its submerged, small, and scattered convict foundations.

While Henry Dumaresq had seen Canada, parts of Europe, and Mauritius as a British Army officer and colonial official, Caroline Chisholm had spent six years in India during her husband's tenure in the East India Company army. Here, too, they represent many of their fellow settlers. 'Migration' to the Australian colonies has often been presented as though one-way migrants sailed directly from Britain to the Antipodes with little exposure to anywhere else. Yet, not only were settlers mobile and often transient, they brought with them first- and second-hand know-ledge of places ranging from North America and the Caribbean, to India, and

---

[1] 'Mrs Chisholm's Lecture', *Sydney Morning Herald* 9 July 1859, p. 7.

southern Africa. They knew about slavery, and some had enjoyed the privileges of white masters and mistresses in slavery colonies. Even more had seen daily life in racially divided societies. They were familiar with Britain's frequent deployment of its army and navy to claim expanding colonial territories. Indeed, the significant number of settlers who had been in the army or navy lent Australia's emerging colonies a decidedly militarist character, helped by the garrison-like nature of many of its first towns and settlements.

Like land, labour was fundamental to settler society: the settlers' desire for inexpensive labourers to clear their land, to help build their houses and huts, and to tend their stock and crops led them to embrace a diverse mix of non-white labourers alongside convict workers and indentured labouring Europeans. Early Australia was built by a labour force that comprised a broad mix of the free and the unfree, European, Indian, Chinese, and Aboriginal, in a whole variety of combinations and thus cultural interactions that might well warrant the Australian colonies being considered 'creole'. Along with the expanses of land, inexpensive labour was a considerable attraction, providing at least some settlers with more workers for land and household, as well as the status of supervising them, than they could command in Britain. For settler men, who asserted their moral authority in judging how different kinds of labourers should be compensated, the status of master of unfree and non-white labour augmented their patriarchal authority. It contributed to evolving definitions of independent settler manliness and settler men's political claims, which in turn were deployed to argue for representative and responsible government. As David Neal has argued, magistrates who oversaw the convict labour system and the relatively harsh colonial master and servant law enjoyed expansive powers that they may have been inclined to overuse due to their own military and naval backgrounds.[2]

Despite this diversity among labourers and their own previous observation of racially hierarchical places, settlers' racial views were not necessarily straightforward. For example, amateur scientist and artist Fanny Macleay, who was better educated than most people of her day, was an avowed conservative who, in her letters to her brother William, freely disparaged 'Negroes' and convicts. Yet in 1836 she married Thomas Cudbert Harington, a mixed-race man of English and Indian parentage, a marriage of which her brother George at least disapproved. While the mature and opinionated Macleay may have been more willing to take this step than other women, the fact that most of her family accepted the marriage suggests that 1830s Sydney had a certain cosmopolitanism—not surprisingly for a port where ships called from around the world.

Even the planned and supposedly more idealistic Wakefieldian colonies of South Australia and Australind embraced racial mixing, both in their founders' schemes for colonial labour recruits and in the daily interactions of settlers from first arrival. These 'systematic' ventures, considered bold and experimental in the 1830s and early 1840s, contributed theoretical dimensions to the Antipodean settler colonies,

---

[2] David Neal, *The Rule of Law in a Penal Colony: Law and Power in Early New South Wales* (Cambridge: Cambridge University Press, 1991), p. 134.

despite not living up to at least South Australia's aspirations to interracial harmony. Moreover, their supporters saw a degree of colonial autonomy as necessary to them. Wakefield's land sales scheme on which they were based was intended to maximize their self-sufficiency. Though that part of their *raison d'etre* may have had limited success, his belief that settlers should acquire political rights as soon as possible augmented the views of other radicals. The radical roots of these southern and western planned settlements helped to swell the wider movement towards colonial democracy.

The achievement of representative and responsible government in the mid-century Australian colonies is at the centre of this history and the heart of this book. From the first surge of free settlers in the 1820s to the height of the movement for their own fully fledged parliaments was only three decades. As settlers disembarked, moved inland, claimed tracts of land, and built huts, houses, and homesteads, their rapid establishment of towns and civic amenities easily turned to demands for colonial self-government. Availing themselves of the Canadian model and promoting the significance of the Durham Report, settlers sought political rights and representation in order to assert control of matters of import to them. Even while they were divided over them, such matters included access to land, closing down the convict system, their regulation of labourers, and their treatment of indigenous people and new arrivals such as Chinese gold prospectors.

'First-wave feminism' is usually thought to have taken off in the Australian colonies in the 1880s. But the widespread debate over the gendering of political citizenship in the 1850s shows that we need to see the era of the attainment of responsible government as an important moment when the possibility of women as political citizens, and their claims for better employment opportunities, were widely aired. In the 1850s and 1860s women voted in some municipal elections in the Australian colonies, thus holding an anomalous status that underscored the timeliness of this issue in the context of overseas debates about women's rights and women's movements. Individual women spoke up about their rights in public meetings, the press, and fiction of the day. Far from women's exclusion from political citizenship being quietly accepted, rather it was hotly contested, as was their exclusion from professions and other higher-status and better-paid areas of employment.

Perhaps above all else, to comprehend these small but expanding British colonies we have to grasp the fact that settlers often knew Aboriginal people personally, relied on their labour, and, at the same time, could accept violence towards them as supposedly necessary, even if regrettable. While men may have carried out more of the violence, even middle-class women learnt directly about the costs of settler society, such as the incarceration of Aboriginal people and their desperate reactions. When Kathleen Lambert left Sydney in the 1850s with her sisters to go to manage their brother's station household in remote Wellington in central New South Wales, the church they attended every Sunday was that of the nearby Aboriginal mission, where Aboriginal residents sang in the choir. She describes the local Aboriginal people as individuals, albeit in patronizing ways, relating stories about them. Further, she argues for their employability when mission-educated, describing in evidence the literate workers at one friend's house. One Aboriginal worker whose story she briefly relates was Franky, who had spent time in a Sydney prison for killing another Aboriginal. Once released, Franky walked the two hundred miles back to Wellington virtually without a rest. Lambert comments:

> He arrived nearly dead from exhaustion, and then took to the 'Bush.' While in prison he had forgotten nearly all the English he had ever learned. Poor creature! It is easy to realise how this child of nature suffered, caged up in stone walls, under prison discipline; and no wonder to us now that he disliked staying in the kitchen to take his meals, and would merely come to the door for them.[3]

But like other settlers, Lambert in New South Wales and Louisa Clifton in southern Western Australia must have known that incarceration was only one aspect of the tragedy unfolding for Aborigines.

The violence settlers wielded against Aborigines was one key part of the wider violence of the Australian bush. From the late eighteenth century, bushrangers, mostly escaped convicts desperate to survive, contributed to a culture of lawlessness and fear. The establishment of Mounted Police, Border Police, and Native Police from the 1820s onwards helped to contain the lawlessness, but at the same time became part of the violence. If the violence was worst in the further reaches of the bush, it permeated settler culture in the towns, the cities, and the halls of politics. To understand fully the meanings of settler self-government in the mid-century decades, we need to recognize the congruency between frontier violence and respectable manhood, as male suffrage became a keystone of colonial self-government.

Perhaps integral to that congruency was the settlers' knowledge of colonial wars elsewhere, not least in their own region. If in recent decades Australians have been reluctant to acknowledge the bloodshed between settlers and Aborigines across the continent as the warfare that it was, in the nineteenth century there was greater realism, even when warfare was not openly discussed. The religious and racial vitriol Australians expressed towards Indians—Hindu and Muslim—during the 1857–58 war in India shows that settlers identified strongly as part of the British Empire's colonizing rulers, and supported the full use of force against revolt. While there was more sympathy and ambivalence expressed towards Maori during the New Zealand Wars of the 1860s, in this nearby war, too, in which many of the troops had departed from Australian soil, support for the British cause was resolute. If military victory and the British assertion of sovereignty in New Zealand spelled doom for the Maori people, that may be a matter for some sadness, but the colonial press agreed it was inevitable. Australian settlers commonly expressed the view that Aboriginal people were less advanced towards civilization than Maori. Moreover, the connections drawn between Aboriginal people in 1857–58 Queensland and the Indian fighters explicitly justified that episode of bloody frontier warfare. Violence against Aboriginal people was seen as a harsh necessity. Settlers were determined to

---

[3] Kathleen Lambert ['Lyth'], *The Golden South: Memories of Australian Home Life, 1843–1888* (London: Ward and Downey, 1890), p. 64.

stake their claims to the land, just as others were doing elsewhere in the empire in the same decades.

Settlers understood themselves and their world in imperial and global terms. While the terms 'Australia' and 'Australians' were common, federation into one nation was not yet envisaged. They were British, settlers, living in Van Diemen's Land, or New South Wales, or Victoria, with direct connections to Britain. Their colonies were expanding and their towns burgeoning at an astonishing rate. They were part of the British Empire's ascendancy, and the spread of civilization. They saw their colonies as progress, places of possibility and opportunity. The smaller 'systematic colonies' in the south and west were planned experiments that showed colonialism's political and theoretical potential—even if they fell short of their grand aspirations. Reformers such as Caroline Chisholm extolled colonialism's benefits for the British poor, and linked it to social reform. Individual 'settlers', men and women, were themselves often mobile, taking chances as they saw them, chances that many considered more abundant in the Antipodean colonies, despite their rawness, physical challenges, and moral complexities.

Bibliography

MANUSCRIPTS

Clark family papers, PRG 389, State Library of South Australia.

Chapman, Eichelbaum, and Rosenberg Families: Papers, Series 2/3 Henry Samuel Chapman—Tasmanian and Victorian Papers, MS—Papers 8670–066, Archives, Alexander Turnbull Library, National Library of New Zealand.

Colonial Office papers CO 13/24, Reel 588; CO 201/318, Reel 338; CO 201/356, Reel 364; CO 201/397, Reel 392; CO 201/467, Reel 645; CO 201/508, Reel 674; CO 210/332, Reel 347; CO 210/344, Reel 356; CO 210/498, Reel 666, Australian Joint Copying Project (AJCP), Public Record Office (PRO).

Correspondence and Associated Papers of the Dumaresq, Darling, and Boissier Families, NS953, Tasmanian Archives.

Diary of Margaret Menzies, MS 3261, National Library of Australia.

Governors' Despatches to the Secretary of State for the Colonies, Vol. 71, 1852, A1260 (CY 1944), Mitchell Library, State Library of New South Wales (SLNSW).

Letters of Lady Charlotte Bacon and Mrs Nora Burney Young, PRG 541, State Library of South Australia.

Macleay Family Letters 1834–40, Macarthur Family Papers, ML A4303 [CY2388], Mitchell Library, SLNSW.

William Sharp Macleay papers, Macarthur Family Papers, ML A4301 [CY1012], Mitchell Library, SLNSW.

Sir Henry Thoby Prinsep, 'Three Generations in India, 1771–1904', Vol. II, MssEur C97/2, British Library.

Thomas Lodge Murray-Prior, ML MSS 3117/6–7, CY Reel 1248 [NLA mfm G28187], Mitchell Library, SLNSW.

Thomas Lodge Murray-Prior, 'Diaries' 1863–1864, MSS 3117/ 4, CY Reel 495, Mitchell Library, SLNSW.

Thomas Lodge Murray-Prior, Diary, Murray-Prior Family Papers, Box 3, Folder 14, MS 7801, National Library of Australia.

Thomas Murray-Prior memoir, OM64-1/3/1/1, Rosa Caroline Praed Papers, John Oxley Library, State Library of Queensland.

UNPUBLISHED THESES

Bishop, Catherine, 'Commerce Was a Woman: Women in Business in Colonial Sydney and Wellington', PhD thesis, School of History, Australian National University, 2012.

Brent, Peter, 'The Rise of the Returning Officer: How Colonial Australia Developed Advanced Electoral Institutions', PhD thesis, Political Science, Australian National University, 2008.

Denholm, David, 'Some Aspects of Squatting in New South Wales and Queensland, 1847–1864', PhD thesis, Australian National University, 1972.

Durrer, Rebecca, 'Changing British Imperial Ideology: Edward Gibbon Wakefield and the Colonization of New Zealand', PhD thesis, University of Houston, 2000 (Proquest, Ann Arbor, MI, microform).

King, Anita, '"Conveniently Kept": Aboriginal Imprisonment on Rottnest Island, 1838 to 1904', Honours thesis, School of History, Australian National University, 2011.

Lee, Tai-Sook,'Edward Gibbon Wakefield and the Movement for Systematic Colonization, 1829–1850', PhD thesis, University of California, Berkeley, 1986 (University Dissertation Information Service Xerox, 1988).

Merritt, Adrian Suzanne, 'The Development and Application of Masters and Servants Legislation in New South Wales—1845 to 1930', PhD thesis, Australian National University, 1981.

Miller, K. R., 'Henry Samuel Chapman: Colonizer and Colonist', MA (Hons) thesis in History, Canterbury University College, University of New Zealand, 1956.

LEGISLATION

An act to consolidate and amend laws relating to the Corporation of the City of Adelaide and to enable towns and places within the province of South Australia to be incorporated under provisions thereof 1861.

13 & 14 Victoriae c.59 An Act for the better Governance of Her Majesty's Australian Colonies (Imperial) 1850.

18 & 19 Victoriae c.55 An Act to enable Her Majesty to assent to a Bill as amended of the legislature of Victoria to establish a constitution in and for the Colony of Victoria (Imperial) 1855.

NEWSPAPERS

Age
Argus
Australasian Chronicle
Brisbane Courier
Courier (Hobart)
Empire (Sydney)
Hobart Town Daily Courier
Hobart Town Mercury
Launceston Examiner
Moreton Bay Courier
New Zealand Spectator and Cook's Strait Guardian
Queanbeyan Age and General Advertiser
Queenslander
South Australian Advertiser
South Australian Gazette and Colonial Register
South Australian Register
Sydney Herald
Sydney Morning Herald
Wellington Independent

PRINTED SOURCES

A holograph memoir of Captain Charles Hervey Bagot of the 87th Regiment (Adelaide: The Pioneers Association of South Australia, 1942).

'A Walk through Taranaki in 1844. Described by the Hon. Mr. Justice Henry Samuel Chapman, of the Supreme Court of New Zealand. A Lecture Delivered at New Plymouth. By the Hon. Mr. Justice Frederick Revans Chapman, of the Supreme Court of New Zealand, Under the auspices of the Victoria League, December 11th, 1922' (Taranaki Herald and Budget Print), British Library.

Archer, Thomas, *Recollections of a Rambling Life* (Brisbane: Boolarong Publications, 1988).

Arthur, Edward, *A Journal of Events from Melbourne, Port Phillip, to Mount Schank in the District of Adelaide, New Holland, a distance of 400 miles undertaken in 1843 by Messrs Edward and Fortesque Arthur, sons of Captain Arthur, RN, with a Flock of 4000* (first published Sheerness, *c.*1844; Hobart: Sullivan's Cove, 1975).

Barnes, Phyllis et al. (eds), *The Australind Journals of Marshall Waller Clifton 1840–1861* (Victoria Park, Western Australia: Hesperian Press, 2010).

Barton, Robert D., *Reminiscences of an Australian Pioneer* (Sydney: Tyrrell's Ltd, 1917).

Baxter, Annie, *Memories of Tasmania and of the Macleay River and New England districts of New South Wales and the Western District of Port Phillip, 1834–1838* (Adelaide: Griffin Press Ltd, 1980).

Boldrewood, Rolf [Thomas Alexander Browne], *Old Melbourne Memories* (first pub. 1884; republished Melbourne: William Heinemann, 1969).

Brown, Margaret Emily, *A Port Fairy Childhood 1849/60* (Port Fairy, Victoria: Port Fairy Historical Society, 1990).

Burgess, H. T. (ed.), *The Cyclopedia of South Australia* Volume II (Adelaide: Cyclopedia Co., 1909).

Chapman, H. S., 'Canada', *Monthly Repository* September 1835.

Chapman, H. S., *The New Zealand Portfolio; Embracing a series of papers on subjects of importance to the colonists* (London: Smith, Elder, & Co., 1843).

Chapman, H. S., *Parliamentary Government; or Responsible Ministries for the Australian Colonies* (Hobart: Pratt and Son, 1854).

Chapman, H. S., 'Progress of Events in Canada', *London and Westminster Review* January 1837.

Chapman, H. S., 'Recent Occurrences in Canada', Hansard's *Monthly Repository* February 1836.

Chapman, Henry S., *The New Settlement of Australind* (London: Harvey and Darton, 1841).

Conigrave, Mrs J. Fairfax, *My Reminiscences of the Early Days* (Perth: Brokensha and Shaw Ltd, 1938).

Cumberland, R. B., *Stray Leaves from the Diary of an Indian Officer* (London: Whitfield, Green and Co., 1865).

Dawson, Robert, *The Present State of Australia* (first published London, 1830; Alburgh: Archival Facsimiles Ltd, 1987).

Deakin, Alfred, *Temple and Tomb in India* (Melbourne: Melville, Mullen and Slade, 1893).

Denison, Sir William, *Varieties of Vice-regal Life* (London: Longman Green and Co., 1870).

Earp, G. B. (ed.), *What we did in Australia: being the practical experiences of three clerks* (London: George Routledge and Co., 1853).

Friell, P., *The Advantages of Indian Labour in the Australian Colonies, As Shewn by Certain Details in Regard to the Indian Labourers* (Sydney: Richard Thompson, 1846).

Gill, Alfred, *Western Australia, containing a Statement of the Condition and Prospects of that Colony, and some account of the Western Australian Company's Settlement at Australind . . . Compiled for the use of settlers* (London: Smith, Elder, & Co., 65 Cornhill, 1842).

Harrison, Robert, *Colonial Sketches: or Five Years in South Australia, with hints to capitalists and emigrants* (first published 1862; Hampstead Gardens, South Australia: Austaprint, 1978).

Hawker, James C., *Early Experiences in South Australia* (Adelaide: E. S. Wigg and Son, 1899; facsimile ed. 1975).

Henderson, John, *Excursions and Adventures in New South Wales* (London: W. Stroberl, 1851).

Hughes, Mrs F. [Alice], *My Childhood in Australia* (London: Digby, Long, and Co., 1892).

Hussey, H., *More than Half a Century of Colonial Life and Christian Experience* (Adelaide: Hussey and Gillingham, 1897).

Kirkland, Katherine, 'Life in the Bush: By a Lady', *Chambers's Miscellany of Useful and Entertaining Tracts* Vol. 1, No. 8 (Edinburgh: William and Robert Chambers, 1845).

Landor, Edward Wilson, *The Bushman: Life in a New Country* (1847; republished Twickenham, UK: Senate, 1998).

'Lyth' [Kathleen Lambert], *The Golden South: Memories of Australian Home Life from 1843 to 1888* (London: Ward and Downey, 1890).

Mahoney, Eliza Sarah, 'The First Settlers at Gawler' [MS dated 1898], *Proceedings of the Royal Geographical Society of Australasia, South Australian Branch* Vol. 28 (1926–27).

Manning, Geoffrey H. (ed.), *Memoirs of Thomas Frost 1825–1910* (Adelaide: Gillingham Printers, 1985).

McConnell, Mary, *Memories of Days Long Gone By* (Brisbane, 1905; self-published).

Memoirs of Simpson Newland CMG, sometime treasurer of South Australia, with foreword by Sir Langdon Bonython (Adelaide: F. W. Preece and Sons, 1926).

Musgrave, Sarah, *The Wayback* (1926; republished West Wyalong, NSW: Bland District Historical Society, 4th Edition, 1979).

Praed, Mrs Campbell, *Australian Life: Black and White* (London: Chapman and Hall, 1885).

Praed, Rosa, *Outlaw and Lawmaker* (London: Pandora, 1988).

Praed, Rosa Campbell, *My Australian Girlhood* (London: Fisher Unwin, 1902).

Praed, Rosa Campbell, *Policy and Passion* (London: Richard Bentley and Son, 1881).

Prinsep, Mrs A. (ed.), *The Journal of a Voyage from Calcutta to Van Diemen's Land: comprising a Description of that Colony during a Six Months' Residence, from original letters* (London: Smith, Elder, and Co., Cornhill, 1833).

Sanders, C. S. (ed.), *The Settlement of George Sanders and His Family at Echunga Creek from the Journal of Jane Sanders* (Adelaide: Pioneers Association of South Australia, 1955).

Stuart, Anthony (ed.), *A Miller's Tale: The Memoirs of John Dunn of Mt Barker* (Kingswood, South Australia: Waterwheel Books, 1991).

The Spectator: Journal of Literature and Art For the Cultivation of the Memorable and the Beautiful.

The Story of the Life of Mrs. Caroline Chisholm, The Emigrant's Friend, and Her Adventure in Australia (London: Trelawney Saunders, Charing Cross, 1852).

Walsh, Richard (ed.), *A Voyage to Australia 1838–39: Private Journal of James Bell* (Sydney: Allen & Unwin, 2011).

Watts, Jane Isabella, *Family Life in South Australia* (Adelaide: W. K. Thomas and Co., 1890).

ARTICLES

Allbrook, Malcolm, '"A Triple Empire . . . United Under One Dominion": Charles Prinsep's Schemes for Exporting Indian Labour to Australia', *South Asia: Journal of South Asian Studies*, 14 August 2012, DOI: 10.1080/00856401.2011.649676: 1–23.

Broome, Richard, 'Aboriginal Workers on South-Eastern Frontiers', *Australian Historical Studies* No. 103 (1994): 202–20.

Burgess, E. L.,'The Settlement at Australind', *Western Australian Historical Society: Journal and Proceedings* New Series Vol. 11 (Oct. 1939).

Burton, Canon, 'The Diary of Anne Whatley', *Western Australian Historical Society: Journal and Proceedings* Vol. 1, 1930 (Part VII).

Clifton, E., 'Australind: The Founding of Australind', *Western Australian Historical Society: Journal and Proceedings* Vol. 1, Part 1 (1927).

Cullen, Rose, 'Empire, Indian Indentured Labour and the Colony: The debate over "coolie" labour in New South Wales, 1836–1838', *History Australia* Vol. 9, No. 1 (April 2012).

Doust, Janet L., 'Exploring Gentry Women on the New South Wales Frontier in the 1820s and 1830s', *Women's History Review* Vol. 18, No. 1 (Feb. 2009): 137–53.

Doust, Janet L., 'Kinship and Accountability: The Diaries of a Pioneer Pastoralist Family, 1856 to 1898', *History Australia* Vol. 2, No. 1 (2004): 04.1–04.14.

Doust, Janet L., 'Setting up Boundaries in Colonial Eastern Australia: Race and Empire', *Australian Historical Studies* Vol. 35 (2004).

Doust, Janet L., 'Two English Immigrant Families in Australia in the 19th century', *The History of the Family* Vol. 13, No. 1 (2008): 2–25.

Dwight, Alan, 'The Use of Indian Labourers in New South Wales', *Journal of the Royal Australian Historical Society* Vol. 62, Part 2 (September 1976).

Elbourne, Elizabeth, 'The Sins of the Settler: The 1835–36 Select Committee on Aborigines and Debates over Virtue and Conquest in the Early-Nineteenth Century British White Settler Empire', *Journal of Colonialism and Colonial History* 4: 3 (2003).

Foster, Heather, 'The First Indians: The Bruce and Gleeson Indentured Labourers in Nineteenth Century South Australia', *Journal of the Historical Society of South Australia* No. 39 (2011): 21–30.

Goodall, Heather, Devleena Ghosh, and Lindi Renier Todd, 'Jumping Ship: Indians, Aborigines and Australians Across the Indian Ocean', *Transforming Cultures eJournal* Vol. 1, No. 3 (University of Technology, Sydney, 2008).

Hannah, Mark, 'Aboriginal Workers in the Australian Agricultural Company, 1824–1857', *Labour History* No. 82 (May 2002).

'Harington, John Herbert (1764/5–1828)', entry in *Oxford Dictionary of National Biography* (Oxford: Oxford University Press, 2004–13), http://www.oxforddnb.com.virtual.anu. edu.au/view/article/12329, accessed 4 October 2013.

Henderson, Kelly, 'Adelaide: The ideal city of the philosophic radicals, and the great experiment in the art of colonization', *South Australian Geographical Journal* Vol. 105 (2006): 138–50.

Hetherington, Penelope, 'Aboriginal Children as a Potential Labour Force in Swan River Colony, 1829–1850', *Journal of Australian Studies* No. 33 (June, 1992).

Hogg, Robert, ' "The Most Manly Class that Exists": British Gentlemen on the Queensland Frontier', *Journal of Australian Colonial History* Vol. 13 (2011), 65–84.

Hogg, Robert, 'The Unmanly Savage: "Aboriginalism" and Subordinate Masculinities on the Queensland Frontier', *Crossings* Vol. 10.3/11.1 (March 2006).

Ilbery, E. S., 'The Battle of Pinjarra, 1834: I. The Passing of the Bibbulmun', *Western Australian Historical Society: Journal and Proceedings* Vol. 1, Part 1 (1927): 24–30.

Lake, Marilyn, 'The Gendered and Racialised Self who Claimed the Right to Self-Government', *Journal of Colonialism and Colonial History* Vol. 13, No. 1 (Spring 2012).

Love, Ngata, 'Edward Gibbon Wakefield: A Maori Perspective', in Friends of the Turnbull Library Symposium, *Edward Gibbon Wakefield and the Colonial Dream: A Reconsideration* (Wellington: GP Publications, 1997).

Merritt, Adrian, 'The Historical Role of Law in the Regulation of Employment—Abstentionist or Interventionist?', *Australian Journal of Law & Society* Vol. 1, No. 1 (1982).

Mitchell, Jessie, ' "Are We in Danger of a Hostile Visit from the Aborigines?" Dispossession and the Rise of Self-Government in New South Wales', *Australian Historical Studies* Vol. 40, No. 3 (2009): 294–307.

Mitchell, Jessie, ' "Great difficulty in knowing where the frontier ceases": Violence, governance, and the spectre of India in early Queensland', *Journal of Australian Colonial History* Vol. 15 (2013), 43–62.

Moles, I. N., 'The Indian Coolie Labour Issue in Queensland', *Historical Society of Queensland Journal* Vol. V, No. 5 (1957).

Neale, R. S., 'H. S. Chapman and the "Victorian" Ballot', *Australian Historical Studies* No. 48 (1967): 506–21.

Newman, Terry, 'Tasmania and the Secret Ballot', *Australian Journal of Politics and History* Vol. 49, No. 1 (2003): 93–101.

Richards, Eric, 'Wakefield and Australia', in Friends of the Turnbull Library Symposium, *Edward Gibbon Wakefield and the Colonial Dream: A Reconsideration* (Wellington: GP Publications, 1997).

Robinson, Shirleene, 'The Unregulated Employment of Aboriginal Children in Queensland, 1842–1902', *Labour History* No. 82 (May 2002): 1–15.

Scalmer, Sean, 'Containing Contention: Reinterpretation of Democratic Change and Electoral Reform in the Australian Colonies', *Australian Historical Studies* Vol. 42, No. 3 (2011): 337–56.

Staples, A. C., 'The Prinsep Estate in Western Australia', *Western Australian Historical Society: Journal and Proceedings* Vol. V, Part 1 (1955): 16–19.

Twomey, Christina and Andrew J. May, 'Australian Responses to the Indian Famine, 1876–78: Sympathy, Photography and the British Empire', *Australian Historical Studies* Vol. 43, Issue 2 (June 2012): 233–52.

Wood, Rebecca, 'Frontier Violence and the Bush Legend: The *Sydney Herald*'s Response to the Myall Creek Massacre Trials and the Creation of Colonial Identity', *History Australia* Vol. 6, No. 3 (2009).

Woollacott, Angela, 'Frontier Violence and Settler Manhood', *History Australia* Vol. 6, No. 1 (April 2009): 09.1–09.15.

Wright, Clare, 'Golden Opportunities: The Early Origins of Women's Suffrage in Victoria', *Victorian Historical Journal* Vol. 79, No. 2 (Nov. 2008), 210–23.

Wright, Clare, ' "New Brooms They Say Sweep Clean": Women's Political Activism on the Ballarat Goldfields, 1854', *Australian Historical Studies* Vol. 39, No. 3 (2008): 305–21.

Wynd, Ian, 'Labour—Supply and Demand in the 1840s', *Investigator: Magazine of the Geelong Historical Society* Vol. 14, No. 1 (March 1979).

BOOKS

Adams, David (ed.), *The Letters of Rachel Henning* (Harmondsworth: Penguin Books, 1969).

Adelaide, Debra (ed.), *A Bright and Fiery Troop: Australian Women Writers of the Nineteenth Century* (Ringwood, Victoria: Penguin Books, 1988).

Alexander, Alison, *Tasmania's Convicts: How Felons Built a Free Society* (Crows Nest: Allen & Unwin, 2010).

Allbrook, Malcolm, *Henry Prinsep's Empire: Framing a Distant Colony* (Canberra: ANU Press, 2014).

Atkinson, Alan and Marian Aveling (eds), *Australians 1838* (Sydney: Fairfax, Syme & Weldon Associates, 1987).

Atkinson, Alan et al. (eds), *High Lean Country: Land, People and Memory in New England* (Sydney: Allen and Unwin, 2006).

Atkinson, Anne, *Asian Immigrants to Western Australia 1829–1901* (Nedlands: University of Western Australia Press, 1988).

Australian Dictionary of Biography (Melbourne: Melbourne University Press, 1966–2012 and Online Edition).

Ballantyne, Tony, *Orientalism and Race: Aryanism in the British Empire* (New York: Palgrave Macmillan, 2002).

Battye, J. S., *Western Australia: A History from its Discovery to the Inauguration of the Commonwealth* (Oxford: Clarendon Press, 1924).

Belich, James, *Replenishing the Earth: The Settler Revolution and the Rise of the Anglo-world, 1783–1939* (Oxford: Oxford University Press, 2009).

Belich, James, *The Victorian Interpretation of Racial Conflict: The Maori, the British, and the New Zealand Wars* (Montreal: McGill-Queen's University Press, 1989).

Bloomfield, Paul, *Edward Gibbon Wakefield—Builder of the British Commonwealth* (London: Longmans, Green, and Co., 1961).

Bradbury, Bettina, *Wife to Widow: Lives, Laws, and Politics in Nineteenth-Century Montreal* (Vancouver: UBC Press, 2011).

Burns, A., G. Bottomley, and P. Jools (eds), *The Family in the Modern World* (Sydney: George Allen & Unwin, 1983).

Chesterman, John and Brian Galligan, *Citizens Without Right: Aborigines and Australian Citizenship* (Cambridge: Cambridge University Press, 1997).

Clarke, Patricia, *Pen Portraits: Women Writers and Journalists in Nineteenth Century Australia* (Sydney: Pandora, 1988).

Clarke, Patricia, *Rosa! Rosa!: A Life of Rosa Praed, Novelist and Spiritualist* (Carlton, Victoria: Melbourne University Press, 1999).

Cochrane, Peter, *Colonial Ambition: Foundations of Australian Democracy* (Carlton, Victoria: Melbourne University Press, 2006).

Crawford, Patricia and Philippa Maddern (eds), *Women as Australian Citizens: Underlying Histories* (Carlton, Victoria: Melbourne University Press, 2001).

Crowley, F. K., *Australia's Western Third: A History of Western Australia from the First Settlements to Modern Times* (Melbourne: Heinemann, 1960).

Damousi, Joy and Katherine Ellinghaus (eds), *Citizenship, Women and Social Justice* (Melbourne: History Department, University of Melbourne, 1999).

Daunton, Martin and Rick Halpern (eds), *Empire and Others: British Encounters with Indigenous Peoples, 1600–1850* (Philadelphia: University of Pennsylvania Press, 1999).

Dawson, Graham, *Soldier Heroes: British Adventure, Empire and the Imagining of Masculinities* (London: Routledge, 1994).

deFalbe, Jane, *My Dear Miss Macarthur: The Recollections of Emmaline Maria Macarthur (1828–1911)* (Kenthurst, NSW: Kangaroo Press, 1988).

deGaris, B. K. (ed.), *Portraits of the South West: Aborigines, Women and the Environment* (Nedlands, Western Australia: University of Western Australia Press, 1993).

Deacon, Desley, *Managing Gender: The State, the New Middle-Class and Women Workers 1830–1930* (Melbourne: Oxford University Press, 1989).

Deacon, Desley, Penny Russell, and Angela Woollacott (eds), *Transnational Ties: Australian Lives in the World* (Canberra: ANU E-Press, 2008).

Dickens, Charles, *Bleak House* (1853; London: Oxford University Press, 1948).

Drew, Pamela Statham, *James Stirling: Admiral and Founding Governor of Western Australia* (Crawley: University of Western Australia Press, 2003).

Earnshaw, Beverley and Joy Hughes (eds), *Fanny to William: The Letters of Frances Leonora Macleay 1812–1836* (Glebe, New South Wales: Historic Houses Trust of New South Wales and Macleay Museum, University of Sydney, 1993).

Edmonds, Penelope, *Urbanizing Frontiers: Indigenous Peoples and Settlers in 19th-Century Pacific Rim Cities* (Vancouver: UBC Press, 2010).

Elkins, Caroline and Susan Pedersen (eds), *Settler Colonialism in the Twentieth Century: Projects, Practices, Legacies* (New York: Routledge, 2005).

Evans, Julie, *Edward Eyre: Race and Colonial Governance* (Dunedin: University of Otago Press, 2005).

Evans, R., K. Saunders, and K. Cronin, *Exclusion, Exploitation and Extermination: Race Relations in Colonial Queensland* (Sydney: Australian and New Zealand Book Co., 1975).

Ferry, John, *Colonial Armidale* (St Lucia, Queensland: University of Queensland Press, 1999).

Fletcher, Brian H., *Ralph Darling—A Governor Maligned* (Melbourne: Oxford University Press, 1984).

Ford, Lisa, *Settler Sovereignty: Jurisdiction and Indigenous People in America and Australia, 1788–1836* (Cambridge, MA: Harvard University Press, 2010).

Foster, Robert, Rick Hosking, and Amanda Nettelbeck, *Fatal Collisions: The South Australian Frontier and the Violence of Memory* (Adelaide: Wakefield Press, 2001).

Foster, Robert and Paul Sendziuk (eds), *Turning Points: Chapters in South Australian History* (Kent Town, South Australia: Wakefield Press, 2012).

Frank, Christopher, *Master and Servant Law: Chartists, Trade Unions, Radical Lawyers and the Magistracy in England, 1840–1865* (Farnham, Surrey: Ashgate, 2010).

Frost, Lucy (ed.), *No Place for a Nervous Lady: Voices from the Australian Bush* (Melbourne: McPhee Gribble Publishers, 1984).

Gill, Thomas, *A Biographical Sketch of Colonel William Light, The Founder of Adelaide and the First Surveyor-General of the Province of South Australia* (Adelaide: Royal Geographical Society of Australia, South Australia Branch, 1911).

Golder, Hilary, *Evidence and Accountability: Revisiting and Reading the Public Record* (Royal Exchange: History Council of New South Wales, 2006).

Gothard, Jan, *Blue China: Single Female Migration to Colonial Australia* (Carlton, Victoria: Melbourne University Press, 2001).

Grimshaw, Patricia, Marilyn Lake, Ann McGrath, and Marian Quartly, *Creating a Nation* (Ringwood, Victoria: McPhee Gribble Publishers, 1994).

Hall, Catherine, *Civilizing Subjects: Metropole and Colony in the English Imagination, 1830–1867* (Chicago: University of Chicago Press, 2002).

Hall, Catherine (ed.), *Cultures of Empire: Colonizers in Britain and the Empire in the Nineteenth and Twentieth Centuries: A Reader* (New York: Routledge, 2000).

Hay, Douglas and Paul Craven (eds), *Masters, Servants, and Magistrates in Britain and the Empire, 1562–1955* (Chapel Hill: University of North Carolina Press, 2004).

Hetherington, Penelope, *Settlers, Servants and Slaves: Aboriginal and European Children in the Nineteenth-Century in Western Australia* (Crawley: University of Western Australia Press, 2002).

Hirst, John, *The Strange Birth of Colonial Democracy: New South Wales 1848–1884* (Sydney: Allen & Unwin, 1988).

Hollis, Patricia, *Ladies Elect: Women in English Local Government 1865–1914* (Oxford: Clarendon Press, 1987).

Hopkins-Weise, Jeff, *Blood Brothers: The Anzac Genesis* (Kent Town, South Australia: Wakefield Press, 2009).

Inglis, K. S., *The Australian Colonists: An Exploration of Social History 1788–1870* (Carlton, Victoria: Melbourne University Press, 1974).

Irving, Helen (ed.), *A Woman's Constitution? Gender and History in the Australian Commonwealth* (Sydney: Hale and Iremonger, 1996).

Irving, Terry, *The Southern Tree of Liberty: The Democratic Movement in New South Wales before 1856* (Sydney: Federation Press 2006).

Isaac, Rhys, *Landon Carter's Uneasy Kingdom: Revolution and Rebellion on a Virginia Plantation* (New York: Oxford University Press, 2004).

Isaac, Rhys, *The Transformation of Virginia 1740–1790* (Chapel Hill: University of North Carolina Press, 1982).

Jayasuriya, Laksiri, David Walker, and Jan Gothard (eds), *Legacies of White Australia: Race, Culture and Nation*, 1st ed. (Crawley, Western Australia: University of Western Australia Press, 2003).

Jupp, James (ed.), *The Australian People: An Encyclopaedia of the Nation, Its People and Their Origins* (Cambridge: Cambridge University Press, 2001).

Keese, Oline [Caroline Woolmer Leakey], *The Broad Arrow, Being Passages from the History of Maida Gwynnham, a 'Lifer'* (first published London, 1859; London: Richard Bentley, 1887).

Kercher, Bruce, *Outsiders: Tales from the Supreme Court of NSW, 1824–1836* (Melbourne: Australian Scholarly Publishing, 2006).

Kiddle, Margaret, *Caroline Chisholm* (Carlton, Victoria: Melbourne University Press, 1950).

Kociumbas, Jan, *The Oxford History of Australia: Possessions, 1770–1860* Volume 2 (South Melbourne, Victoria: Oxford University Press, 1992).

Laidlaw, Zoe, *Colonial Connections, 1815–45: Patronage, the Information Revolution and Colonial Government* (Manchester: Manchester University Press, 2005).

Lambert, David, *White Creole Culture, Politics and Identity during the Age of Abolition* (Cambridge: Cambridge University Press, 2005).

Lambert, David and Alan Lester (eds), *Colonial Lives Across the British Empire: Imperial Careering in the Long Nineteenth Century* (Cambridge: Cambridge University Press, 2006).

Larcombe, F. A., *The Origin of Local Government in New South Wales* Volume 2 (Sydney: Sydney University Press, 1976).

Levine, Philippa (ed.), *Gender and Empire* (Oxford: Oxford University Press, 2004).

Lloyd Prichard, M. F. (ed.), *The Collected Works of Edward Gibbon Wakefield* (Glasgow: Collins, 1968).

Lorimer, Douglas A., *Colour, Class and the Victorians: English Attitudes to the Negro in the Mid-nineteenth Century* (Leicester: Leicester University Press, 1978).

Lorimer, Douglas A., *Science, Race Relations and Resistance: Britain, 1870–1914* (Manchester: Manchester University Press, 2013).

Macintyre, Stuart, *A Concise History of Australia*, 3rd ed. (Cambridge: Cambridge University Press, 2009).

Macintyre, Stuart and Richard Mitchell (eds), *Foundations of Arbitration: The Origins and Effects of State Compulsory Arbitration 1890–1914* (Melbourne: Oxford University Press, 1989).

Magarey, Susan, *Unbridling the Tongues of Women: A Biography of Catherine Helen Spence* (Sydney: Hale & Iremonger, 1985).

Malouf, David, *Every Move You Make* (London: Chatto & Windus, 2006).

Malouf, David, *Remembering Babylon* (New York: Pantheon Books, 1993).

Mar, Tracey Banivanua and Penelope Edmonds (eds), *Making Settler Colonial Space: Perspectives on Race, Place and Identity* (Houndmills, Basingstoke: Palgrave Macmillan, 2010).

Martin, A. W., *Henry Parkes: A Biography* (Melbourne: Melbourne University Press, 1980).

McLaren, John, A. R. Buck, and Nancy E. Wright (eds), *Despotic Dominion: Property Rights in British Settler Societies* (Vancouver: UBC Press, 2005).

McMichael, Philip, *Settlers and the Agrarian Question: Foundations of Capitalism in Colonial Australia* (Cambridge: Cambridge University Press, 1984).

Morgan, Cecilia, *Public Men and Virtuous Women: The Gendered Languages of Religion and Politics in Upper Canada, 1791–1850* (Toronto: University of Toronto Press, 1996).

Morgan, Sharon, *Land Settlement in Early Tasmania: Creating an Antipodean England* (Cambridge: Cambridge University Press, 1992).

Neal, David, *The Rule of Law in a Penal Colony: Law and Power in Early New South Wales* (Cambridge: Cambridge University Press, 1991).

Nicholas, Stephen (ed.), *Convict Workers: Reinterpreting Australia's Past* (Cambridge: Cambridge University Press, 1988).

Nile, Richard (ed.), *The Australian Legend and Its Discontents* (St Lucia, Queensland: University of Queensland Press, 2000).

Nolan, Melanie, *Kin: A Collective Biography of a Working-Class New Zealand Family* (Christchurch, NZ: Canterbury University Press, 2005).

Offen, Karen (ed.), *Globalizing Feminisms 1789–1945* (London: Routledge, 2010).

Oldfield, Audrey, *Woman Suffrage in Australia: A Gift or a Struggle?* (Cambridge: Cambridge University Press, 1992).

Paxton, Nancy L., *Writing Under the Raj: Gender, Race, and Rape in the British Colonial Imagination, 1830–1947* (New Brunswick, NJ: Rutgers University Press, 1999).

Pike, Douglas, *Paradise of Dissent: South Australia 1829–1857* (Carlton, Victoria: Melbourne University Press, 1967).

Potter, Simon J., *News and the British World: The Emergence of an Imperial Press System, 1876–1922* (Oxford: Clarendon Press, 2003).

Provis, Selkirk and Keith A. Johnson, *Cadman's Cottage: The Life and Times of John Cadman in Colonial Sydney 1798–1848* (Sydney: J. S. Provis & K. A. Johnson, 1972).

Pybus, Cassandra, *Black Founders: The Unknown Story of Australia's First Black Settlers* (Sydney: University of New South Wales Press, 2006).

Reid, Gordon, *A Nest of Hornets: The Massacre of the Fraser Family at Hornet Bank Station, Central Queensland, 1857, and Related Events* (Melbourne: Oxford University Press, 1982).

Reid, Kirsty, *Gender, Crime and Empire: Convicts, Settlers and the State in Early Colonial Australia* (Manchester: Manchester University Press, 2007).

Reynolds, Henry, *Black Pioneers* (Ringwood, Victoria: Penguin Books, 2000).

Reynolds, Henry, *Why Weren't We Told? A Personal Search for the Truth about Our History* (Camberwell, Victoria: Penguin Books, 1999).

Reynolds, Henry, *With the White People: The Crucial Role of Aborigines in the Exploration and Development of Australia* (Ringwood, Victoria: Penguin Books, 1990).

Richards, Jonathan, *The Secret War: A True History of Queensland's Native Police* (St Lucia, Queensland: University of Queensland Press, 2008).

Robinson, Shirleene, *Something like Slavery? Queensland's Aboriginal Child Workers 1842–1945* (Melbourne: Australian Scholarly Publishing, 2008).

Russell, Lynette, *Roving Mariners: Australian Aboriginal Whalers and Sealers in the Southern Oceans, 1790–1870* (Albany, NY: State University of New York Press, 2012).

Russell, Penny, *Savage or Civilised? Manners in Colonial Australia* (Sydney: University of New South Wales Press, 2010).

Rutherford, Jennifer, *The Gauche Intruder: Freud, Lacan and the White Australian Fantasy* (Carlton South, Victoria: Melbourne University Press, 2000).

Ryan, Mary P., *Women in Public: Between Banners and Ballots, 1825–1880* (Baltimore: Johns Hopkins University Press, 1990).

Saunders, Kay, *Workers in Bondage: The Origins and Bases of Unfree Labour in Queensland 1824–1916* (St Lucia, Queensland: University of Queensland Press, 1982).

Sawer, Marian (ed.), *Elections: Full, Free & Fair* (Leichhardt, New South Wales: Federation Press, 2001).

Scott, Joan Wallach, *Gender and the Politics of History* (New York: Columbia University Press, 1999).

Scully, Pamela and Diana Paton (eds), *Gender and Slave Emancipation in the Atlantic World* (Durham, NC: Duke University Press, 2005).

Sharpe, Jenny, *Allegories of Empire: The Figure of Woman in the Colonial Text* (Minneapolis: University of Minnesota Press, 1993).

Shaw, A. G. L. (ed.), *Great Britain and the Colonies 1815–1865* (London: Methuen, 1970).

Smith, Philippa Mein, *A Concise History of New Zealand* (Cambridge: Cambridge University Press, 2005).

Spence, Catherine Helen, *Clara Morison* (first published by John W. Parker and Son, 1854; Adelaide: Rigby Ltd, 1971).

Spence, Catherine Helen, *Mr. Hogarth's Will* (first published London: Richard Bentley, 1865; Ringwood, Victoria: Penguin Books, 1988).

Spiller, Peter, *The Chapman Legal Family* (Wellington: Victoria University Press, 1992).

Steiner, Marie, *Servants' Depots in Colonial South Australia* (Kent Town, South Australia: Wakefield Press, 2009).

Temple, Philip, *A Sort of Conscience: The Wakefields* (Auckland: Auckland University Press, 2002).

Thorpe, Bill, *Colonial Queensland: Perspectives on a Frontier Society* (St Lucia, Queensland: University of Queensland Press, 1996).

Victorian Parliamentary Debates Vols. 9 & 11 (Melbourne: W. Fairfax, 1858–65).

Walker, David and Agnieszka Sobocinska (eds), *Australia's Asia: From Yellow Peril to Asian Century* (Crawley, Western Australia: UWA Publishing, 2012).

Wall, Barbara, *Our Own Matilda: Matilda Jane Evans, 1827–1886, Pioneer Woman and Novelist* (Kent Town, South Australia: Wakefield Press, 1994).

Ward, J. M., *Colonial Self-Government: The British Experience 1759–1856* (London: Macmillan, 1976).

Ward, Russel, *The Australian Legend* (first published 1958; Melbourne: Oxford University Press, 1978).

Webby, Elizabeth (ed.), *Colonial Voices: Letters, Diaries, Journalism and Other Accounts of Nineteenth-Century Australia* (St Lucia, Queensland: University of Queensland Press, 1989).

Webling, Rae, *A Song for Australia: Caroline Carleton—Her Poems and Biography 1820–1874* (Kadina, South Australia: Mrs. R. Webling, 1977).

Westrip, Joyce and Peggy Holroyde, *Colonial Cousins: A Surprising History of Connections Between India and Australia* (Adelaide: Wakefield Press, 2010).

Wilcox, Craig, *Red Coat Dreaming: How Colonial Australia Embraced the British Army* (Cambridge: Cambridge University Press, 2009).

Williams, Stephan (compiler), *The Book of a Thousand Bushrangers* (Woden, ACT: Popinjay Publications, 1993).

Windschuttle, Elizabeth, *Taste and Science: The Women of the Macleay Family* (Glebe: Historic Houses Trust of New South Wales, 1988).

Wright, Christine, *Wellington's Men in Australia: Peninsular War Veterans and the Making of Empire c.1820–40* (Basingstoke: Palgrave Macmillan, 2011).

Wright, Clare, *The Forgotten Rebels of Eureka* (Melbourne: Text Publishing, 2013).

Index

Charles Seale-Hayne Library
University of Plymouth
(01752) 588 588
LibraryandITenquiries@plymouth.ac.uk